How to Succeed at Scho

CW00661834

This book shines a light on the best research into learning and the brain development that makes it all possible. Written by two distinguished education journalists, it provides an invaluable guide to the latest information for parents seeking to help their children to make the best use of their potential and steer a true course through an often confused, noisy and crowded learning landscape where ideas compete and nothing can seem clear.

Summarising the most up to date and significant research in a jargon-free and understandable way, this book provides readers with simple and clear access to knowledge and information about what really helps children learn and flourish. Drawing on expert analysis, interviews and example studies, the chapters tackle common misconceptions and myths, and explore crucial topics including:

- The use of neuroscience in education;
- The role of parents and how *all* parents can help their children learn;
- What works in the classroom and the best ways of teaching a child.

The first of its kind, this seminal text is a unique resource for parents, carers, primary and secondary teachers, student teachers, policymakers and anyone interested in the development of children and how they learn.

Wendy Berliner is an award-winning former senior *Guardian* journalist. She specialises in education and has also worked at *The Independent*, edited the *Times Educational Supplement* and been Director of Parental Engagement for one of the world's largest international school groups.

Judith Judd is a former editor of the *Times Educational Supplement* and former education correspondent of *The Observer*, *The Independent* and *The Independent on Sunday*. She was Pro Chancellor of the University of Essex and Chair of its Council until August 2019.

How to Succeed at School

Separating Fact from Fiction
What Every Parent Should Know

Wendy Berliner and Judith Judd

Routledge
Taylor & Francis Group

LONDON AND NEW YORK

First published 2020
by Routledge
2 Park Square, Milton Park, Abingdon, Oxon OX14 4RN

and by Routledge
52 Vanderbilt Avenue, New York, NY 10017

Routledge is an imprint of the Taylor & Francis Group, an informa business

© 2020 Wendy Berliner and Judith Judd

British Library Cataloguing in Publication Data
A catalogue record for this book is available from the British Library

Library of Congress Cataloging-in-Publication Data
Names: Berliner, Wendy, author. | Judd, Judith, author.
Title: How to succeed at school : separating fact from fiction / Wendy Berliner and Judith Judd.
Description: Abingdon, Oxon ; New York, NY : Routledge, 2020. | Includes bibliographical references and index.
Identifiers: LCCN 2019036242 (print) | LCCN 2019036243 (ebook) | ISBN 9780367186456 (hardback) | ISBN 9780367186463 (paperback) | ISBN 9780429197369 (ebook)
Subjects: LCSH: Academic achievement--Psychological aspects. | Cognition in children. | Brain--Growth. | Education--Parent participation.
Classification: LCC LB1062.6 .B47 2020 (print) | LCC LB1062.6 (ebook) | DDC 371.26/4--dc23
LC record available at https://lccn.loc.gov/2019036242
LC ebook record available at https://lccn.loc.gov/2019036243

ISBN: 978-0-367-18645-6 (hbk)
ISBN: 978-0-367-18646-3 (pbk)
ISBN: 978-0-429-19736-9 (ebk)

Typeset in Palatino
by Taylor & Francis Books

MIX
Paper from
responsible sources
FSC
www.fsc.org   FSC® C013056

Printed and bound in Great Britain by
TJ International Ltd, Padstow, Cornwall

For Tristan, Madita Felix and Anna

Contents

Parents can and do make or break their children's education by what they do in the home – the research is clear. But how do you distinguish fact from fake in the ocean of information that's out there. The answer is simpler than you may think.

Neuroscience research is beginning to change what we thought we knew about learning and the news is good for children and adults alike. There is almost nothing we cannot change about our brain, but we need to use it in the right way.

The study of twins and rapid advances since the mapping of the first human genome has brought us closer to beginning to know how far our genes impact on our ability to learn. Reading, exam success and how long you stay in education are all affected. But they aren't responsible for everything.

Children prosper in their education if they come from a home that encourages learning. If parents play their part at home and choose a good preschool, children get a flying start. But how do you choose a good preschool and do the benefits last?

How can you tell that your child is ready for school particularly if they are very young in their school year? Should you try to keep them at nursery longer to let them grow up a little bit more or will this do them no favours in the long run? The evidence reviewed.

A child's first year in the classroom can decide how well they succeed at school. A major long term-study in England has found that only a tiny minority of first year classes are making a positive difference to children's long-term school prospects. Similar evidence also reviewed.

Forget the idea that the type of school your child attends makes a difference. It's a myth. It's the quality of the teaching and how well the school teaches children of all abilities that matters. Setting and streaming works for the brightest but disadvantages everyone else.

When are there too many children in a class, what's the best way of learning to read and how much does a good teacher improve the performance of children in one year? Also, find out why getting your sums wrong is good for you and why 10/10 is not good enough.

The labels attached to many children who struggle at school are suspect or just plain wrong. New research is reviewed and myths debunked. Children with special needs are getting a raw deal at school because they spend too much time with teaching assistants and not enough with teachers.

How do you motivate your children to do their best work and feel good about themselves? Forget bribing them or punishing them. It doesn't work in the long term. You need to provide the right kind of conditions to get the best kind of motivation.

Children are born curious and can ask hundreds of questions a day when they are little but more or less stop asking them when they get to school. Why? Curiosity is the superhero of learning. Children who stay curious do better at school. How can parents keep the curiosity flame alive?

Acknowledgements

We would like to thank all the academics who have worked on the huge range of research we looked at for this book. We would especially like to thank those who gave particularly generously of their time to us – Professors Peter Blatchford, Robert Coe, Stephen Gorard, Robert Plomin, Iram Siraj, Michael Thomas, Peter Tymms, Dieter Wolke, Judy Ireson, and Drs Katharine Bailey and Claire Crawford.

Any mistakes are our own and if there are any, we will be glad to learn from them. By the end of this book you will know that's one of the best ways to learn.

Wendy would also like to thank her partner, the author J.D. Davies, for his unerring support and for his uncanny ability to listen to huge amounts of arcane detail with interest when it isn't even his subject. Judith would like to thank her husband, Peter, for his support throughout a career in education journalism and for his boundless curiosity about the world.

Preface

We've known each other a long time. Since long before we were parents and now, grandparents. We've worked together since the day we first met as reporters on the *Birmingham Post* – Wendy specialising in school education, Judith in higher education. In time we moved to London and Judith became news editor of the *Times Higher Educational Supplement* – as it was then called, and Wendy worked across the corridor in the same building in Gray's Inn Road as a reporter on the *Times Education Supplement*.

After that our paths diverged for a while: Judith worked at *The Observer*, *The Independent* and then *The Independent on Sunday*; Wendy went to *The Guardian*, eventually working with Judith again at *The Independent* before returning to *The Guardian*. We specialised in education, reading reams and reams of education research and writing reams and reams of stories about it. Eventually we both became editors of the TES – Judith first and then Wendy.

As the years have gone by, both of us have noticed how people can be full of questions when they know what our line of expertise is. Probably as doctors get asked for medical advice when they are off duty, walking the dog or dropping off a child at Cubs, we get asked about how to choose a good school, or how much class size matters. Or we listen to worries about a child being late to read, or being in the bottom set for maths, or not getting enough homework.

We've got used to dispensing honest advice, rooted in good research and told without the distancing jargon education is very good at and in a nutshell that is what this book is all about: a go-to guide for anyone who cares about the education of their children or grandchildren – or nephews or nieces, or whatever the relationship is, but told in the way journalists tell important but complex stories – simply and straightforwardly.

Anyone who believes, like we do, that education can be transformative, and that our children and their children deserve the best possible one, should read this. Anyone who wants a book steeped in the truth about what really works in education, without any of the flights of fancy you might pick up from the wilder shores of the mass media and the internet, should read this.

To write it we've interviewed distinguished academics and searched out the best academic evidence from across the world of what works at home, before school and in the classroom and we've also cast our net wider and looked at the latest eye-popping research on the brain and genetics. We've examined the huge importance of motivation and curiosity to developing a love of learning – and so much more

In this noisy, busy world we are exposed to dizzying amounts of information wherever we choose to look. Every couple of days we create as much information as we did from the dawn of human civilisation to 2003, or that's what Eric Schmidt when CEO of Google estimated way back in 2010. Goodness knows how quickly we do it now.

We live in an amazing world, in amazing times, but it is also a world of fake news and social media that tells you only half a story. A world of wildly conflicting information available in a millisecond on your phone or laptop. Being a parent can still be a solitary and confusing experience in all this noise as myth and rumour masquerading as truth float alongside disregarded fact in a never-ending snowstorm of material

Millions of true words have been written about great education research but they mostly reside in arcane specialist journals that most people never see. They are written by academics in academic language which can be like a foreign language to people unused to it. The people who could really benefit from reading it – the parents of children and teenagers – don't get to read it because it's largely inaccessible to them, on many levels.

This book, which we think is a first of its kind, puts that right. It isn't a compendium of every bit of education research that has ever been published but it is a look at the best mainstream research, supported by excellent evidence, that throws light on some of the burning education issues of the day. We hope it will bust some myths and release the fresh air of reality into some of the half-truths and fake facts that abound about education.

We also hope you enjoy it. But, most of all, we hope the children in your lives flourish that little bit more because of it.

Wendy Berliner and Judith Judd
June 2019

Chapter 1

In the beginning

What parents do with their children at home through the age range, is
much more significant than any other factor open to educational influence.
Professor Charles Desforges with Alberto Abouchaar,
The Impact of Parental Involvement, Parental Support and
Family Education on Pupil Achievements and
Adjustment, published in 2003

Normal human instinct makes us want the best for our children because,
at the most primitive and unsentimental level, we want them to survive
and perpetuate our genes or that's at least what a gene centred view of
evolution would argue. But at the deepest level, we love them and want
the best for them.

We know they need enough food to eat, a safe place to live and the
opportunity to learn well. For most people it's really obvious what enough
food to eat means, it's enough of the right kind to help the child thrive
and that includes being neither too fat nor too thin; we know about BMI,
we know what a healthy weight should be. The same goes for a safe place
to live. It has to be somewhere warm and dry and protected from physical
and moral dangers; where parents are unable or unwilling to provide that,
society should step in to support the child.

But what about the opportunity to learn well? There are schools, of
course, where bodies of knowledge deemed significant by society are
transmitted to children by professional teachers, along with the means to
assimilate that knowledge. And parents are bombarded with advice on
how to turn their children into geniuses or at least super learners, some of it
as wildly conflicting as the advice given to parents of at least one new-born
baby we know by two health visitors in the same clinic, sequentially – "Why
not try swaddling?" "No! Don't tell them that. We don't swaddle anymore."

But how do children – and for that matter we adults that care for
them – learn best? What does the research science say? A child born in the
nineteenth century, when national education systems promoting literacy
and numeracy for the masses began to emerge would have had a very

different experience, at least of school learning, than a child of today yet those teachers from the past would have thought they were doing the right thing.

Those nineteenth century children would have been taught by rote how to read and write and do some basic arithmetic in large classes. Only in very rural areas where pressure of numbers was not so heavy would any one-to-one tuition have been possible. Their teachers would more likely have been authoritarian and, at least in more rural areas, untrained – perhaps a literate farm worker who could no longer work on the land because of injury.

The teachers would have been aided in many parts of the world by pupil monitors, abler and slightly older children who had already learned the lesson being delivered. The pupil monitors would sit at the end of the rows and reinforce what the teacher said to the children who didn't quite get what was being barked at them. Poor behaviour, or any difficulty with learning, may well have been met with humiliation, some of it ritual – think of the Dunce's Cap – and or physical violence, a modus operandi that extended long into the twentieth century.

Schools in the developed world are now very different, in part because of how children's place in society has altered for the better but also because of the findings of education research that has been going on world-wide into children's learning for the last 150 years or more.

But research findings that were once seen as a key to good learning for all can be overturned as something else arrives on the scene contradicting it. The last 30 or 40 years are littered with what once were seen as miracle boons for learning but were later dismissed by researchers or scientists as fads of little or no consequence or merit.

Perhaps you remember a brain gym craze at the end of the twentieth century when there were water bottles on primary school children's desks so the children would never get dehydrated. During their lessons, children might do rapid intermittent exercise such as star jumps on the spot to exercise their brains and pressed "brain buttons" – varied parts of their anatomy – to improve blood supply to their brains. This would all help children learn anything faster and more easily said the commercial schemes which schools across the world paid for.

Regardless of the fact that the brain isn't a muscle, so the idea of giving it a quick gym work out seemed somewhat bizarre, it was also an idea which has subsequently been debunked by scientists who understand how blood flows to the brain. Significantly, it has lacked high quality, peer reviewed research supporting it. Peer review involves scientists independent of the research checking on whether an academic study has been set up fairly and correctly and so can pass the tests of quality academic inquiry which will support the credibility of its findings. Yet the idea of gym for your brain was one which quickly caught on and blazed a trail around the world.

You don't need a great memory to remember all this. Today if you google the words brain and gym you will get helpful videos about it. In one from the United States a grown up asks a child to demonstrate his "brain buttons." He obliges by putting his right palm apparently above his heart, as if pledging allegiance to the US flag first thing in the morning at elementary school, rather than putting his finger on the "brain button" in his neck. Maybe he was more patriotic as a result. Or more honest – there is actually Polish research which has found that we are likely to speak more honestly if we put our hand over our hearts. Who knows, maybe the human instinct to do that to persuade the person you are talking to that what you are saying – however unlikely – is true, may be a very old one.

But returning to a much newer idea, gym for the brain, some elements of it make plenty of sense – we all know quick exercise breaks can be a good idea to help anyone doing some concentrated work to improve focus, even if it's just a walk to get a cup of tea from the canteen or the kitchen. We also know water is good in reasonable amount because homo sapiens needs it to keep hydrated. But if reputable scientists say blood circulation doesn't work this way and a learning approach doesn't pass scientific tests for efficacy, in other words there is insufficient scientific proof it works, why do people keep doing it?

Going back to the beginning of this chapter, when it comes to children's education, maybe because teachers and parents want to do their best for children and if something looks like a simple activity that will help children learn better that no-one over the last few thousand years of human evolution has spotted before, they may well want to give it a go – particularly if at least some of it sounds like common sense. And particularly if they go online and find lots of testimonials from people saying how well it has worked for their children. After all, scientists are making potentially life-changing discoveries all the time so why shouldn't this be one of them?

Because experts tell you it isn't.

The elixir of education

In December 2018, Amanda Spielman, the chief inspector of schools in England, launched her annual report as head of the Office for Standards in Education (Ofsted) with advice to teachers and policymakers to get the basics right rather than relying on the latest educational gimmicks. The top basic she cited was early literacy.

The London office of *The Guardian* newspaper reported Spielman advising against "gimmicks like brain gym" and when asked later to elaborate on other gimmicks, she came up with a list including interactive whiteboards, adherence to learning styles – more to come on that later – and a growing enthusiasm for "fidget spinners," a small hand held toy which children can fiddle with that is meant to help concentration. It became a craze. Some schools banned them.

The Guardian report quoted Spielman telling an audience of education professionals and policy experts in London's Westminster, that although many fashionable educational gimmicks had been debunked, there was still an appetite among educationalists to find the next "great white hope." She went on:

> Some policymakers and practitioners are constantly looking for the next magic potion that will infallibly raise standards. Indeed, despite the history of snake oil, white elephants and fashionable gimmicks that have in the main been debunked, there remains a curious optimism that the elixir of education is just around the corner.
>
> But the truth is, we don't need an elixir to help raise standards, because we already have the tried and tested ingredients that we need ... Instead, to put all children on the path to success, the most important thing is to get the basics right, which begins with early literacy.

We'll come back to early literacy but perhaps the education gimmicks have the space to catch on because education researchers as a whole are less good at marketing than commercial organisations. Neither are they often as successful as academics from other key disciplines in communicating and promoting their work and they sometimes struggle to influence schools and policy makers.

Scientists from a leading discipline like medicine, for example, have access to world renowned journals in which peer reviewed research of the highest quality is published. If a piece of research appears in *The Lancet*, for example, and has a particularly populist appeal – a new cure for cancer say, newspapers and broadcasters all over the world will cover it so if you follow general news on a daily basis you are likely to know about it whether you work in the medical profession or not, even if you don't subscribe to *The Lancet*.

That's because *The Lancet*, which is published weekly in London and New York, is the leading general medical journal in the world and journalists know that. If there could be a polar opposite to snake oil, this would be it. It's as far removed as you can get from one of those ads you don't click on that pop up from nowhere on your computer screen telling you how you can banish back pain with a simple method the mystics knew all about. *The Lancet* is an authoritative source that can be trusted implicitly.

How does it do it? It's trusted where it counts. It's one of the oldest publications of its kind in the world. By aiming to publish the highest quality research on all aspects of human health from across the globe, *The Lancet* gives physicians world-wide a reliable source with which they can build their subject knowledge and better help their patients.

Of course, if a researcher chooses to produce fraudulent evidence to back up findings, bad research can end up published even with this trusted seal of approval. This happened when research claiming to prove a link between the MMR (measles, mumps and rubella) vaccination and autism and bowel disease was published in *The Lancet* in 1998. MMR vaccination levels dropped across the world because of the scare that followed. More children got sick; some of them died. In 2010 the research paper was fully retracted by *The Lancet* after the UK's General Medical Council ruled that Andrew Wakefield, the lead author of the research, was guilty of serious professional misconduct during his research for the paper. He was subsequently struck off the register as a UK doctor.

But this inaccurate story – that there was a link between the MMR vaccine and autism and bowel cancer – has developed a life of its own on social media and there are still large numbers of people across the world who believe this particularly pernicious piece of fake news, and refuse to let their children be immunised, despite governments and medical professionals trying to get the truth across.

Millions of children around the world have missed MMR vaccination and cases of highly contagious measles, which can kill or seriously disable, rose by an estimated 300 per cent in the first four months of 2019, compared with the same period in 2018.

There are even now outbreaks of measles in countries like America and the United Kingdom which have high overall vaccination rates because of the refusal of increased numbers of parents to allow their children to be vaccinated. The UK was one of four European countries, along with Greece, Albania and the Czech Republic to lose their "Measle Elimination Status" in August 2019. The US narrowly averted losing its measle elimination status in 2019 with the ending of measles outbreaks in New York City and New York State. Had they lost it, measles would have been endemic in the country for the first time in a generation. Measles breaks out among the unvaccinated, usually young children who can be very hard hit by the illness. It can be a killer. You have to be careful about who you believe.

This kind of falsified research is, thankfully, rare. You have to be very good to be published in *The Lancet*. Only about five per cent of submissions are chosen for publication and the research it publishes is acknowledged as ethical and credible and of the highest quality. There is nothing approaching that as a world resource for general education research.

There are some very fine education journals but they generally specialise and there isn't one for all aspects of human learning with the profile of *The Lancet*. It is reassuring that there is a journal of such prestige for health but learning, and being able to fulfil your potential because of that learning, is arguably as important as being healthy. Regardless, education research is more scattered and less well communicated to the general public despite real efforts by academics, journalists and publishers to tackle this.

Successful communication of education research is often down to the skills of a particularly media savvy education researcher or university press office with an education specialist – and they are thinner on the ground than you would expect. A reduction in the number of skilled journalists covering education in significant parts of the mainstream media, and thus fewer education stories published, hasn't helped either.

But the communication problems are not just because education research findings get a low or non-existent profile in the national mainstream media when they are released. Sometimes complex and nuanced findings are just not properly understood. As with all kinds of new technologies, some early adopters of new education research can be almost messianic about it and the word can quickly spread exponentially by word of mouth that there is a kind of education nirvana abroad, even when the truth is something different. Teachers want the best for the children they teach and they will try things if lots of other teachers swear by them. Can you blame them?

A new education idea can become a craze like those fidget spinner toys. Indeed, there can be a cycle of birth and decay of an idea which begins with early adopters proselytising, continues as large numbers of schools embrace the idea, falters as critics emerge questioning it and ends when it finds its proper place after the original researcher hits back and says their findings have been misinterpreted anyway.

It is also not unheard of for findings from one academic to become conflated with other research because the complexity of a theory is not fully grasped by the people implementing the ideas. Then original ideas can lose their true meaning altogether. The fault need not be in the research but in the wrong-headed application of it. Learning styles which were on Amanda Spielman's list of fads is one of the bigger and more recent ones of these so let's take a look and see what that exemplifies for understanding what really works in education – what the evidence actually is.

Learning styles

The idea of learning styles goes back a long way, perhaps as far as the 1920s when some psychologists classified the three most common ways that people learn new things which, in essence, were:

1 **Looking** – at written words, pictures or graphs, for example, to help you learn;
2 **Hearing** – listening to someone such as a parent or teacher, explaining;
3 **Hands on** – using something you can touch such as beads to learn to count.

If you think you probably use two of these or all three when you learn something new, you are not alone, but the argument was that we have a dominant preference – or think we have.

As the twentieth century wore on there were different theories on how learning styles should be defined (and how many there were) but the common core remained – that people have differences in the way they learn best and teachers who respond to that in the way they teach and the materials they use will be helping children learn more easily.

With the switch to more individualised learning, certainly in schools in the developed world, the last 20 or 30 years of the twentieth century saw the learning styles approach begin to sweep through classrooms, despite a growing backlash from some academics who disputed the value of it. Where teachers embraced it most fully, classrooms were turned into spaces where children had the opportunity to learn in different ways, sitting at a desk, lying on the floor, roaming around the classroom and so on. Some teachers went as far as labelling children with badges saying, for example: "I'm a kinaesthetic learner." We remember going into schools during those years where children would tell us proudly what kind of learner they were.

Yet neuroscientists, people who specialise in the brain and its association with learning and behaviour, said the idea didn't make sense. They branded it a neuromyth. Yes, they said, it was true that the brain processed certain things in different parts of the brain but the brain is so joined up that it didn't matter what part of the brain was processing which input – as soon as one part was activated, other parts would activate too. If, for instance, sight was in use so was hearing – unless you'd jammed noise cancelling headphones on or you had hearing difficulties. That doesn't just make neuroscience sense, of course, it should make common sense to any human being from personal experience.

There are other myths about the brain, for example whether being "right brained" or "left brained" – creative or logical – causes learning differences, but there is lots more to come on that in the following chapter on the brain.

In the case of learning styles perhaps what was most important in the fall from grace was that increasing amounts of research evidence suggested they didn't work. There was no evidence that children taught using their preferred learning style did any better than they did before and there was no evidence that once a child's learning style had been identified, perhaps using one of the many questionnaires you can still find online, that they actually used it solely to learn new things. You may, for instance, think you're an auditory learner but when the methods you use to learn are analysed you might be found to learn in a variety of different ways, not just by hearing an explanation.

When we tried one of the well-known online tests, we both came out as using "multimodal strategies." In other words, we don't just use one approach to learn but all of the ones in that test list – visual, aural, read/write and kinaesthetic.

In the middle of all this brouhaha, enter Howard Gardner, an American development psychologist, and his theory of multiple intelligences laid out in a book he published in 1983 called *Frames of Mind: The Theory of Multiple Intelligences*. This suggested a new model of human intelligence which went beyond the traditional view that we have a single intelligence which can be measured in standardised tests such as the IQ test.

His original theory identified seven intelligences at work and working together in the human brain which were:

Linguistic – able to use words particularly well, both when writing and speaking. Good at writing stories, memorising information, reading and capable of making persuasive speeches;

Logical-mathematical – good at reasoning, recognising patterns, and logically analysing problems. Tends to think conceptually about numbers, relationships, and patterns. Good in areas like maths, science and engineering;

Musical – good at thinking in patterns, rhythms, and sounds. Have a strong appreciation for music and are often good at musical composition and performance;

Bodily kinaesthetic – good at movement and physical control of the body, hand to eye co-ordination and dexterity. Tends to remember by doing and can be particularly good at dance, sport or creating things with their hands – like sculpture;

Spatial – strong in visualising things, understanding three-dimensional images and shapes. Good at things like reading maps, giving good directions, building or engineering projects, jigsaw puzzles and the visual arts;

Interpersonal – good at understanding other people and interacting with them. More able than others to assess how people around them are feeling or what they want. Good at seeing the other person's point of view and in communicating non-verbally, resolving conflict, creating a positive atmosphere;

Intrapersonal – particularly self-aware and self-reflective. More likely than others to understand what is triggering their own feelings and motivations. Enjoys analysing theories and ideas.

Later Gardner was to add an eighth intelligence which he called **naturalist**. People with this type of intelligence are more in tune with nature and often interested in nurturing, exploring the environment, and learning about other species. These individuals are said to be highly aware of even subtle changes to their environments. Gardner, who is Professor of Cognition and Education at the Harvard Graduate School of Education, University of Harvard in the US, says there may be more intelligences.

The theory was a breath of fresh air for teachers because if there were different types of intelligence, it meant their pupils could succeed in the classroom in different ways, not just the academic. It was embraced by teachers in the US, and then across the world, and more and more children found out they were kinaesthetic learners.

But in real life there is no "Get out of jail free" card. Learning styles and multiple intelligences were two very different things but there was perhaps just enough similar language used about them by non-academics to allow the two gradually to become synonymous for some educators in a kind of global game of Chinese Whispers, much to Gardner's intense irritation.

Gardner does believe that teachers should get to know their pupils so that they individualise learning as much as they can for them, and that they should use as many different ways of getting information over as possible to maximise good learning. But he thinks labelling children as a particular kind of learner can do harm rather than good.

There were academics who disagreed with his theory of multiple intelligences and he was willing and able to defend his theory when it came to it – remember it was an academic theory; it wasn't based on experimental research, it was derived from academic thinking on a wide variety of sources by a leading education mind of his generation. Even so it was much harder to lay the ghost floating around the machine that whispered that multiple intelligences *were* learning styles.

In a blog post published by the *Washington Post* in 2013, Gardner took robust issue with the misinterpretation. In defending his own idea of multiple intelligences, he painted a picture of the brain as a series of specialist computers working on different types of information received. What it wasn't was an all-purpose computer deciding how we perform in every part of our lives.

He castigated the proponents of learning styles for their lack of evidence about what the styles amounted to, where they came from, how they could be recognised and how they could be assessed or used in teaching, adding:

> In contrast, there is strong evidence that human beings have a range of intelligences and that strength (or weakness) in one intelligence does not predict strength (or weakness) in any other intelligences. All of us exhibit jagged profiles of intelligences.

What does work?

If academics get misinterpreted and their ideas used wrongly, how do you as an interested parent, grandparent or carer who has a great deal of influence over the children you are involved with, know what works?

How do you navigate the maze of education research – some of it poorly publicised – dodge the snake oil and the white elephants and find out what *really* works in education. What does the most up to date well founded science say about learning?

In this book we will be looking at the things that the best research proves matter to learning as well as at some of the ones that matter perhaps less than you think. We will look at big picture brain development and genetics, basic learning skills, reading, writing and numbers, what age a child should start school, whether academic selection works and how important hot topics like class size and homework really are. Along the way we will be busting quite a few myths but by the end, you should have a clearer picture of what really works in education. What really helps a child to learn well.

We will be doing this through considered analysis of key pieces of education research and theory whether it is new research, standing the test of time research or good to know about research because it throws light on how thinking about learning has evolved. We will be highlighting important, one-off studies as well as milestone investigations done over long periods of time with the same children as they grow up which have thrown brilliant light on learning. We will also look at research on important issues where the evidence conflicts.

We will examine what are known as meta analyses – work which looks at the findings of many independent pieces of research on a similar theme to establish trends over time sometimes in very large numbers of children. We will only turn the spotlight on high quality research from around the world which has used the best possible research standards to set up their investigations and reach conclusions which can be relied upon.

But before we move on to looking at the detail of all that, and because this is principally a book written for parents, we are going to touch on the research about you. Because, from the start, you need to know how important you are to the educational development of your children and that there is much research to prove this. The parent effect is no gimmick. It can be the difference between a child's success or failure at school.

Amanda Spielman, England's Chief Inspector of Schools was right to highlight the importance of early literacy to long term success at school. That is a genuine elixir for all children. If you can't read or write fluently, if you are functionally illiterate in the twenty-first century, you are condemned to the fringes of the human herd as anyone who wasn't good at killing animals or collecting berries probably was in our hunter gatherer past.

Homo sapiens wasn't very special when we evolved, we were probably somewhere in the middle of the food chain. Now we dominate the planet so dangerously that an international group of scientists reported under the auspices of the United Nations in May 2019 that one million of the world's eight million species were at risk of extinction because of us.

We've already denuded the world's mammals, birds, fish and reptiles in the lifetimes of anyone over 50. A WWF (World Wide Fund for Nature) report in October 2018 found that human activity had eradicated 60 per cent of other vertebrates – *since 1970*. We risk our own extinction through climate change and would take much other life with us through our own actions.

How on earth did we manage to do this from not very special beginnings? Almost certainly because of language. Our rise has been aided and abetted by the development of complex language which is at the root of everything we do. Many specialists believe it is our language development, which is unique in the animal world, plus the ability to encode what we talk about – write information down that can be stored and shared – which was most important in getting us as a species to where we are today. It is language, and the ideas we can express with it, that will be needed to put right what we've done wrong.

If literacy is at the heart of everything we do as humans, families and the people who care for children can play a big hand in helping that literacy along, particularly before school, in the way they talk to children and introduce them to the written word in a playful and enjoyable way. We will look at this in greater depth in later chapters.

What about things other than literacy? Let's take a brief first look at some of the big picture stuff – the meta-analysis that can be so useful in discovering the true effects of varying approaches to learning over the years because it takes many pieces of research involving big numbers of children into account.

The largest study of recent years is *Visible Learning* published in 2008 by Professor John Hattie when he was Professor of Education at the University of Auckland in New Zealand. To produce it, Hattie spent 15 years looking at more than 800 separate meta-analyses of research involving millions of children across the world, all related to what works best to stimulate school achievement. By doing this he was able to produce one mega meta-analysis designed to spell out the effects on school achievement of a wide range of things in education from class size, to teachers, to parents via many stops in between.

His conclusions on the impact of parents are revealing. It was, he found, the expectations and aspirations of parents for their children to do well in the education system which had the highest effect. Talking to children about their progress in school and helping with homework, had a moderate effect, while a parental supervision approach – restricting things like watching TV (now it would be screen time as a whole) had the least effect and sometimes a negative effect.

Just to be clear, what Hattie found out about parents from 15 years of researching education research, was that they have their biggest effect on the positive educational outcomes of their children simply by wanting them to do well and expecting them to. They want their children to do well when they go to school and they expect them to. The fact that you are reading this book suggests you are a parent like this.

In homes where it is the norm to think like this and *talk* about it so the children know their parents are fully behind them in their learning, parents can have the biggest effect. And although research shows these ideas are more prevalent in affluent homes, they are also held in the homes of families suffering disadvantage. Parents, grandparents and carers can be a tremendous force for good in the development of children's education potential. We will touch on more of Hattie's findings later in the book.

Second, let's mention the *Effective Pre School, Primary and Secondary Education,* or EPPSE, project, which began following the progress of nearly 3,000 English three-year-olds in different nurseries and preschools in 1997. It was the first major longitudinal study in Europe to investigate the impact of preschool provision on a national sample of children and is now Europe's largest study of its kind. Initially designed to work out what effective preschool and primary schools did, it carried on with the same job when the children reached secondary school, in the end following the children until they were 18. Numerous reports and books have been written using the evidence.

This extraordinary piece of long-term research was undertaken by a team from the universities of London and Oxford and has provided a wealth of information about the importance a good preschool and school experience has on children's learning. But it has also looked carefully at home as well as school, doing some seminal work on the importance of what it dubbed the "home learning environment" – establishing, for example, that children who were read to by their parents in the years before school did better in public examination results as teenagers. Again, we will look at that in more detail in later chapters.

Lastly for now, let's touch on a very significant meta-analysis for parents, grandparents and carers. One which concentrated solely on research into the effect of parental involvement in the education of children and looked at all the research literature to that date in an effort to try to establish the effect of parents.

Undertaken by Professor Charles Desforges with Alberto Abouchaar, published in 2003 and now seen as a landmark study, *The Impact of Parental Involvement, Parental Support and Family Education on Pupil Achievements and Adjustment* was carried out for the UK government's Department for Education and Skills in London.

One of its most striking findings was that parents could have such a positive impact on how well their children did at school and also on how well they behaved were in class, that they could cancel out the effect of them going to a "bad" school. The scale of the impact was present in all social classes and all ethnic groups.

Put simply, some parents could have more impact than some schools on their children's achievements – regardless of how advantaged or disadvantaged they were.

What were these parents doing? What did the researchers find that was so important? One of the things "safely established" by the researchers, as they put it, was that "parental involvement in the form of interest in the child and manifest in the home as parent-child discussions can have a significant positive effect on children's behaviour and achievement." In other words, parents who took an interest in their child and talked to them in a meaningful way, not just shouted instructions at them, had children who did better at school. Not exactly rocket science but not every parent actually does it. And does it remind you of what Hattie found?

Taking an interest in your child shouldn't really need any further explanation and neither should the importance of talking to them but it can benefit from some unpacking and perhaps the best way of tackling it is looking at one highly significant piece of research into the importance of conversation, or talk, in the home.

Talk

In the later years of the last millennium, a pair of American researchers frustrated by the lack of progress in language skills being made at school by poor children, despite high quality learning programmes designed to help them, decided to switch the spotlight into the home for their next study. Their theory was that if schools weren't reducing the skills gap between the poor and the affluent, despite having the best tools for the job, something may be happening at home that was interfering.

In an ambitious project the research team listened in on the conversations of 42 families, selected from all kinds of social backgrounds, to see what adults were saying to their children so they could work out how the home was impacting on those all-important language skills. They began their fly-on-the-wall project when the children were seven-month-old babies and they kept going back with their recording equipment for one hour a week for three years.

What they found was the most alarming language gap. On average, the children in the most affluent homes had heard at least *30 million words more by their fourth birthdays* than children in the least affluent homes.

This is what the researchers found:

- The average child in a professional family heard *2,153* words per waking hour;
- The average child in a working-class family heard *1,251* words per hour;
- The average child in a family on welfare benefits heard *616* words per hour.

Children in the most affluent families were hearing more than three times the amount of words than children in the poorest families.

What they were hearing made a difference to what the children were saying as they grew. The children in the most affluent homes were typically adding around *two new words a day* as they began to build their vocabulary between their second and third birthdays; working class children were adding *a word a day* over the same period and the children from the poorest families were adding about *a word every two days*.

Moreover, the children in the most affluent homes were hearing a lot more praise than the poorer children. Children of professional families heard, on average, six encouraging comments for every discouraging one, while children of families living on social benefits got one encouraging comment for every two discouraging ones. They heard a lot of discouraging comments.

And the speaking style of parents was different with more affluent parents adopting a more conversational style with the child and poorer parents using language more often just to give instructions. Significantly though, the child with the largest vocabulary in their study came from a lower socio-economic class family with a highly interactive conversational style

By the age of three, up to 98 per cent of the words the children were using were derived from their parents' vocabularies. The children's speech patterns were very similar to their parents too and, crucially, so were the numbers of words they used. If their parents didn't go in for long sentences and use lots of vocabulary, neither did they.

And when the researchers checked on the children when they were nine and ten years-old they found that their progress at three years-old on various vocabulary, language development, and reading comprehension measures was highly indicative of their progress six years later. Those early conversations – or lack of them – were affecting their progress at school. Those with less conversation in the home were doing less well at school.

The researchers, and other researchers who have built on their work, suggest that this word deficit may explain, at least partially, the longstanding general underachievement of children in less affluent families in the American education system, something that bedevils the UK and other developed education systems too.

That's what good educational research does – it gets a handle on some of the more intractable learning problems, allows other researchers to build on the work and encourages solutions to be sought.

It doesn't solve everything immediately. It's more than 20 years since that language research was published which became known as the "30 million word catastrophe" from an article about it written by the researchers Betty Hart and Todd R. Risley from Kansas State University in the United States. There are always outliers but poor children are still not doing anything like as well at school as children from affluent families.

However, programmes that seek to develop language preschool, for example, continue to be developed and refined as more research becomes available.

Early development in the first five years of life lays the foundations for lifelong learning – multiple research projects confirm that. Children who are read to regularly by adults and talked to conversationally do better at school and in their public examinations.

Good preschools help but children spend far more time in the care of their parents and other carers than they do at preschool. If their parents and carers are not talking to them, encouraging their language and intellect by having conversations with them and taking an interest in what interests them, children lose out on golden and life enhancing opportunities right from the word go. They arrive at school behind the children whose parents and carers did all those things and most of them never catch up. They are more likely to leave school at the earliest possible opportunity, often with poor qualifications which affects far more than the jobs they can do.

People with higher education don't just on average earn more, they are healthier and live longer. They have higher levels of trust in society, are more interested in politics and less likely to be hostile to immigrants – research confirms all this and more about the positive effects of a good education. It all starts with you the parents and your backups in the family – perhaps the grandparents or the carers you use to look after your children when you are at work.

Look back at the quote at the beginning of this chapter. You really matter. You are your child's first and longest serving teacher so talk to them, read to them until they can read themselves and answer their questions or they will stop asking them and learning from the answers. And use the following chapters to understand the best of educational research and help you, and them, along the exciting road ahead, starting with a look at something we all use to learn with – the brain.

References

Weale, S. (2018) 'Ofsted warns teachers against gimmicks such as Brain Gym.' *The Guardian*, 4 December. Available from www.theguardian.com/education/2018/dec/04/ofsted-teachers-gimmicks-brain-gym-schools (downloaded 6 June 2019).

Gardner, H. (1983) *Frames of Mind: The Theory of Multiple Intelligences*. New York: Basic Books.

Gardner, H. (2013) '"Multiple intelligences" are not "learning styles".' *Washington Post blog. Available from*www.washingtonpost.com/news/answer-sheet/wp/2013/10/16/howard-gardner-multiple-intelligences-are-not-learning-styles/?noredirect=on&utm_term=.ed196cfa963f (downloaded 6 June 2019).

'IPBES 2019 global assessment report on biodiversity and ecosystem services.' (2019) *UN News*. Available from https://news.un.org/en/story/2019/05/1037941 (downloaded 6 June 2019).

World Wide Fund for Nature. 'Our living planet report 2018.' (2018) Available from www.wwf.org.uk/updates/living-planet-report-2018 (downloaded 6 June 2019).

Hattie. J.A.C. (2009) *Visible Learning: A Synthesis of Over 800 Meta-Analyses Relating to Achievement*. London and New York: Routledge.

Taggart, B., Sylva, K., Melhuish, E., Sammons, P. and Siraj, I. (2015) 'How pre-school influences children and young people's attainment and developmental outcomes over time: effective pre-school, primary and secondary education project (EPPSE 3–16+).' Department for Education. Available from https://assets.publishing.service.gov.uk/government/uploads/system/uploads/attachment_data/file/455670/RB455_Effective_pre-school_primary_and_secondary_education_project.pdf.pdf (downloaded 6 June 2019).

Sylva, K., Melhuish, E., Sammons, P.Siraj, I., Taggart, B. with Smees, R., Tóth, K., Welcomme, W. and Hollingworth, K. (2014) 'Students' educational and developmental outcomes at age 16: effective pre-school, primary and secondary education (EPPSE 3–16) project research report.' Department for Education. Available from https://assets.publishing.service.gov.uk/government/uploads/system/uploads/attachment_data/file/351496/RR354_-_Students__educational_and_developmental_outcomes_at_age_16.pdf (downloaded 6 June 2019).

Desforges, C. and Abouchaar, A. (2003) *The Impact of Parental Invodlvement, Parental Support and Family Education on Pupil Achievements and Adjustment*. Department for Education and Skills. Available from https://dera.ioe.ac.uk/6305/1/rr433.pdf (downloaded 6 June 2019).

Hart, B. and Risley, T.R. (1995) *Meaningful Differences in the Everyday Experience of Young American Children*. Baltimore, MD: Paul H. Brookes Publishing Company.

Hart, B. and Risley, T.R. (2003) 'The early catastrophe: the 30 million word gap.' *American Educator*, Vol. 27, No. 1, pp. 4–9.

Chapter 2

The brain

Individual brains, like individual bodies, are different from each other but there is almost nothing that you cannot improve or change.
Sarah-Jayne Blakemore, University College, London.

The idea that the growth of your brain is in your hands is thrilling.
Carol Dweck, Professor of Psychology Stanford University, United States.

Today's grandparents grew up with the idea that people reached the peak of their intellectual achievement in their late teens. As a university student, one of us remembers gloomily discussing with other students the idea that our brain cells were starting to "die" as she came to the end of her degree course.

There was more to this than ill-informed speculation. Professor Chris Frith, Emeritus Professor of Psychology at University College, London, recalled being taught as a science student that the brain stopped developing around the age of 16 and that the neurons (nerve cells that carry electrical impulses and process information – a kind of messaging system) began to die: no more structural change in the brain was possible. No new cells grew. No new connections between them were made and the ability to learn new skills and information therefore diminished. Adult brains were in a downward spiral.

Some of the most remarkable discoveries of recent years have shown how mistaken this was. Professor Frith is sometimes called the founder of modern neuroscience, and his research and that of his fellow neuroscientists has helped overturn theories about the brain held by their predecessors. Thanks to advances in scanning technology, scientists are now able to view the inside of our brains through "neuroimaging." Just as MRI body scanners have revolutionised medicine, so these techniques have revolutionised what we know about the brain.

Neuroscience, the exploration of how the brain and nervous system function, is about much more than brain scanning. It is a multidisciplinary branch of biology that includes anatomy, psychology and mathematical modelling. One of the main findings of modern neuroscience is that the brain is much more flexible and adaptable than we thought. The belief that 20-year-olds' brains are already starting to deteriorate has been replaced by the belief that we can go on learning throughout our lives. We are beginning to discover more about the process of learning and that may have big implications for how we educate children and adults.

The brain is plastic

The term "plasticity" used by neuroscientists is a way of describing the fact that the brain changes all the time and everything we do changes it. When people are talking to friends, looking out of the window or even sleeping, neurons fire. When neurons fire together, the connections between them become stronger, "neurons that fire together wire together." This process does not stop after we become adults but carries on throughout life. The brain is able to adapt to the environment and to retain memories so that our experience prepares us for the future.

The research suggests that, though changes continue in adults, there are particularly important or "sensitive" periods for brain development. These are not confined to childhood. The brain continues to change into the mid-twenties and possibly even the early thirties.

The latest studies of adolescents have shown that this is a particularly significant time. Professor Sarah-Jayne Blakemore of the Institute of Cognitive Neuroscience at University College, London has found the parts of the brain that are still developing are those that control self-awareness, impulses, feelings of guilt and embarrassment and the ability to put things in perspective. It may be the case that changes in adolescents' brains affect their ability to learn.

There is certainly no evidence to support the old theory that you cannot learn effectively after the teenage years. Blakemore has also done research that shows that older teenagers and young adults improve their maths and reasoning skills more quickly than younger teenagers if they have some training. The study of more than 600 teenagers and young adults aged between 11 and 33 compared the effect of training between three age groups. They were given three tests and then 20 days of online training before they were tested again. On one test – face recognition – the performance of the three age groups remained the same after training but on non-verbal reasoning and number judgments those in the older groups progressed more rapidly after training.

The brain's plasticity does decrease with age for some skills. For instance, the mastery of a second language, its vocabulary and grammar, is easier before puberty but changes in the wiring of the brain continue for a surprisingly long time. Even after adolescence, concentration on particular activities causes "plasticity" as the brain adapts to new circumstances.

The best-known example of this is a study of London taxi drivers from University College London. The drivers aim to acquire The Knowledge, or a mental map of the complicated web of the city's streets, so that they can earn the right to drive a black cab. They learn 320 routes covering 25,000 streets and 20,000 landmarks. The research used magnetic resonance to examine their brains and found that the volume of their hippocampi, a complex part of the brain that plays an important part in memory and learning, was larger than that of a control group of non-taxi drivers, including bus drivers who took the same routes every day. Those taxi drivers with the most experience had the largest hippocampi.

Other studies have shown similar findings. When researchers compared the brains of 20 professional musicians with 20 amateur musicians and 20 adults who had never played an instrument with brain imaging scans, they found that the "grey matter" was largest in the professional musicians. Grey matter affects, among other skills, movement and muscle control, seeing, hearing and memory. The amateurs had the next largest grey matter and the non-musicians the smallest. All the musicians were keyboard players.

Studies of violinists have found that the part of their brains that controls the fingers of their left hands is larger. By contrast, the researchers noticed no enlargement of the area of the brain that controls the right hand, which holds the bow and requires no special finger movements. Non-musicians do not show these differences.

Because the brain continues to be plastic in adults, learning really can be lifelong. Many studies show that the parts of the brain used for our senses and movement can adapt, depending on how they are used, in only five days. Brain cells can change their function because of use. When blind people read Braille, the part of their brain that would normally be used for vision is used for touch. The brain is capable of "relocation of function" – brain cells change the specific job they perform depending on their usage. This strategy makes use of part of the cortex that would otherwise be redundant.

There are limits to the brain's plasticity. New skills need to be practised if they are to be maintained. We need to use them or lose them. The researchers found that, when taxi drivers retired, their ability to navigate London's streets declined. And about half of taxi drivers failed The Knowledge test. Some skills, such as the fine motor skills required for playing the piano, are harder to acquire as we age.

A Royal Society review of research in 2011 concluded:

Plasticity tends to decrease with age and this is particularly evident when we consider learning of a second language: mastery of speech sounds and grammatical structure is generally better in those introduced to a second language before puberty compared to later in life.

Adults and children learn in different ways. Adults build on their previous knowledge and skills: for instance, a chess player might use their knowledge of chess to learn to play another game. Children's brains are like sponges, absorbing information and experiences.

Despite these caveats, neuroscientists' discoveries provide new opportunities for anyone involved in education and underline the importance of giving children the right support at home and at school.

Is three too late?

I do believe that the brain has a certain clump of neurons firing, and that by the time [my baby] is five, it will be too late.
American consumer of educational toys for babies

The first three years of a child's life are uniquely important because this is the most sensitive period for brain development.
Zero to Three, early years movement in the US

Some of the biggest misconceptions to be overturned by the research into brain plasticity relate to the first years of a child's life. Neuroscience confirms that infants' brains are very active. They grow rapidly and produce twice as many synapses (connections between nerve cells or neurons) as adults' brains. As they grow older, the synapses are "pruned."

Scientists originally assumed that the development of the brain in humans was the same as in monkeys whose brains are mature by the age of three (Rakic, 1995). The assumption had a big impact on parents, teachers and policy-makers and is reflected in the first two quotations at the beginning of this section.

The first is from a mother, an educated professional, who spoke to journalist Alissa Quart for an article published in *The Atlantic* magazine in 2006 about the commercial exploitation of the belief that young children need as much stimulation as possible if they are to succeed in life. The article, called "Extreme Parenting," describes the many companies producing toys that claim to boost children's learning. It quotes the marketing pitch on the cover of one DVD for babies: "Did you know that you can actually help to enhance the development of your baby's brain? The first 30 months of life is the period when a child's brain undergoes its most critical stages of evolution."

One of the most quoted examples of attempts to improve babies' brain power is the result of a research study carried out in 1993 by Gordon Shaw and Frances Rauscher of the University of California at Irvine which built on the findings of a preliminary pilot study which suggested that music training of three-year-olds provided long-term enhancements of nonverbal cognitive abilities.

A group of college students listened to ten minutes of a Mozart sonata, a relaxation tape, or silence. Then they took a paper-folding-and-cutting test. Those who had listened to Mozart performed better than those who had not. Shaw and Rauscher concluded that listening to Mozart improved the students' short-term spatial thinking.

Though no other study managed to replicate the findings, companies made classical music videos and suggested they should be played to babies or even foetuses. *The Mozart Effect* became a trademark. An article in *Nature* magazine in 1999 by a professor of psychology who had tried and failed to replicate the findings made a persuasive case against Shaw and Rauscher's findings. It was headlined "Prelude or Requiem for the Mozart Effect" and it proved to be a requiem. The idea that listening to Mozart improved your brainpower was laid to rest.

The second quote is from the Zero to Three movement in the United States, which aims to change parents' attitudes to early years development and to shape government policy. The Centre for Educational Neuroscience (CEN), part of the University of London, brings together researchers from Birkbeck, University College and the Institute of Education, and has this to say about Zero to Three:

> There is ... a general idea that the first three years of life are a critical period for children's brain development, and that deprivation over those years will result in persistent deficits in cognitive, emotional and even physical health. This idea was first propounded in the late 90s in America, and became the "zero to three movement." The policy implications have been huge, especially in the States, and the idea is based on some key findings in neuroscience, and yet it's still not clear cut what's true and what's hype.

In the UK, successive governments have invested money in early years, funding more and more nursery places first for four-year-olds, then for three-year-olds and, most recently for two-year-olds. Few people question the advantages of a good preschool education and the UK has been slow compared with other European countries to address the needs of this age group.

But researchers are now pointing to the need for high quality education and sensitive parenting at every stage of a child's life. Paul Howard Jones, Professor of Neuroscience and Education at the University of Bristol, has pointed to flaws in an economic analysis that suggests that it is more cost effective to invest money in early years education than in later periods of schooling. Will the lack of stimulation in the early years really permanently damage a child's brain development?

The CEN analysis says that neuroscience supports the idea that there are "sensitive periods" – a time in a young animal's life when the brain and behaviour are especially susceptible to change. Birds, for instance, must learn their own particular song early in life and researchers observe sensitive periods in all young animals. But that does not mean if we do not learn things early, we cannot learn them at all.

Professor Sarah-Jayne Blakemore says that the study of monkeys' brains may be misleading because monkeys reach sexual maturity at around the age of three. Humans are not sexually mature until 12 or 13 so the period of rapid brain development in monkeys may be shorter. Professor Michael Thomas, Director of the Centre for Educational Neuroscience, Birkbeck College at the University of London, says it is mistake to focus mainly on the early years.[1] He says:

> You create potential in the early years but you need to reinforce it in primary pupils and teenagers.

The comforting message for parents is that, as the CEN analysis puts it, "to go wrong you have to go really wrong." Only the most basic human skills have sensitive periods. So, a child would have to experience extreme neglect to miss out on them.

Professor Thomas says:

> If you put a child in a dark cupboard, can it still see when it comes out? If you restrain movement by tying its feet together, will it be able to move normally? These are the skills we are talking about. So, if your child has a squint or needs a cochlear implant in an ear, get it fixed early. Otherwise good enough parenting really is good enough. If you give a child more stimulation it doesn't mean that they will make huge gains.

Some specialised skills, such as the fine motor skills required for becoming a top gymnast or pianist are best taught early, he says:

> But you have to take the risk that intense coaching will make them unhappy, that they may be more likely to have broken relationships or mental health problems in the future. Parents may feel it is more important to make young children feel emotionally and socially secure.

Blakemore says that the stimulus a toddler needs is available in ordinary homes. Studies of rats in normal and deprived environments appear to show that those deprived of toys, wheels, ladders and playmates were not as clever (for example, quick to navigate mazes) as those kept in "normal" conditions. But the normal conditions were very similar to those rats'

1   The quotations in this chapter from Professor Michael Thomas are taken from an interview with Judith Judd, 6 October, 2018.

experience in the wild. There is no evidence to show that young children benefit from extra enrichment activities.

Patterns on curtains, colours in pictures or on mugs and plates and everyday objects such as saucepans and wooden spoons to bang are enough to ensure a child's brain develops normally. The interactive alphabet games and videos for babies described by Alissa Quart are unnecessary. What matters is talk and communication between child and adult. Playing with a baby helps. Hothousing doesn't. The evidence about this age group suggests that what really matters is not learning but loving. A child who feels emotionally secure is well placed for a life of learning.

The story of the Romanian orphans

One of the reasons that researchers are able to evaluate the importance of emotional security for young children is the result of a tragedy. After the fall of the Ceausescu regime in Romania in the early 1990s, people from across the world offered homes to some of the thousands of children who were found in the country's orphanages. When they were rescued, the orphans were dirty, under-nourished and starved of love and attention. They had no toys to play with and no adult had bothered to talk to them. They were living in a state of extreme neglect and deprivation.

What did that mean for their future? Were they irreparably damaged emotionally and intellectually? A group of researchers at Southampton University and at King's College, London began to investigate. They followed 165 Romanian orphans who were adopted by UK families and who had spent between two weeks and 43 months in institutions.

The UK families were comfortably off, stable and caring. The study used questionnaires, tests and interviews with the children and their parents to compare them with 52 children who were adopted by similar families in the UK. This was done at the ages of six, 11 and 15 and finally, when the group were young adults, at the age of 22 and 25. It monitored the children's social and emotional development and their progress in learning. It also compared those who were adopted before the age of six months with those who were adopted later.

In their new, stable families, the Romanian children improved rapidly but a substantial minority of those who were adopted after the age of six months had problems that were very uncommon in the UK children such as autism, relating to others, difficulty concentrating and hyperactivity. A third of these children needed special help and their problems continued as young adults even though they had lived in caring families for 20 years. Equally, a substantial minority of the Romanian adoptees were coping just as well as the UK children at the age of 11.

More than one in five of the adopted children who spent more than six months in Romanian institutions had no mental health problems throughout their young lives. However, the research does show that it is difficult for even the most committed adults to compensate for an extended period of extreme social and emotional deprivation in early life.

The picture for the development of children's learning is somewhat different. As children, most of the adopted orphans who lived in Romanian institutions for more than six months had an IQ of less than 80, but this recovered to normal levels by the time they were young adults. That suggests that the deprivation of their early years was not a permanent barrier to their ability to learn. The findings give strong support to the idea discussed earlier in this chapter that the brain continues to change and develop well into adulthood. Writing in the medical journal, *The Lancet*, the report's authors wrote:

Our results provide compelling evidence of long-term neuroplasticity in human beings.

For parents, the Romanian orphans' story emphasises the need to provide the love and support that will help children to become emotionally secure adults who can form relationships with adults and their peers. Every parent wants their child to do well at school and hopes to lay the foundation for a life of learning but hothousing and constant stimulation with educational toys are not necessary.

Myths about neuroscience and education

Discoveries about the brain may have exciting implications for education. Education depends on the mental process of learning so research into the brain must surely be useful in finding out how children learn and how teachers should shape their lessons? The idea is enticingly simple but it has led to some unfortunate consequences. Teachers have been eager to provide a scientific basis for their classroom practice but they have sometimes misunderstood scientific evidence or twisted it to fit their own views, as we have already touched on in the opening chapter.

A number of myths about the brain – neuromyths – have been widely accepted. Neuroscientists have begun to challenge these and to work with teachers to find the best way to apply their findings in the nursery, the classroom and beyond.

Paul Howard Jones collaborated with academics in four other countries (the UK, the Netherlands, Turkey, Greece and China) to survey teachers and established that many neuromyths ran across cultures (2014). These are some examples:

Myth

- You only use 10 per cent of your brain – believed by around half of teachers;

- Children learn better in their preferred learning style (e.g. by listening, looking or doing) – believed by more than 90 per cent;
- Differences between left brain and right brain help explain developmental differences among learners – believed by 70 per cent in China and more than 90 per cent in the UK;
- Children are less attentive after sugary drinks and snacks – believed by around half (57 per cent in the UK);
- In the UK, 29 per cent of teachers even believed that drinking less than between six and eight glasses of water a day causes the brain to shrink, though for Chinese teachers the figure was only 5 per cent.

Fact

- Water makes you cleverer

Professor Howard Jones says that the myth that drinking six daily glasses of water boosts children's performance has no foundation in scientific fact but some studies have shown that dehydration can affect the ability to learn.

- You only use 10 per cent of your brain

You can see the attraction of the idea that we only use 10 per cent of our brains. Wouldn't it be fantastic if we could work out how to use just a fraction more? If one part of the brain were damaged surely the remainder could easily cope with the loss? Sadly, not. It is true that different parts of the brain control movement, memory, language and other functions but these are all closely integrated. Loss in one area causes damage. Images of sleeping brains show that all the different areas are active. This myth seems to have arisen from a misunderstanding of early work by neuroscientists who said that they only knew 10 per cent of how the brain worked.

People have different learning styles

The most popular myth and the one that has had most influence on how children are taught is the one about learning style which we remarked on in the opening chapter. It seems to arise from the neuroscientific fact, mentioned above, that different parts of the brain are responsible for different functions, in this case, seeing, hearing and doing. If you discover which part of a child's brain works best, that suggests you can tailor your teaching to suit it by developing visual, auditory and kinaesthetic styles.

In the early 2000s, the idea even won government approval in England: "Through an understanding of learning styles, teachers can exploit pupils' strengths and build their capacity to learn," said a Department of Education pamphlet. The department no longer supports this as the comments of Amanda Spielman, Chief Inspector of Schools for England, in the opening chapter make clear.

In some schools, children wore those labels we talked about earlier showing whether they were visual, auditory or kinaesthetic learners. Auditory learners supposedly learned best by listening to the teacher rather than looking at a diagram on the board, for example, while kinaesthetic learners absorbed information and skills more quickly through an activity such as a role play.

More recent studies suggest that different parts of the brain are closely connected and cannot be separated in this way. There may be visual and auditory areas but we do not fully understand what happens to information after the brain receives it.

In 2004, a team of researchers at Newcastle University led by Professor Frank Coffield found that none of the most popular learning styles theories were supported by independent research or by laboratory studies. A report from the thinktank Demos, by respected academics on brain-based learning found that the evidence was "highly variable."

It may be true that preferences exist and that teachers should consider a mix of styles. That is all.

The right brain is creative. The left is logical.

Are you right-brained or left-brained? If you are the former, the thinking goes, you might describe your house as cosy, bright and welcoming. If you are the latter you might say that it has three bedrooms, gas central heating and faces south-west. You can go online to do one of the many brain tests that will tell you which you are. We both tried this. One of us was congratulated on using both sides of her brain and told that she was 60 per cent right-brained and 40 per cent left-brained; the other was congratulated on using both halves equally. Does that make us unusual? Read on to see why it doesn't.

Teachers are sometimes advised to find out whether their pupils are right-brained or left-brained. Some American universities even supply a test for this so that teachers can discover at the start of a course how their students' brains work. Examples abound of right-brain and left-brain teaching techniques: for right-brain use plenty of visual aids, for left just lecture and use abstract concepts, play music for the former as they are intuitive and like to be in touch with feelings, keep the room quiet for the latter.

So why does Professor Howard Jones list this concept among his myths? As we have seen, different parts of the brain are responsible for different functions but there is no evidence that any particular area influences personality traits or causes some people to behave more intuitively and others more rationally.

A 2013 study at the University of Utah showed that activity is similar on both sides of the brain and is not related to personality. Researchers looked at brain scans of more than 1,000 young people between the ages of seven and 29 and divided different areas of the brain into 7,000 regions to find out whether one side of the brain was more active than the other. It wasn't.

The brain's responses depend on networks of neurons (nerve cells) working with chemicals. If you damage one site, its function may be lost, temporarily or permanently, but it does not mean that that site alone was responsible for a particular function.

Neuroscience and education

Some brain-based ideas and techniques in education that claim to be based on neuroscience are either the result of misinterpretation or rest on shaky scientific foundations. But neuroscience has also begun to point to some new opportunities to improve education for people of all ages. Do people learn better if they are physically fit? Would teenagers get higher exam grades if they were allowed to sleep in longer and start school later in the day? Why do our minds go blank when we are stressed? Why can we remember that we are frightened of spiders but not the name of the capital of Hungary?

The idea that neuroscience can help to address educational problems has its critics but potential connections between neuroscience and education are being explored throughout the world. Professor Michael Thomas believes that neuroscience can support teaching and learning in the way that science helped to change public health in the nineteenth century, a change from trial and error experiments (plus some fads and quackery) to an understanding of biology, anatomy and biochemistry.

He expects neuroscience to explain how learning ability changes as we get older and whether training in one skill is likely to transfer to another because the same mechanism of the brain is involved. It will also address the way in which physical fitness, sleep and stress affect the brain. None of this is a quick fix. Knowledge about the implications of neuroscience for education is in its infancy but some neuroscientists are optimistic about the possibilities.

A healthy brain

So, what do we know so far? Professor Thomas has reviewed the evidence and says:

> The brain is a biological organ. It does better when the body gets nutrients, sleeps well, is free of stress and does exercise.

Sleep is vital if the brain is to consolidate knowledge. We know that sleep is connected to the hippocampus, the part of the brain where episodic memories (the collection of past personal experiences that happened at a particular time or place such as a birthday party) are stored but there is only room there for around 50,000 memories and if they all remained it would fill up in about three months. While we sleep, the brain transfers some of these memories out of the hippocampus so that they can be stored more permanently. While we sleep, we take out important memories and we reinforce skills. So, sleeping well is important especially when we're learning something new.

Professor Thomas cites the example of a study of adolescents who had only five or six hours sleep for several nights in a row and then found it harder to use "working" or short-term memory, and therefore to reason. He says:

> We always knew that it makes sense to have a good night's sleep – it's the kind of thing our grandmothers told us – but neuroscience is helping us to find out how much sleep and how it helps learning.

Other studies show that teenagers have a different sleep pattern from many adults - they are biologically predisposed to go to sleep around midnight and are not fully awake until between 9 and 10 a.m. Researchers at the University of Oxford are tracking around 32,000 GCSE students to monitor the effects of a 10 a.m. school start. A small trial at Monkseaton High School in North Tyneside found that the percentage of pupils getting five good GCSEs rose from 34 to 50 per cent when school start times were shifted from 08:50 to 10:00. Among disadvantaged pupils, the increase was from about 19 per cent to about 43 per cent.

Exercise is also good for the brain. Regular and intense bursts of physical exercise during the school day improve academic performance and test scores.

Meditation, studies suggest, improves behaviour, though there is no published research yet on the effect of meditation on academic achievement,.

Pollution may delay children's ability to think about and understand the world, recent research on 2,700 primary school children in 39 schools in Barcelona (Sunyer, et al. 2015) has suggested.

Adolescence is a time when the brain is still developing – as we have seen, this is one of neuroscience's big discoveries. We used to think that children's IQ stayed the same after the age of ten, justifying the 11-plus examination used in the past to decide which type of school you should go to. Now we know that IQ scores go up and down during adolescence and that these fluctuations are mirrored by changes in the brain so they are not simply the result of errors in the tests or in motivation. It is possible that poor performance in some skills may be explained by the nature of the developing teenage brain.

Neuroscience is also supplying new insights into the reasons why teenagers sometimes worry and puzzle their parents and teachers. The region of the brain associated with reward develops more quickly than the ones protecting people against social anxiety and risk-taking so adolescents may understand that risk-taking is rewarding and be unable to stop themselves taking a risk.

Sarah-Jayne Blakemore suggests that this may explain why intelligent adolescents ignore advice about drug-taking or drinking too much. It may also explain why the fear of being excluded from a group is so strong at this age and why teenagers are particularly vulnerable to peer pressure. It may be that schools should look for more ways of involving peers and mentors more actively in learning.

How we learn

The brain involves eight systems of learning and each is different. That's why people are much more likely to forget the name of a capital city than they are that they are frightened of dogs or spiders says Professor Thomas.

Phobias involve the amygdala, the part of the brain that detects threats, and which responds to emotions rather than facts and it does not forget. Factual learning is stored in the cortex and works more on a "use it or lose it" basis. Says Professor Thomas:

> Each system has a different rate of learning. I learned to ski in three weekly sessions at the ages of 15, 26 and 30. You couldn't learn a language like that because there is a different rate of consolidation.

Another region of the brain helps us acquire skills by watching other people so imitation is a useful learning tool. Observing someone performing, say, a dance step, involves the same part of the brain as performing the action oneself. So, your brain is mimicking the step even if you are not. That is obviously important in learning to dance, act or play sport but it may mean that we are generally inclined to imitate people around us. Some neuroscientists believe that children may copy the values and beliefs of those who care for them or teach them. Parental example may play a big part in children's development.

Neuroscience shows us that you can improve skills associated with different regions of the brain by training them. The London taxi drivers who memorised the intricate map of London streets are one example of this. But training one area of the brain does not improve the skills associated with the others. As Professor Thomas says:

> You get better at what you are practising but training someone in the rote learning of poetry doesn't improve your ability to do anything else.

Some studies have examined the thinking and learning skills that are used across the school curriculum, for example in literacy and numeracy, by investigating "executive function," the ability to get things done or manage one's thoughts, actions and emotions.

Researchers know that "executive function" is a good predictor of academic success and accounts for up to a third of the difference in achievement in maths and reading scores. It also influences children's readiness for school, determining whether they can follow instructions, hold a pencil and join in lessons.

The latest evidence suggests that it is possible to improve executive function skills in young and old but it is not clear how long the benefit lasts or how much they can be improved (Diamond and Ling, 2016). Their review of the research in this area also concluded that the chances of improvement were greatest if people's social, emotional and physical needs were also met. The brain, they said, was not isolated from the rest of us. Everything that makes us human is connected.

That, Professor Thomas says, is one of the key messages about learning:

> Learning depends on the emotional context. Relationships between people matter. That is why children develop maths anxiety. There are hundreds of teachers in primary schools who are not confident about their ability to teach maths. They pass on that anxiety.

However much we understand about the brain, the way that parents and teachers relate to young people seems likely to remain at the heart of education. We will come back later to this in the book when we look at motivation.

Neuroscience and the classroom

It is not easy to translate research into how learning happens in the brain into higher achievement in the classroom but some recent projects have begun to explore the possibilities.

In 2014 the Education Endowment Foundation, a London-based charity that aims to raise the academic attainment of the poorest children, and the Wellcome Trust, set up a series of collaborative projects between educators and neuroscientists. One of these is the investigation mentioned earlier into the effect of sleep on teenagers' achievement. Another is to study whether it is possible to train primary children in "inhibitory control," that is the ability to control natural but incorrect responses, for instance resisting the temptation to eat a cream cake while you are on a diet. This ability to control yourself is important in learning maths and science too.

Counter intuition – the earth is round

To progress in maths and science, children have to learn "inhibitory control" and that things are not always as they seem. Everyday knowledge can be misleading. Our ancestors thought the earth was flat. Maths can be confusing in a similar way. We learn that four is bigger than two but a quarter is smaller than a half.

A team from Birkbeck College and the Institute of Education in London, led by Professor Denis Mareschal, is investigating whether you can train pupils to suspend pre-existing beliefs, for example, the idea that a heavy object falls more quickly than a light one.

Researchers gave a series of 48 maths and science tests to 90 pupils at a secondary school. Pupils read a statement about science or maths and pressed one of two keys to indicate whether they thought the statement was correct or incorrect. They found that those who took *longer* to respond were more likely to get the right answer. The researchers carried out brain imaging on the pupils while they were doing the tests and confirmed that the part of the brain used for "inhibitory control" – the ability to stop and think, an essential part of learning – was involved.

The findings suggest that pupils should be encouraged to take their time if we want them to understand and correct their misconceptions. It may be a mistake for teachers to ask for an immediate response to a question. This was a pilot project. A bigger study is in progress to assess whether the initial findings are supported.

The brain continues to astonish us as it gives up its secrets to researchers. Probably the best thing we have learned so far is the ability of the brain to go on learning into old age. It's not on a downward spiral from our teens which we once thought. We learn best when we feel safe and secure – whether we are children or adults – but that extraordinary organ sitting inside our skull can be changed and improved by our own activities which is a glorious thought. Is the same true of our genes? Read on to the next chapter to find out.

References

Blakemore, S.J. and Frith, U. (2005) 'The learning brain: Lessons for education: a précis.' *Developmental Science*, Vol. *8*, No. 6. doi:10.1111/j.1467-7687.2005.00434.x

Dweck, C. (2011) Brain Science and Education on BBC Radio 4.

Blakemore, S.J. (2008) 'The social brain in adolescence.' *Nature Reviews Neuroscience*, Vol. *9*, No. 4, pp. 267–277.

Adams, R. (2016) 'Older teenagers "quicker to improve maths and reasoning skills".' Available from www.theguardian.com/society/2016/nov/04/olderteenagers-quicker-to-improve-maths-reasoning-skills-survey (downloaded 20 May 2019).

Blakemore, S.J. and Mills, K.L. (2014) 'Is adolescence a sensitive period for sociocultural processing?' *Annual Review of Psychology*, Vol. *65*, pp. 187–207.

Knoll, L.J., Fuhrmann, D., Sakhardande, A.L., Stamp, F., Speekenbrink, M. and Blakemore, S. (2016) 'A window of opportunity for cognitive training in adolescence.' *Psychological Science*, Vol. *27*, No. 12, pp. 1620–1631. Available from https://pdfs.semanticscholar.org/2d7f/2c6ac28a1d45b09cfce1da6c01538d038d23.pdf (downloaded 7 June 2019).

Woollett, K., Spiers, H.J., and Maguire, E.A. (2009) 'Talent in the taxi: a model system for exploring expertise.' *The Royal Society*, Vol. *364*, No. 1522.

Elbert, T. et al. (1995) 'Increased cortical representation of the fingers of the left hand in string players.' *Science*, Vol. *270*, Issue 5234, pp. 305–307. doi:10.1126/science.270.5234.305

Sadato, N., Pascual-Leone, A., Grafman, J., Ibanez, V., et al, (1996) 'Activation of the primary visual cortex by Braille reading in blind subjects.' *Nature*, Vol. *380*, No. 6574, pp. 526–528.

Gaser, C. and Schlaug, G. (2003) 'Brain structures differ between musicians and non-musicians.' *Journal of Neuroscience*, Vol. *23*, No. 27, pp. 9240–9245. doi:10.1523/JNEUROSCI.23-27-09240.2003

The Royal Society (2011) 'Brain Waves Module 2: neuroscience: implications for education and lifelong learning.' Available from https://royalsociety.org/-/media/Royal_Society_Content/policy/publications/2011/4294975733.pdf (downloaded 26 September 2019).

Rauscher, F.H., Shaw, G.L., Levine, L.J. and Wright, E.L. (1993) 'Pilot study indicates music training of three-year-olds enhances specific spatial reasoning skills.' Paper presented at the Economic Summit of the National Association of Music Merchants, Newport Beach, CA.

Steele, K.M., et al. (1999) 'Prelude or requiem for the Mozart effect?' *Nature*, Vol. *400*, No. 6747, pp. 827–828.

Sonuga-Barke, J.S., Kennedy, M., Kumsta, R., Knight, N., Golm, D. and Rutter, M. (2017) 'Child to adult neurodevelopmental and mental health trajectories after early life deprivation: the young adult follow-up of the longitudinal English and Romanian adoptees study.' *The Lancet*, Vol. *389*, No. 10078, pp. 1539–1548.

Howard-Jones, P.A. (2014) 'Neuroscience and education: myths and messages.' *Nature Reviews Neuroscience*, Vol. *15*, pp. 817–824. doi:10.1038/nrn3817

Nielsen, J.A., Zielinski, B.A., Ferguson, M.A., Lainhart, J.E. and Anderson, J.S. (2013) 'An evaluation of the left-brain vs. right-brain hypothesis with resting state functional connectivity magnetic resonance imaging.' *PLOS One*, Vol. *8*, No. 8, p. e71275. doi:10.1371/journal.pone.0071275

Sunyer, J., Esnaola, M., Alvarez-Pedrerol, M., Forns, J., Rivas, I., López-Vicente, M., Suades-González, E., Foraster, M., Garcia-Esteban, R., Basagaña, X., Viana, M., Cirach, M., Moreno, T., Alastuey, A., Sebastian-Galles, N., Nieuwenhuijsen, M. and Querol, X. (2015) 'Association between traffic-related air pollution in schools and cognitive development in primary school children: a prospective cohort study.' *PLoS Med.*, Vol. *12*, No. 3, p. e1001792. doi:10.1371/journal.pmed.1001792

Diamond, A. and Ling, D.S. (2016) 'Conclusions about interventions, programs, and approaches for improving executive functions that appear justified and those that, despite much hype, do not.' *Developmental Cognitive Neuroscience*, Vol. *18*, pp. 34–48. doi:10.1016/j.dcn.2015.11.005

Thomas, M.S.C., Ansari, D. and Knowland, V.C.P. (2019) 'Educational neuroscience: progress and prospects.' *Journal of Child Psychology and Psychiatry*, Vol. *60*, No. 4, pp. 477–492. doi:10.1111/jcpp.12973

'How the Brain Works.' (n.d.) A website for parents and the general public prepared by the University of London Centre for Educational Neuroscience. Available from www.howthebrainworks.science/ (accessed 26 September 2019).

Chapter 3

Genetics

A devil, a born devil on whose nature nurture can never stick, on whom my pains, humanely taken, all, all lost, quite lost.
Prospero, Act 4, Scene 1, *The Tempest* by William Shakespeare.

Give me the child for the first seven years and I will give you the man.
Jesuit maxim widely attributed to both Aristotle and Saint Ignatius of Loyola.

How well you do in your education can be affected by many things including how much your parents can support you, how effective are the schools you attend and the teachers in them, who your friends are and often how much your family earns. But the set of genes you inherit at conception – your genetic inheritance – can play a significant part too.

Just how big a part has been the subject of controversy which has travelled across the centuries about whether nature or nurture make a human what they are. But research including the systematic and long term studies of the development of twins during and since the twentieth century, followed by the DNA mapping of the first individual human genome in 2003 has seen discoveries by scientists working with genetics coming thick and fast and new evidence clothing the bones of an old argument whilst, of course, creating new ones.

There is no suggestion that a single gene is responsible for intelligence. It's much more complicated than that. Recent genetic finds have associated nearly 1,000 of our 24,000 human genes with intelligence but science is only at the beginning of this particular journey. What all these genes actually do and how they interact with your other genes remains a mystery – at least for the time being. But they're crucially important. For example, individuals with particular gene clusters appear to be more likely to learn to read more easily than others who don't have them, or be better at maths, or public exams or stay in education longer. Or more likely to suffer from learning difficulties such as dyslexia.

Based on the study of twins' development, there is evidence that up to half of personality differences are heritable – in other words up to half of the differences between people in a given population are genetic. Also, the effect of those differences strengthens with age – we become more different from one another as we get older, perhaps as our youthful drive to fit in ebbs away and we become more like our true selves.

Some genetic differences and similarities anyone can see. Physical similarities – we tend to look a bit or a lot like our parents, and we can inherit eye colour and height from them and body types that might make us better at netball or swimming or even getting a good job and rising in it. Research shows taller and/or more attractive people doing better in the job market across cultures.

Then there are the things we assume might be inherited because they seem to run in our families. Scientists have confirmed plenty of these from research. We inherit heightened or lowered potential for getting many diseases of the body or the mind from arthritis, cancer and obesity to schizophrenia, anxiety and depression and many other conditions – very few have been pinned down to a single gene though. Knowledge such as this can be helpful because it means monitoring can lead to earlier diagnosis and treatment but it can cause personal upset and worry for individuals even though a heightened potential for something doesn't mean you will definitely get it.

But it's the area of inherited intelligence and the ability to learn well that provokes the most controversy – not the health findings. Any suggestion that human life cannot be a level playing field no matter how hard schools and families work and that it is our genes that limit us in education, not our home backgrounds for example, is strongly disputed by experts within education and also in areas of relevant science.

And the idea that our lives are determined by genes that we can do nothing about would be a shocking one – if it were true.

To begin with these are possible genetic outcomes not definite ones. But, for the sake of argument, just because an individual inherits fewer genes associated with intelligence, doesn't mean they won't do well in life. They may have other things in spades that are essential to success like motivation, determination or resilience. Regardless of the size of their intellectual endowment it's up to them what they make of it. And it may not be the number of genes associated with intelligence that determines how intelligent you are but patterns of genes you inherit that are important. Science hasn't worked that out yet. It's still early days in the development of the science.

And that brings us to the other important proviso. If half the differences between peoples are due to their genes, half the differences aren't. Other things make a difference. That could, of course, be poverty or affluence in childhood, or how your parents treat you, or your friends, or a job that bores you rigid or delights you, a bad relationship or a great one, an accident or serious illness, a life changing personal discovery, a chance meeting or any manner of things that you can encounter in life.

Which brings us back to nature and nurture and the inspirational research of the last 40 years, and particularly the last 20 years since we first mapped human DNA comprehensively, which is throwing fresh light on the old argument.

Nature and nurture

The nature versus nurture debate goes back a very long time. Is it what we are made of or how we are influenced by our upbringing that makes us who we are? Or is it a bit of both, nature and nurture, which most educators believe. And if they both play a part – is it equal shares or does one part have more effect?

From the early humans who gave up hunter gathering in favour of farming and the selective breeding of crops and animals for food, through the recorded words of early Greek philosophers to the arguments of modern history and today, we know people have reflected on the relative strengths of nature and nurture across time.

But it wasn't until the mid-nineteenth century that experiments – using pea plants – led a Moravian monk called Gregor Mendel to deduce that genes came in pairs and were inherited from each parent plant. At the time his research was ignored but at the beginning of the twentieth century it was rediscovered and research continued. Later in the twentieth century there were decades of research into the differing genetic outcomes of identical and non-identical twins and then finally in 2003 the human genetic code was cracked with the first mapping of a full human genome.

Since then new research has been pumping out helped by increasingly large samples of genetic data becoming available and increasingly powerful computers to crunch all that data, but there is still a long way to go.

How much do key attitudes to learning – like motivation, curiosity and conscientiousness – matter and how far are they inherited or learned? What if our nature has a role in influencing how we are nurtured so that nature is pre-eminent even over nurture? Perhaps we are intensely curious and our parents encourage that and treat us differently to a brother or sister who asks fewer questions and prefers running around and climbing trees or singing and dancing round the house. What if our parents are genetically pre-disposed to nurture a child to be sporty or academic or creative?

And what if how we turn out is just down to how we use the genes we have and chance happenings which some experts do believe?

Professor Robert Plomin, the prominent psychologist and behavioural geneticist who leads the Twins Early Development Study at King's College, London has spent a lifetime investigating the genetics of human behaviour and is convinced that our genes and chance happenings make us who we are.

He thinks parents and teachers need to accept that there are genetic differences in children's appetite for learning and that there are also genetic differences in parents that will make them more or less likely to support their children's learning at home. Even more controversially, he believes genes are more influential than schools and families put together and that society's attempts to provide equal education for all simply highlights genetic differences between children. He favours using children's DNA to plan more personalised learning for them.

Over many years studying the development of twins he has been looking for stable versions of non-shared environmental influences – the stuff that happens to us aside from our genetic make-up that is responsible for the non-genetic half of differences between people in a given population at a particular time. He hasn't found any yet. He calls these influences "unsystematic, idiosyncratic, serendipitous events without lasting effects."[1]

Respect your children's differences

Robert Plomin is professor of behavioural genetics at King's College, London and author of *Blueprint. How DNA Makes us Who we Are.*

Genetic differences in children affect the extent to which they take advantage of educational opportunity. Genetic differences in parents may also affect the extent to which parents offer educational opportunity in the home.

Genetic differences, of which there are millions, are predictions. They are not deterministic or fatalistic but they are predictions based on thousands of tiny inherited differences in our individual DNA which makes you more or less likely to be or do something – tall, for example, or successful in public examinations. You can't find anything that doesn't show a genetic influence – we know that from the studies of twins and adopted children.

Twin studies in England have shown a 60 per cent genetic influence in the results of national curriculum tests. Education is still focused on a one-size-fits-all approach and if genetics tells us anything it's that children are different in how easily they learn and what they like to learn. Forcing them into this one academic approach is going to make some children confront failure a lot and it doesn't seem a wise approach. It ought to be more personalised.

Why do children differ in their GCSE scores? People say it's down to the teaching they get in school but if schools accounted for all the variance in performance between children then children in one classroom would all get the same results. Schools have little effect compared with genes.

1   Unless stated otherwise, the quotations in this chapter from Professor Robert Plomin are taken from an interview with Wendy Berliner, 1 March, 2019.

Genetics emerges as such a strong influence on exam scores because the schooling system aims to give all children the same education. The more school and other factors are made equal, the more genetic differences can be seen in children's performance.

The same thing would happen if everyone had a healthy diet and ate the right number of calories for their lifestyle and body type. Differences in body weight would then be more down to genetic variation, instead of being dominated by lifestyle. Obesity is heritable. So is an appetite for learning. Some children find it easier to learn than others do, and I think it's appetite as much as aptitude. There is a motivation, maybe because you like to do what you are good at.

All personality traits are 40 to 50 per cent heritable which means that up to half of the differences in a population between children in say curiosity and conscientiousness, things that might help feed an appetite for learning, are caused by genetic differences not the environment they grow up in.

The other half is down to chance events that we have no control over.

Parents do have an influence and can make a difference but they don't have as much control as they thought they had. They don't control all the levers and to some extent the child is moulding the parent by their responses to them. The message is that parents should be more tolerant of their children and respect them for their differences. Parents shouldn't beat themselves up over those differences. Some children will like to be read to for a long time, others who are brothers and sisters in the same family won't – because of their genetic differences, not because of the family environment.

Brothers and sisters can be more genetically different to each other than they are to random strangers.

It's been said before that parents are environmentalists and think the way their children behave is down to the way they bring them up, until they have a second child who is totally different even though they are treated the same. The difference is in their genes.

The National Health Service in Britain is moving towards human genome sequencing as part of its disease prevention strategy. Why shouldn't you eventually use DNA in a similar way to predict a child's likelihood to find it harder to learn to read and put in appropriate help early so they are not disadvantaged? Why would anyone who thinks it is right to use DNA to predict a genetic propensity for heart disease, and offer early measures to counter that, think it could be wrong to predict a genetic propensity to find it harder to learn to read and offer early and tailored support?

A brief history of genetics research

There are many experts who hotly contest the conclusions Robert Plomin has drawn from his research and argue that the environment we grow up in and experience has an effect on us – sometimes a profound effect – that our outcomes are not just down to our DNA and chance.

What does all this mean for a parent trying to do the best they can for their children particularly when experts can fundamentally disagree? How do you know where you are?

The important thing to remember is that a lot of genetics research is still relatively young and some of it is in its infancy. The first hints that there was a genetic link with education attainment (the highest level of education an individual completes) came in the 1970s in a study of twins which showed the identical twins getting exam grades that were more similar to one another when compared with the results of non-identical twins.

Identical twins share virtually the same genes but non-identical ones share only half the same genes so the differing school outcomes for different types of twins were identified as genetic by researchers. If you had almost identical genes – as identical twins do – your school results were more similar. If you were non-identical, you shared only half the same genes so you were as different from your twin as you would be from any other brother or sister born at a different time, and the result was that your grades were not necessarily going to be that similar to those of your twin.

Before the human genome was cracked, decoding genes was expensive and took a long time. Sequencing the first human genome cost £2 billion and took hundreds of scientists 13 years. Today it typically takes just one day to sequence an individual's genome and the opportunity is available to the public, not just scientists. It's affordable enough to make it routine for a lot of people really interested in trying to research their family history to take a DNA test to find out who they are related to, both now and in the past. Some firms claim they can now read an individual's DNA in an hour.

The massive drop in the time it takes and how much it costs to decode DNA, coupled with the growing amount of genetic profiles available to researchers through health studies and the rise of genealogy DNA services, has led in just a few short years to a huge upsurge in academic studies into what we may be inheriting through our genes. But as we said, there was plenty of research going on before, the bedrock of it being the study of twins.

The value of twins

Twins are incredibly useful to science because their genetic structure allows researchers to separate genetic influences from environmental ones. As a research method, it has its critics because not everyone agrees it can do what it says. Regardless of this, the findings of twin studies are among the most replicable – other academics can get the same results from them – which means that readers should be confident of the results.

Identical twins are born with virtually the same DNA because they come from one egg and one sperm. Non-identical twins, also known as fraternal twins, share only half the same DNA – the same as single brothers and sisters sharing parents – because in their case, two different eggs are fertilised by two different sperms. Non-identical twins are just conceived, developed and born at the same time but they are as genetically different as individual siblings conceived and born years apart.

The theory underpinning twin research is that because twins are the same age and are usually brought up together in the same family, they will share very similar environments. If a pair of identical twins are more similar in a behaviour – an ability to learn to read easily, for example – than a pair of fraternal twins, the difference will be genetic not environmental.

They learn to read more easily and take broadly the same amount of time, because they share virtually 100 per cent of the same genes, which includes a genetic pre-disposition to learn to read easily, and not because their parents bought them the same alphabet colouring books. The fraternal twins who learn to read at different rates, one perhaps being quicker than the other, despite having the same alphabet colouring books are also exhibiting their different genetic make-up, in their case because they only share half of the same genes and may have inherited different reading abilities.

One of the longest running studies of its kind is the Twins Early Development Study based at King's College, London, led by Professor Robert Plomin who we have just heard from in this chapter. The study has been following the lives of thousands of pairs of twins since 1994 and has accrued vast amounts of data.

There are critics who query the value of twin studies because they believe there is no such a thing as a completely shared environment. They say that children in the same family can be treated differently both at home and at school, even if they are twins, and you can't rule out those environmental influences playing a part in their behaviours. It's not nice but some parents have favourites among their children and treat them differently. Also, identical twins are always the same sex whereas roughly half of fraternal twins are opposite sex. Some parents still treat boys and girls differently.

Researchers of twins acknowledge that the ideal is to study identical twins who have been brought up apart which means they still share the genes but not the environment. That way, they say, no-one can cast doubt that similar traits – like that ability to learn to read quickly – are genetic rather than environmental.

Proportionately few separated identical twins have been studied compared with twins brought up together but when they are researchers have found remarkable similarities in them. For example, the Minnesota Twin Family Study reported on Jim Lewis and Jim Springer who were identical twins raised separately in different families from the age of four weeks. Reunited in 1979 when they were 39, they found each suffered from tension headaches, bit their nails, smoked cigarettes (the same brand), drove the same type of car and even went on holiday to the same place in Florida, among many other startling similarities.

Then there is the impact of social class. In 2003 Eric Turkheimer, a psychology professor at the University of Virginia in the United States, noticed most of the studies that found IQ is largely due to genetics involved twins from middle-class backgrounds. He decided to look at identical twins from poorer families and he found their IQs were much more varied than those of middle-class identical twins. They were more like those of fraternal twins who in turn are, as we have already learned, individually different as any other brothers and sisters born at different times.

Twin studies have produced huge amounts of research but it was the ability to unlock the secrets of human DNA in its entirety with the final mapping of the first human genome – a full set of genes and genetic material – in 2003 that produced a tipping point in genetic research and launched so many more research studies. Even so, our genetic raw material is still a largely uncharted map of a vast new world still to be explored by scientists not unlike, in some respects at least, the adventurers of old who searched for fortune in the new worlds.

Big research money in genetics is following medical research into diseases that blight human life and cause suffering on an epic scale. Pharmaceutical companies need advances in medical research to bring new treatments to market which can alleviate suffering for millions, whilst making big revenues.

More than 350 biomedical advances using just the draft genetic code published in 2000, and the variances in that code which were linked to human diseases such as cancer, had already reached clinical trials only three years later when work on mapping that first human genome was completed. In comparison with all that activity, education research using genetics has a long way to go even though much work is happening.

There is an old adage that if you think education is expensive, you should try the cost of ignorance -however, health is a very expensive commodity. Taking heart and blood circulation disease as one example and the UK as one country which provides free health care to its citizens through a national insurance scheme and National Health Service, healthcare costs relating to heart and circulatory diseases are estimated at £9 billion each year rising to £19 billion a year if you add in the wider costs and losses to the economy of disability and premature death. In the US with its much bigger population, the cost of cardiovascular disease is around $110 billion annually.

Little wonder that the UK government has an ambition to sequence the genomes of five million people in the UK. From 2019 the NHS offered all seriously ill children whole genome sequencing as part of their care, as well as adults with certain rare diseases and hard to treat cancers. The more genetic information is available the earlier doctors can predict, diagnose and treat illnesses and, in the long run, potentially cut costs as researchers bring on stream new treatments.

But the more data that is collected, the more it will help research into the genetics of intelligence and learning. Health questionnaires used in medical studies routinely ask what education level the participant reached giving education researchers more data to work with.

But as we have touched on before there is sensitivity to research into the genetics of intelligence and learning. It has a pre-history shadowed by the eugenics movement which linked intelligence with race and believed in selective breeding of humans to produce a "master race." Eugenics took off in America early in the twentieth century and saw compulsory ster-ilisations first of people in mental hospitals but later of people with low IQ and poor non-white women. The idea crossed the Atlantic and reached its appalling nadir in Nazi Germany and the war time genocides of Jews and others in the concentration camps.

As late as the 1970s women's rights groups and other activists found some American doctors coercing poor non-white women and people with learning disabilities into forced sterilisations. Then in 1994 came an American book called *The Bell Curve* written by Richard J. Hernnstein and Charles Murray which argued that poor people, and particularly poor black people, score on average less well in IQ tests than white or Asian people. They said they had corrected their findings for social and financial circumstances and acknowledged that the gap between the IQs of black and white people was shrinking. But they argued for reduced immigration to stop a lowering of the American IQ. They were accused of racism and their conclusions rebutted as flawed. Professor Robert Plomin was one of 52 leading researchers who signed a statement in the Wall Street Journal at the time that largely endorsed the data in the book, though not the authors' conclusions.

Other signatories included the American Professor Arthur Jensen and the influential, but controversial, German-born psychologist, Professor Hans Eysenck, who lived and worked in Britain. Jensen, who had been a post-doctoral student of Eysenck, had published a paper in 1969 conclud-ing that 80% of variance in IQ scores was genetic and attempts to boost African-American scores through pre-school intervention would fail. Fur-ious students laid siege to his office in California. Eysenck was punched on the nose while lecturing at the London School of Economics.

In the prologue to his book, *Blueprint. How DNA Makes us Who we Are*, Plomin says he delayed writing the book for 30 years, in part because of what he describes as "cowardice." He writes:

> It might seem unbelievable today, but 30 years ago it was dangerous professionally to study the genetic origins of differences in people's behaviour and to write about it in scientific journals. It could also be dangerous personally to stick your head up above the parapets of academia to talk about these issues in public.

There is a significant attainment gap in education across the developed world with far more disadvantaged children faring poorly at school. Educators point to unequal home lives and educational opportunities as the cause and there will be programmes going on world-wide as you read this trying to help the children who fall behind at school to catch up.

Any suggestion that it is their genetic inheritance – not the tough circumstances the children find themselves in – that is causing them to under achieve, is a red rag to a bull for those who think this is incorrect.

Small changes, big differences

With the exception of identical twins, every human is unique. We inherit the genetic differences of our parents with some differences all of our own. It's the variances, or differences, that are written into our genetic code when it is copied from those of our parents at conception that make us different. If there were no differences – sometimes described as copying mistakes – in our DNA, every human would be identical.

Even in all the variety of human life we have on earth, every human is still almost identical. Just look at us. We are only different at the margins of all those bones and organs. We are genetically similar to other mammals too – 80 per cent genetically similar to dogs, 60 per cent genetically similar to bananas and we share a common ancestor with Zebrafish. With our chimpanzee "cousins," the similarity is around 96 per cent. But look how different we are to chimps. That 4 per cent makes for a big difference. As can the minute differences in individual human DNA in the way we look and behave.

It's genetic diversity that strengthens any species. Genetic diversity, the total number of genetic characteristics in a species, allows for adaptation to changing circumstances which could threaten life itself. Climate change or infection that could wipe everyone out if we were identical and couldn't cope with extreme weather or an illness none of us could resist.

We know incest can lead to birth abnormalities that, over time, has wiped out families or in the case of royal families, dynasties. That's because the gene pool becomes less diverse and deformities linger within the pool and are passed increasingly through the generations. It's the depth of our genetic diversity which makes us strong.

But just because we have decades of research from twin studies and have made enormous strides very recently in reading the human genome, this should not lead us to under estimate the complexity and enormity of the task for scientists seeking to understand what they are reading in our genetic code.

As we said earlier in the chapter, when it comes to how humans learn it is impossible to point the finger at one gene for this or that and the latest thinking is suggesting thousands of the tiniest influences across many genes are at play to create one learning problem or advantage. Because of this, researchers need access to a huge amount of DNA to get results that are trustworthy – studies need to be big and researchers need access to huge computing power.

It takes time to amass a huge amount of genetic profiles. In the early twenty-first century scientists looked for a link between particular genes and schooling, but their efforts were largely unsuccessful then. One of the most important reasons was the small size of their studies. It's the size of the more recent studies which is uncovering gene associations with what are known as traits – whether it's intelligence, heart disease, eye colour, how long you stay in education or something else – across vast amounts of data.

But even when scientists eventually discover the clusters of genes that have an impact on learning, that is only the beginning. Even if they manage to work out what every strand of human DNA does and what each variant does, how do they then disentangle the effects of, say, an inherited ability to learn to read easily and all the support (or lack of it) a child may have in learning to read?

And there is an awful lot of DNA in each and every one of us – 2.8 billion letters in our DNA code to be reasonably exact and six billion nucleotide bases – the building blocks of DNA.

That is not to say education researchers haven't already made important discoveries. They are finding links between genes and education attainment, reading ability and exam performance, for example, that may in time see learning difficulties pinpointed early, and precision help offered in the classroom. But even that has the potential to be controversial.

Dyslexia and DNA

In the American district of New Haven, Connecticut, children starting school with the lowest literacy scores are being given intensive reading support while being monitored by a team of education, genetics, and neuroscience researchers from nearby Yale University.

Some 450 children are involved in the study which began in 2015 and will last for six years. Towards the end of the study the children's DNA will be mapped. The researchers will then look for any differences in DNA between the children whose literacy improves and children who continue to find it hard to read despite intensive support.

But the $20 million project is controversial. While the New Haven study includes students from different racial groups, it draws students from the overwhelmingly Black and Latino New Haven public schools. In 2018 new members of the New Haven school board queried why the children had to be DNA mapped and argued that it could stigmatise children or even create a self-fulfilling prophecy which said, in effect, "there is no point trying, I don't have the right genes." The board did vote to continue with the project despite the misgivings of some members.

Jeffrey Gruen, Professor of Paediatrics and Genetics at Yale, who is leading the New Haven study, was quoted in *Education Week* (10 September 2018) as saying: "Probably the bigger barrier is we're all sensitized to the idea of using genetics (in education), because people have misused these terms in ways that are totally inappropriate."

What's the evidence?

Let's turn now to some highlights of the more recent research to be reported, research which is offering tantalising glimpses of what our genes influence when it comes to learning. Let's start with reading ability which is at the heart of accessing school curricula.

Reading ability

Researchers from King's College, London used a genetic scoring technique to predict reading performance throughout school years (Selzam et al. 2017). Using the DNA of 5,825 individuals who are part of the Twins Early Development Study they mapped education achievement genetic scores against reading ability between the ages of seven and 14. The achievement scores were developed by looking for genetic variants between the participants in the study – variations which are already known to be associated with educational attainment, also known as years spent in education. They then mapped these scores against reading ability between the ages of seven and 14.

A report published in *Scientific Studies of Reading* (28 March 2017), found there was a correlation between children's DNA and their reading ability and that the genetic scores explained up to five per cent of the differences between children in their reading ability. That might not sound much but the children with the highest and lowest genetic scores for education achievement had reading abilities almost two years apart. The link remained significant even after cognitive ability and family wealth was taken into account.

Given that good reading ability is strongly associated overall with high levels of academic achievement you can see how useful a two-year head start in it can be – how much easier it is for that child to get ahead with their learning compared with a child who struggles to learn to read. How much easier it is for a child who really struggles to learn to read to fall behind and be turned off education.

The researchers proposed that genetic scoring in education could be used as an early screening tool to help identify those at particular genetic risk of reading problems so that they could receive early tailored support, not unlike the project being worked on in New Haven, Connecticut mentioned earlier.

Maths

Many of the genes that affect how well a child can read at secondary school have an impact on their maths skills too. A research team from University College London, Oxford University and King's College, London reported in 2014 their findings that around half of the genes that influenced the literacy of 12-year-olds also played a role in their mathematical abilities.

In the study, 12-year-old twins and unrelated children from around 2,800 British families were assessed for reading comprehension and fluency and tested on mathematics questions from the English national curriculum. This information was then analysed alongside the children's DNA.

The study did not identify specific genes linked to numeracy or literacy, and researchers do not know what the various gene variants do. But they may affect brain development and function, or other biological processes that are important for learning both skills.

How long you stay in education.

An enormous study from a team of international scientists, published in Nature Genetics in 2018 and involving the DNA of 1.1 million people, discovered 1271 genetic variations in DNA associated with how many years you stay in education.

The newly discovered gene variants, or differences in DNA, are only responsible for a very small amount of the differences in levels of education observed between groups of people but, nonetheless, matter. The longer you stay in education, the more you are likely to achieve in terms of qualifications and subsequently the job market. Someone who leaves as soon as compulsory school ends is less well set than someone with a good higher education degree.

Fascinating as the findings sound, the researchers found that the effect of each gene was weak and some differences only implied people spending a few more days in education than others, not years. Crucially, the data did not predict educational achievements for individuals.

However, the *New York Times* (23 July 2018) reported that researchers had gone on to use the findings to calculate a genetic score for educational success. The more gene variants an individual had that were linked to staying in education longer, the higher that individual scored.

The researchers then calculated a score for a group of 4,775 Americans, using their education attainment scores to rank them into five groups.

Only 12 per cent of people whose scores put them in the lowest fifth of the rankings finished a college education whereas 57 per cent of the people in the top fifth, the ones with the most gene variants linked to staying longer in education, did.

When the researchers then looked at people who had repeated a grade at school because they had been unsuccessful first time, they found that 29 per cent of the individuals in the lowest ranked group had repeated a grade compared with only 8 per cent in the top group.

The study is limited because the genetic profiles are all of people who are over 30 and of European heritage so further research would be needed to include younger people and people from other ethnic backgrounds to see whether that would affect the results. When researchers calculated scores for a group of African-Americans, they failed to predict how well different groups had done in education. One likely reason is that genetic markers aren't reliable guides to how genes influence traits in different populations.

However, the overall results did show an 11 to 13 per cent gap in time spent in education across this large group and co-author, Robbee Wedow from the Institute of Behavioural Genetics at the University of Colorado Boulder in the US, quoted in *The Independent* newspaper (23 July 2018) said the size of score was as significant as other factors known to improve educational outcomes, such as the amount of education the child's mother has or how affluent the family is.

But he added:

> Having a low polygenic score absolutely does not mean that someone won't achieve a high level of education. As with many other outcomes, it is a complex interplay between environment and genetics that matters.

The huge and interesting study had its genesis in 2011 when Daniel J. Benjamin, a behavioural economist at the University of Southern California, and colleagues, formed a world-wide Social Science Genetic Association Consortium to investigate genetic effects.

Researchers used genetic data from medical research to help them. As we said earlier, people taking part in genetic studies of a medical condition fill in questionnaires about their lives and a common question to answer will be aimed at finding out how much education they've had – better educated people generally enjoy better health. This is golden data for education researchers to mine. They can compare individual genetic codes looking for genetic similarities between people and the time they report spending in education.

By 2016, nearly 300,000 genetic profiles had been studied and 71 gene differences had been linked to education. Next, nearly half a million genetic profiles from anonymous volunteers who are part of the UK Bio-bank, which is funded by government and health research charities, were added in and then nearly 400,000 genetic profiles supplied by 23andMe, the genealogy service providing private DNA testing. The company collects genetic health data for scientific research from customers who volunteer to participate and who want to know their genetic predispositions to diseases.

Studying the DNA of all these people, researchers found a number of genetic variations that were unusually common in people who spent longer in education, and others that were more common in people who left education earlier. In all 1,271 of these variants were linked so tightly that they couldn't be eliminated as chance.

The researchers then scanned the DNA surrounding these influential variants and discovered a pattern. The differences are linked to genes active in the brain which help neurons to form connections – the messaging system of the brain. A key to educational success may not be how quickly information is acquired, but how quickly it can be shared between various regions of the brain.

Underlining the importance of maternal and baby health, many of the differences affect genes active in the brains of foetuses and young babies which have an impact on the creation of brain cells and how they react to new information.

Interestingly the influence of the genes varied from country to country. This may be because education cultures differ, some may prefer a lot of rote learning, for example, over creative problem solving. Different genes may be coming into play for learning jobs involving memory compared with creativity.

The researchers have cautioned that these genetic patterns can only be seen across very large groups, such as the one tested. Genetics on its own will play only a small part in how long an individual child remains in education.

The researchers plan to increase the size of the group studied to two million and expect to find thousands more genetic links to education.

Exam performance

How long you stay in education is often influenced by how well you do in your public examinations and in 2013 an international research team led from King's College, London found that differences in GCSE exam results at the age of 16 were more affected by genes than teachers or families. They were responsible for more than half the grade differences overall.

The authors used data on 11,117 twins born in England and Wales between 1994 and 1996 recruited into the Twins Early Development Study (TEDS) which was set up at King's College, London in 1994. In 2013 they reported finding that 58 per cent of the variation for the overall GCSE per-formance of the twins for compulsory core subjects (English, maths and science) was influenced by genes. By comparison the overall effects of the shared environment, which includes all family and school influences shared by twins growing up in the same family and attending the same school, accounted for only 36 per cent of the variance of mean GCSE scores.

Grades in the sciences had a bigger genetic link than those in huma-nities subjects, such as art and music.

Subsequent research using the data of 12,500 twins published by the Institute of Psychiatry, Psychology & Neuroscience, King's College, London in 2015 analysed grades in other school subjects including second languages, business informatics and art. This found they were affected by the same genes that impacted on the core subjects studied earlier. The shared genetic influence was found even when genetic effects due to gen-eral intelligence were removed.

And when the GCSE subject results were all combined, genes explained an even bigger proportion of the grade differences – as much as 65 per cent – and the home and school environment was found to be even less important – responsible for as little of 14 per cent of the differences in grades across the group of teenagers studied.

Intelligence

In 2017 an international research team of 30 scientists from Vrije Uni-versity Medical Centre Amsterdam and Imperial College London revealed they had discovered 52 genes linked to human intelligence, 40 of which had been identified as such for the first time.

The genes accounted for 20 per cent of the discrepancies in the IQ test results of 78,000 people examined, the researchers reported in the journal *Nature Genetics*. Most of the genes were in brain tissue and involved in the regulation of cell development and the formation of the synapses – the neural information gateways of the brain. The gene clusters appear to influence cognitive function which includes memory, attention, processing speed and reasoning. Crucially, the gene clusters are thought likely to be under the control of master regulator switches.

The team used 13 earlier studies in which detailed genetic profiles and intelligence evaluations – based on IQ tests – had been compiled for 78,000 people, all of European descent.

Many of the genetic variations linked with high IQ also correlated with other attributes: more years spent in education, bigger head circumference in infancy, tallness, and even the ability to stop smoking. It was also linked with autism.

Professor Danielle Posthuma, a geneticist at the Center for Neuroge-nomics and Cognitive Research at Vrije University in Amsterdam, who was the principal investigator of the study, was quoted at the time of publication on the university's website as saying:

> These findings for the first time provide clear clues towards the underlying biological mechanisms of intelligence. The current genetic results explain up to 5% of the total variance in intelligence. Although this is quite a large amount of variance for a trait as intelligence, there is still a long road to go: given the high heritability of intelligence, many more genetic effects are expected to be important, and these can only be detected in even larger samples.

Such is the speed at which genetics research is happening by the following year researchers led by Posthuma had searched another 14 databases of health and genetic records and had identified nearly another 1,000 more genes associated with intelligence. People with these genes also tend to live longer than average and are less likely to have Alzheimer's disease, attention deficit hyper activity disorder (ADHD) or schizophrenia. Research continues.

The education attainment gap

In September 2018 a report from the Fair Education Alliance estimated that in the United Kingdom alone the conservative cost to society of young people who were not in education, employment or training was around £21 billion in lost productivity and welfare payments.

Other economic and personal costs are being racked up too. People who fail in the education system are over represented in the prison population and more likely to be substance abusers than those who succeed at school; as mentioned before, their health is also generally poorer which is a cost to them and the National Health Service.

With all these costs taken into account the Fair Education Alliance put the price to society of educational underachievement at a staggering £76 billion. That dwarfs the cost of day to day spending on schools in England which stood at £42 billion in 2017/2018.

In the UK, along with other developed nations, it is children from impoverished backgrounds who do worst at school on average – those poor enough to qualify for free school meals; those assessed with special educational needs also do poorly on average. There are plenty of disadvantaged children who buck the trend, of course, and always have. In London, home to large numbers of motivated migrant families, some disadvantaged children outperform affluent children who live outside the capital. The lowest performing major group of all nationwide are white boys from financially poor homes.

In England, as elsewhere, the gap is already there when children start school and balloons as the children grow up. By the end of their first year in reception – the year before the national curriculum cuts in – nearly half of disadvantaged English children are already not reaching expected standards of development.

By the end of primary school, an English disadvantaged child is the equivalent of almost an entire school year behind expected levels of development, and they are two years behind by the end of secondary school. A majority leave education without a good standard of recognised qualifications in English and maths, making it harder to do well in further study or work.

This is not without successive governments investing in teachers, systems and techniques to try to reduce the attainment gap. More recently there had been signs of slight improvement but this may be stalling. In 2018 the Department for Education in London published figures which showed the gap had widened for the first time in four years. With this kind of slow progress, the attainment gap is going to last into an indefinite future.

It's not just about how much money a nation puts into its education system that makes the difference either. The United States spends 60 per cent more on its education system than the average of the 34 democracies who make up the Organisation for Economic Cooperation and Development (OECD) yet there is a yawning attainment gap between privileged and less privileged young Americans and between the educational performance of the US as a whole, and other developed countries.

But maybe, just maybe, research into genetics can ultimately help if better ways of teaching and learning can be developed based on what we find out about the impact of our children's DNA on how they do at school.

Genes are a blueprint. They are not our destiny. Other factors are at work including factors we can influence in our approach to problems and opportunities. There is so much we didn't know about our genetic inheritance 30 years ago that we know today. How much more might we know in another 30 years with so many research projects pouring out results, so many technological and scientific advances to help us?

Knowing more about how our genes shape us may bring ethical chal-lenges for the future but not knowing more about them is no longer an option. Knowing more can only help us as we support our children as they grow but research has already told us a lot about what is good to do to help them as they learn. The best place to start is when they are very small as we explain in the next chapter which is about research into learning before children go to school.

References

Plomin, R. (2018) *Blueprint. How DNA Makes us Who we Are*. London: Allen Lane.

Bouchard, T.J., Jr., Lykken, D.T., McGue, M., Segal, N.L. and Tellegen, A. (1990) 'Sources of human psychological differences: the Minnesota study of twins reared apart.' *Science*, Vol. *250*, No. 4978, pp. 223–228.

Turkheimer E., et al. (2003) 'Socioeconomic status modifies heritability of IQ in young children.' *Psychological Science*, Vol. *14*, No. 6, pp. 623–628.

Hernnstein, R.J. and Murray, C., (1994) *The Bell Curve: Intelligence and Class Structure in American Life*. New York and London: Free Press.

Sparks, S.D. (2018) 'What if a DNA test could show how to teach a student with dyslexia?' *Education Week*, Vol. *38*, No. 4, pp. 1–9. Available from www.edweek.org/ew/articles/2018/09/12/scientists-use-dna-testing-to-seek-answers.html (downloaded 20 May 2019).

Zahn, B., (2018) 'New Haven Board of Education concerned about ethics of genetic-based reading intervention program.' New Haven Register. Available from www.nhregister.com/news/article/New-Haven-Board-of-Education-concerned-about-13071036.php (downloaded 20 May 2019).

Selzam, S., Dale, P.S., Wagner, R.K., DeFries, J.C., Cederlof, M., O'Reilly, P.F., Krapohl, E. and Plomin, R. (2017) 'Genome-wide polygenic scores predict reading performance throughout the school years.' *Scientific Studies of Reading*, Vol. *21*, No. 4, pp. 334–349.

Davis, O.S.P., Band, G., Spencer, C.C.A. et al. (2014) 'The correlation between reading and mathematics ability at age twelve has a substantial genetic component.' *Nature Communications*, Vol. *5*, No. 4204.

Lee, J.J., Wedow, R., Cesarini, D., et al. (2018) 'Gene discovery and polygenic prediction from a genome-wide association study of educational attainment in 1.1 million individuals.' *Nature Genetics*, Vol. *50*, pp. 1112–1121.

Zimmer, C. (2018) 'Years of education influenced by genetic makeup, enormous study finds.' *New York Times*. Available from www.nytimes.com/2018/07/23/science/genes-education.html (downloaded 20 May 2019).

'Hundreds of genes that affect academic success identified.' (2018) *Independent*. Available from www.independent.co.uk/news/science/academic-genes-dna-education-success-intelligence-tests-humans-a8460071.html (downloaded 20 May 2019).

Shakeshaft, N.G., Trzaskowski, M., McMillan, A., Rimfeld, K., Krapohl, E., Haworth, A.M.A., Dale, P.S. and Plomin, R. (2013) 'Strong genetic influence on a UK nationwide test of educational achievement at the end of compulsory education at age 16.' *Plos One*. Available from https://journals.plos.org/plosone/article?id=10.1371/journal.pone.0080341 (downloaded 6 June 2019).

Rimfeld, K., Kovas, Y., Dale, P.S. and Plomin, R. (2015) 'Pleiotropy across academic subjects at the end of compulsory education.' *Scientific Reports*, Vol. *5*, No. 11713.

Sniekers, S., Stringer, S., Posthuma, D. et al. (2017) 'Genome-wide association meta-analysis of 78,308 individuals identifies new loci and genes influencing human intelligence.' *Nature Genetics*, Vol. *49*, pp. 1107–1112.

Savage, J.E., Jansen, P.R., Posthuma, D. et al. (2018) 'Genome-wide association meta-analysis in 269,867 individuals identifies new genetic and functional links to intelligence.' *Nature Genetics*, Vol. *50*, pp. 912–919.

Fair Education Alliance Report Card (2018) Available from www.faireducation.org.uk/report-card-2018 (downloaded 20 May 2019).

Chapter 4

Before school

The most important period of life is not the age of university studies, but the first one, the period from birth to the age of six.
Maria Montessori, Italian physician, educator and founder of the Montessori method.

Children have real understanding only of that which they invent themselves.
Jean Piaget, Swiss psychologist known for his influential child development theories.

In 2015, the British TV Channel 4 screened a programme called *The Secret Life of Four-Year-Olds*. The cameras followed a group of nursery children as they talked, played, fought and made friends. Viewers watched them start to learn how to share, how to deal with bullies and how to relate to other children. The programme was a hit. More than two and a half million viewers tuned in to watch children at a remarkable stage in their development.

Maybe one of the reasons for the programme's success was the variety of language, reasoning and emotions that the children displayed. The fights over who rode the bicycle might have been predictable, but the more sophisticated social negotiation was not.

Recent research has shown that this is a stage of intense activity in children's brains. The brain grows in size until it is about 90 per cent of the weight of an adult's brain around the age of five-years-old. There are also big changes in the frontal lobes, the front of the human brain and the part that controls skills such as problem-solving, memory, language and judgement.

Four and five-year-olds produce about twice as many synapses or connections between brain cells (neurons) in some parts of their brains as adults do. As we have heard, these important connections allow signals to pass from one neuron to another. That is why people sometimes talk about the brain being "wired." As we grow older, these connections "prune" themselves spontaneously as they become redundant through lack of use.

The pruning is a natural and healthy process. More connections don't equate with intelligence or superior reasoning power. Nor do they mean that offering preschoolers the maximum number of experiences will make them cleverer or more emotionally intelligent because more of these connections will be maintained.

Instead, the new knowledge about young children's brains suggests that we should search for the kind of environment that provides a use for the kind of connections that we want them to take with them into adult life. They should be encouraged, for instance to explore physical objects, their shape and size and to listen to sounds that lead to the development of language.

These discoveries about young children's brains are comparatively recent. Peter Huttenlocher, one of the founding fathers of cognitive neuroscience, who first described the rapid increase and then slow decline of synapses in the human brain, published many of his findings in the past quarter of a century. But they chime remarkably with earlier research that educators have used to shape the way they teach and nurture preschool children. One of the main ways they do that is through play.

The importance of play

> I thought my son would be an early reader but then he discovered making friends was more fun and spent his last year at nursery having the time of his life. I'm sure if I had sat him down I could have taught him to read but I think they start early enough and as he wasn't pushing it, neither did I, we just read together.
>
> Post on the website for parents www.netmums

The debate between those who favour an early start to academic education and those who believe that young children are better served by more informal learning and play is at least a century old. It divides parents, politicians and is the subject of numerous research studies.

Education has risen up the political agenda in many parts of the world, not least in the UK. Politicians of every complexion have worried about the need to make schools accountable for the public funds that they receive. As we have seen, the early years are a time of intense activity in children's brains and governments are keen to ensure that children are well equipped to start school. But what does that mean?

In 2014, Sir Michael Wilshaw, then chief inspector of Ofsted (The Office for Standards in Education, Children's Services and Skills) in England, called for more formal, structured learning in nurseries to close the attainment gap between rich and poor children. He wanted nurseries to put more emphasis on letters and numbers and how to hold a pen. This echoes the views of many politicians who are in a hurry for children to acquire academic skills. One Conservative Secretary of State for Education said that it was:

> a persistent scandal that we have children starting school not able to communicate in full sentences and not able to read simple words.
> (Damian Hinds, *The Guardian*, 31 July 2018)

Such pronouncements worry many early years educators. As the Professional Association for Childcare and Early Years puts it:

> For a child to be considered school ready … cognitive and academic skills such as reading and writing are not as important as children being confident, independent and curious.
> (Research Report 2013)

Many are concerned about the introduction of a baseline testing system for infants' children in England due in September 2020 and that Ofsted has now encouraged all primary schools to make literacy the core purpose of the reception year.

So, who is right? Should parents and early years teachers encourage children to acquire more academic skills before they start school? One of the most important figures in the debate is Jean Piaget (1896–1980), a Swiss psychologist, whose ideas are still influential. He believed that there were stages of child development and that children should not be taught information or ideas until they are "ready" for them.

Piaget believed that it was pointless trying to teach children letter sounds or addition until they were mature enough to respond. If they were obviously struggling, the parent or teacher should wait and try again at a later date.

He identified four stages of cognitive development. For example, between the ages of two and seven children learned through handling concrete objects and physical activity. Then they could move to the next stage where they learned logical and abstract thinking.

Piaget believed that problem-solving skills could not be taught but must be discovered. It followed that the student must be at the centre of learning and active in discovering new things. The teacher must enable children to make discoveries but should not provide direct teaching. Piaget thought that play enabled children to practise what they had learned but it did not necessarily mean that they learned anything new.

His contemporary, the Russian psychologist, Lev Vygotsky (1896–1934) disagreed. His work was suppressed in Stalin's Russia but since it was published in English in the 1970s it has become very influential. Play, he said, was vital in developing children's language and in helping them to control their thoughts and feelings, to do what psychologists call to "self-regulate."

More recent research (Valloton and Ayoub, 2011) has reinforced his findings by showing that language and self-regulation go hand in hand and predict academic success and emotional well-being (Whitebread, 2011). It's not only children's language skills that depend on play but their ability to deal with other symbols, numbers in maths, notes in music, drawing and dance, according to Vygotsky.

Most parents have watched, fascinated, as their young children play "let's pretend." They imagine they are doctors and nurses, mothers and fathers, teachers and pupils or, as they move the figures round a pirate ship or the animals round a farm, they can imagine they are all kinds of things. Some of us have had fun joining in.

The four-year-old in the opening sequence of Channel 4's *The Secret Life of Four-Year-Olds* says at one point as she picks up a toy telephone: "Stop ringing me Richard. You are not the dad." Vygotsky argues that there is much more to this kind of activity than fun: it sets children on the road to the sort of abstract thinking they will need as adults. At this stage, they need to use real situations and real objects, such as telephones, stethoscopes and cooking pots as they learn how to think.

Finally, what about that mysterious stream of chat as a child plays with a doll or car, completely absorbed in their own world? Vygotsky was right to emphasis its importance. More recent research shows that children (Fernyhough and Fradley, 2005) are using it to solve problems.

Professor David Whitebread, the world's first professor of play from the Centre for Research, Play, Development and Education set up in 2017 at the UK's Cambridge University has reviewed research on play. He suggests that it is crucial to our development as humans. Playful children are happy and secure while those in poverty or with parents who are under stress may be deprived of play.

Children in an Indian orphanage made big strides emotionally and intellectually after the introduction of carefully organised play (Taneja et al, 2002). Equally, some children with affluent parents are so over-supervised and over-scheduled that they, too, suffer from play deprivation. One of the drawbacks of modern living is that parents are so worried about their children's safety that they fail to allow them enough freedom to play. There has been a sharp decline in children's free play throughout the western world (Chudakoff 2007). That affects their independence, resourcefulness and the skills traditionally learnt through play, Whitebread says.

He consulted play researchers from eight European countries. All agreed that, while play was not the only way that children learned, it made a unique and beneficial contribution. There was less agreement about the more complicated question of the role of adults in helping children to play. Some thought it could be counter productive.

Recent developments in psychology and neuroscience have further emphasised how vital play is in helping children to learn and to their emotional well-being. Vygotsky's view that "let's pretend" games with other children promote the ability to control feelings and actions is backed by numerous studies.

For example, a group of children aged between three and seven were asked to stand as still as sentries. They did so for significantly longer when their playmates were watching them than when they were alone, presumably because they felt their fellow pupils were checking on their performance (Manuilenko, 1948, reported in Karpov, 2005). The importance of games of pretence in helping children cope with stress in hospitals, conflict or abuse is well documented.

So, as David Whitebread concludes, the evidence that play is an essential component of young children's development is powerful. But that does not mean children should simply be left to play on their own all the time. Much modern research has confirmed Vygotsky's view (1978) that the right kind of interaction and co-operation with someone more skilful is vital to children's progress. He spoke of the need for an adult to guide children in their "zone of proximal development." That is not the same as being told what to do all the time but means that children benefit and learn by talking to a parent, teacher or another child, and by playing games with them. It is this type of social interaction that offers opportunities to learn language which is the foundation of thought.

The myth of discovery learning

If you find out something yourself you are more likely to have thought deeply about it and to understand and remember it. Surely that's obvious? As it happens, no.

"Discovery learning" has enjoyed huge popularity among teachers of children of all ages. Jerome Bruner, the American psychologist who changed the way we think about education, is the academic often associated with the theory (1961). He believed that education was not about instructing children in facts but about teaching them how to think and solve problems.

Bruner's idea was that children should use their own prior knowledge and experience to solve a problem because this type of learning motivated them more than when they were instructed directly by an adult. It also helped them to become resourceful and independent. Discovery learning meant minimal adult guidance, hands-on activity and little repetition or rote learning.

One study (Ray, 1961) found that children retained more knowledge six weeks after they learned a topic, if they discovered it in this way than if they were taught directly by an adult. Unlike Piaget, Bruner believed that young children were capable of grasping intellectually complex subjects if they were taught in the right way.

The Plowden report, a major government-commissioned report on primary education, published in London in 1967 which influenced teachers for decades, took its cue from Bruner and argued that children should move from discovery to discovery with the teacher as supporter rather than instructor.

Bruner did believe that teachers should provide "scaffolding" to support children. That might mean producing appropriate materials or intervening to correct misconceptions but it was not the same as the "chalk and talk" of the traditional classroom.

Bruner's work led to decades of debate about the role of adults in education. His defenders say that his work has often been misinterpreted by practitioners to support a regime in which children are left too much to their own devices. We have touched on the misinterpretation of evidence before and this would be another classic example if we are to accept what Bruner's supporters say.

However, as we learn more about the brain and how people learn, evidence abounds that the discovery approach does not work. John Hattie, Professor and Director of the Melbourne Education Research Institute at the University of Melbourne, says:

> The idea that secure knowledge emanates automatically from personal discovery is flawed and incorrect. We certainly enjoy solving puzzles. We find enquiry is highly motivating but there is little to suggest that personal discovery within itself assists a person to actually learn.
>
> (Hattie and Yates 2013, p. 77)

Some studies have shown that discovery learning may actually hinder progress of young children who have too little knowledge to embark on this type of problem solving (Alfieri et al 2011). Kirschener, Sweller and Clark (2006) found that children, especially those who were new learners, had to expend so much mental effort in making sense of the information before them that their long-term memory and understanding of what they were doing were overwhelmed. Students were overloaded and unsure where to start.

Working examples in maths, for instance, and problem-solving rules all enhance learning. Repetition helps to reinforce it. Directing, rather than guiding, children – a teacher standing in front of a class and presenting new information or skills – now has persuasive advocates. An analysis of half a century of research on the effect of direct instruction (Jean Stockard et al, 2018) has recently confirmed its benefits across the curriculum.

As we can see, play is very important to the development of young children but it does appear to have some limits when it comes to learning. Interestingly, Northern Ireland which at four years and two months has one of the youngest compulsory school starting ages in the world, has experimented with a play based versus a formal curriculum for its four-year-olds. Over time researchers have found no statistical difference in how the children did whether they began with the formal curriculum or the play based one.

The importance of parents

Young children spend many more hours at home than they do in nurseries and every year research provides more evidence of the role parents play in giving their children a good start in life. Let's look again at Europe's largest longitudinal study on this, the Effective Provision of Preschool Primary and Secondary Education. EPPSE has tracked the progress of nearly 3,000 children from the age of three until they were 18. The study has shown that children from deprived backgrounds can prosper at school if they have a good preschool experience and live in a home that encourages them to learn.

More research carried out for the UK's Equalities Review by Iram Siraj, Professor of Child Development and Education at Oxford University and a principal investigator for EPPSE, looked at 24 families whose children were succeeding against the odds in education. Half were on free school meals, more than half were in single parent families and four out of five lived in deprived areas.

The adult or adults in these families took education and parenting seriously. Many worried that they did not have the skills they needed to help their children but they were not afraid to ask for help from their extended family, other people who lived nearby or the religious communities to which they belonged.

Professor Siraj suggests that the practice of sending home reading books with children that began in the 1980s may have encouraged these parents' belief in education.[1] They and their children believe that success comes from working hard. When they find a task difficult, they are not deterred. By contrast, children from homes where learning is not valued, think success is simply down to ability. They think that if you are not clever, there is no point in trying. She says:

> We know that home influences kids more than school and that the level of educational stimulation that children receive is bound up with the engagement of their parents with them, for instance the amount of attention they get at home.

Despite strong evidence of the importance of parents' educational qualifications in determining their children's academic achievement, all parents can help their children to progress. What really counts is how parents behave. Says Professor Siraj:

> Reading books together, talking about historic buildings, attending free library sessions all support children's education whatever the level of disadvantage.

1   Unless stated otherwise, the quotations in this chapter from Professor Iram Siraj are taken from an interview with Judith Judd, 10 September, 2018.

Another longitudinal study confirms EPPSE's findings about why parents matter. It shows that between a third and a half of differences between deprived children and children in middle-income families in literacy, numeracy and behaviour are the result of parenting styles and the way that parents encourage learning. This research used data from 19,000 UK and 10,000 US children born in 2000 and 2001 analysed by Jane Waldfogel, professor of social work and public affairs at Columbia University in New York and Liz Washbrook, a researcher at Bristol University's Centre for Market and Public Organisation in the UK on secondment in Columbia.

The researchers who observed children in the US found that parenting styles had the biggest impact on the differences in school readiness between low and middle-income children, accounting for 19 per cent of the gap in maths, 21 per cent in literacy and a third in language.

In the UK, the study tracked more than 12,000 children and found that a combination of the home environment and parenting style accounted for around 20 per cent of the difference between low and middle-income children's school readiness. The way parents related to their children was almost as important as activities in the home such as reading and visits to the library or the theatre. The study described the parenting style that worked as "sensitive and responsive." In other words, parents who were warm towards their children and noticed their changing needs made the biggest contribution to their progress.

In the UK, research at Oxford University funded by the government, the Early Learning Partnership Programme, aimed at supporting disadvantaged families also reported changes in parents' behaviour. But the study lasted only 18 months so the long-term effects are unknown.

Preschools make a difference

Most parents of three and four-year-olds in the UK take advantage of government-funded preschooling. From 2018, English children were entitled to 30 hours free a week, though some parents, of course, choose to pay for even more.

Even those parents who feel confident that they can provide the foundations of reading and number at home want their children to learn how to relate to others and how to cope confidently with life outside their homes.

For politicians, the motivation for funding preschool education is somewhat different. The decision by recent governments of all parties to expand and fund preschool education is based on the belief that it gives children a head start at school and that it helps to narrow the academic gap between children from affluent backgrounds and those from poorer homes. There are different views from differing research groups on whether it's working but more on that both later in this and following chapters.

The EPPSE study mentioned earlier is the largest longitudinal study in Europe of the effect of preschool and primary education. The first phase of the study which ran from 1996 to 2003 recruited 2,800 children who attended all types of preschool: publicly and privately funded nursery schools, nursery classes, private and local authority day nurseries and playgroups. Researchers assessed them at the age of three and again as they entered school when they were compared with more than 300 children who had not been to preschool.

They found that children with any type of preschool experience made more progress socially and intellectually than those who had not been to preschool. Their behaviour also improved more. But there were differences according to the type of preschool they attended and how long they spent there. The greater the number of months spent in preschool, the better the outcome. Every month after the age of two led to increased intellectual development, more independence, better concentration and improved social skills. Interestingly, there was no difference between full-time and part-time attendance.

The quality of the education was also important. Children who were taught by better qualified staff, especially trained teachers, did better than those in lower quality preschools. Case studies revealed that the staff who saw educational and social development as equally important helped children achieve better all-round progress. The findings reinforce the belief outlined earlier in the chapter that children learn best when they receive some structured teaching. Teachers in the most successful preschools planned their sessions carefully to encourage children to think about what they were doing.

What about government hope that preschool education will promote social mobility and help close the gap between disadvantaged children and the rest? The EPPSE findings are encouraging. Disadvantaged children who did not attend preschool were less well-equipped to start school, intellectually and socially, than those who did. And they were still behind their peers at the age of seven. Disadvantaged boys in particular benefitted from preschool and all vulnerable children made more progress if they mixed with children from different social backgrounds at nursery.

Child and family case studies carried out by Iram Siraj as part of EPPSE investigated why some children succeeded against the odds of their socioeconomic background. They showed that children were more likely to succeed in education if they came from a home that supported learning and attended a good quality pre-school.

How sensitive parenting and a good preschool helped Martha succeed against the odds

Martha is one of 50 children whose progress was tracked in the EPPSE study from preschool to secondary school. The study looked at children who were "at risk" of not achieving their potential because they came from low-income families and had parents with low educational qualifications, factors that tend to hold children back.

By the time that she reached the early years of secondary school, Martha was achieving much better results than might have been predicted. She was succeeding against the odds of her background.

Martha came from a home where money was tight but her mother enjoyed playing with her. She went to preschool because her mother wanted her to enjoy the company of other children and to learn new skills there. These comments from her mother help to explain Martha's progress at school.

> 'Cos we didn't have a lot of money, so we made things.... Used to make all sorts (laughing). We used to walk up the city and walk to parks, and we used to do art stuff didn't we? We used to make a lot of things. Anything out of nothing (laughing). We made this big dolls' house out of toilet roll and glue and cardboard. We had this big cardboard box (laughing) we put a wooden plank on the bottom, and we made it into a dolls house. And it was really big; it was just out of toilet roll. It's brilliant (laughing).

And on Martha's preschool:

> They learn how to interact with other children ... definitely, erm ... and I think they do pick up a ... it ... slowly ... gets them into going to proper school, rather than just shove 'em in ... into school full-time, and then you're, "oh my god," you know, they slowly learn ... because it's very few hours to start with, and then they increase it until they go to proper school, so they do ... and I think they do teach them a lot, they teach them songs and ... urm ... well they teach them things that you wouldn't believe that they're teaching 'em. 'Cos they do it all through play to start with, in nursery.

> (Siraj et al. 1997–2014)

Researchers are still grappling with the question of whether the effects of attending a good preschool last. The EPPSE study suggests that they do. By the age of 11, children who had attended preschool were better behaved, had better social skills and did better at school work than those who had not. This was especially true for boys, children with special educational needs and those from disadvantaged backgrounds.

However, the quality of the preschool made a difference, particularly in Maths, English and to hyperactive behaviour. Only good or very good preschools had a long-term effect. The influence of home in the early years also continued to affect children's behaviour and academic performance at the end of primary school.

According to this study, the benefits of preschool do not end at 11. Children from all backgrounds who attended preschool are more likely than those who did not to progress to academic examinations in the sixth form. Findings published in 2015 show that they are significantly more likely to take four or more AS-levels. The researchers also found that children from homes where parents encouraged learning before they went to school – nursery rhymes, reading, playing with numbers and letters and visiting the library – were more likely to go on to A-levels.

Professor Siraj says:

> Schools play a role, a very important role and they can help children to catch up but the studies show that the effects of a good home learning environment and a good preschool have a cumulative effect. You build on it and create momentum.

Many of the EPPSE findings are confirmed by John Hattie, Professor of Education at Melbourne University, mentioned before. As we have heard, he spent 15 years surveying research on educational achievement and producing a statistical analysis of a wide variety of studies. He says that preschool intervention does make a difference to academic achievement though the effect lessens over time. Disadvantaged children gain most.

Hattie broadly agrees with the EPPSE findings that the quality of education for the under-fives is important. The most effective programmes are structured, intense and involve at least 15 children for up to 13 hours a week. He also points out that skills vital for academic achievement are often taught in preschool. Children who know for example, about "seriation" – the difference between the biggest and smallest, thinnest and thickest – or about sequencing, what comes first, second and third – are well placed to start school.

Doubts about the lasting effect of preschool have been raised by Lipsey, Farran and Durkin in a study of 2,990 children in Tennessee in the United States (2018). The researchers randomly assigned children to preschool or not. When they entered school the preschool children scored more highly than the rest but even in the first school year the differences began to disappear and by the age of eight or nine, the children who had not attended preschool were scoring significantly higher marks in maths and science and were doing slightly better in reading than those who had. It is a big study and it cannot be easily dismissed.

Note that the Tennessee research measured educational progress not the development of social skills or changes in behaviour. Parents will view the issue of preschools differently from governments who see them primarily as ways of raising standards. They are places where children first learn to be independent, to relate to others and to feel confident away from home. They learn how to cope with new experiences and a new environment.

As Professor Siraj says:

> Preschool offers something different from a good home learning environment. It offers the chance to meet other children, to use materials that may not be so prevalent at home. In science, for instance, children have the opportunity for water play and to learn about melting in cooking. Our studies find that all children benefit from attending preschool.

Whatever the educational outcomes of the decision by the governments of England, Scotland, Wales and Northern Ireland to offer free nursery education, it has eased the burdens of many working parents in the UK. Most researchers agree on the value of good quality education for the under-fives. That will strike a chord with all parents of young children. Parents think carefully about choosing a primary or a secondary school for their children. They talk to their friends and neighbours. They visit schools. They talk to teachers and assess the behaviour of the pupils. Picking the right nursery or preschool is just as important.

How to choose a good preschool

Professor Siraj suggests that, based on the EPPSE findings of what makes a good preschool, there are a number of things parents should look out for on a nursery visit as they observe how the staff relate to the children and what activities are happening. In the best nurseries there will be lots of talk and all research studies show that talk that is "real," for example about rock pools or theme parks, is more valuable than abstract talk about shape and colour.

A checklist of what to look out for could look like this:

- Is the relationship between children and teachers warm as it should be?
- Are teachers paying attention to individual children and treating all of them with respect?
- Are there plenty of child-centred activities going on?
- Are staff looking for opportunities to extend children's knowledge and vocabulary?
- Are staff well qualified? (Some research has found that high quality preschools tend to have at least one graduate on their staff. In Finland's highly successful school system, at least a third of nursery teachers need a degree. But some recent studies suggests that teachers' qualifications make no difference).

What does good nursery teaching look like? Professor Siraj tells the story of a nursery that she visited in Birmingham where the children were outside studying giant African snails. One girl said:

> "They's eating them leaves, again."
> "Yes," said the teacher. "They do seem to particularly like those hosta leaves, don't they?"
> The boys were screaming past on their tricycles paying no attention to the snails so one girl said: "Stop shouting. You'll frighten the snails."
> "Oh," said the teacher, "so you think snails can hear do you?"
> Then all the boys abandoned their tricycles and came to see whether the snails could hear.

That sort of interaction between a teacher and young children helps to set them up for a lifetime of learning. If you and your child's preschool teachers are encouraging that kind of talk and learning from talk before they go to big school, your children will be much more ready for school when they finally make the transition there.

How can you tell when a child is ready for school or not? That's what our next chapter is all about but before we get there, let's remind you that research continues to show the benefits of play first highlighted in studies more than half a century ago, and challenges those who are keen to rush children into formal education.

Let's leave you with an important thought from one of the great researchers into early education, Lev Vygotsky, who said:

> In play a child is always above his average age, above his daily behaviour; in play it is as though he is a head taller than himself.

It's good to feel a head taller than you are when you are very little (or indeed at any age). It makes you more confident and more likely to bravely step forward and learn lots more.

References

Whitebread, D. with Basilio, M., Kuvalja, M. and Verma, M. (2012) 'The importance of play.' TIE (The Toy Industries of Europe). Available from www.csap.cam.ac.uk/media/uploads/files/1/david-whitebread—importance-of-play-report.pdf (downloaded 21 May 2019).

Siraj, I., Taggart, B., Silva, K., Simmons, P. and Melhuish, E. (1997–2014) 'Effective pre-school, primary and secondary education project (EPPSE).' Available from https://www.ucl.ac.uk/ioe/research/featured-research/eppse-publications (downloaded 21 May 2019).

Waldfogel, J. and Washbrook, E.V. (2010) 'Low income and early cognitive development in the UK: a report for the Sutton Trust.' Available from www.sutton trust.com/wp-content/uploads/2010/02/Sutton_Trust_Cognitive_Report-2.pdf (downloaded 21 May 2019).

Hattie, J. (2009) *Visible Learning. A Synthesis of Over 800 Meta-Analyses Relating to Achievement*. London: Routledge.

Hattie, J. andYates, G. (2013) *Visible Learning and the Science of How We Learn*. London: Routledge.

Vallotton, C. and Ayoub, C. (2011) 'Use your words: the role of language in the development of toddlers' self-regulation.' *Early Childhood Research Quarterly*, Vol. *26*, No. 2, pp. 169–181.

Whitebread, D. (2011) *Developmental Psychology and Early Childhood Education*. London: Sage.

Fernyhough, C. and Fradley, E. (2005) 'Private speech on an executive task: relations with task difficulty and task performance.' *Cognitive Development*, Vol. *20*, pp. 103–120. Available from https://community.dur.ac.uk/c.p.fernyhough/Fer nyhoughCogDev05.pdf (downloaded 21 May 2019).

Taneja, V., Sriram, S., Beri, R., Sreenivas, V., Aggarwal, R. and Kaur, R. (2002) '"Not by bread alone": impact of a structured 90-minute play session on development of children in an orphanage.' *Child: Care, Health and Development*, *28*, pp. 95–100.

Chudakoff, H.P. (2007) *Children at Play: An American History*. New York: New York University Press.

Karpov, Y.V. (2005) *The neo-Vygotskian Approach to Child Development*. Cambridge: Cambridge University Press.

Vygotsky, L.S. (1978) 'The role of play in development.' In *Mind in Society* (pp. 92–104). Cambridge, MA: Harvard University Press.

Bruner, J.S. (1961) 'The act of discovery.' *Harvard Educational Review*, Vol. *31*, pp. 21–32.

Ray, W.E. (1961) 'Pupil discovery vs. direct instruction.' *Journal of Experimental Education*, *29*, pp. 271–280.

Alfieri, L., Brooks, P.J., Aldrich, N.J. and Tenenbaum, H. R. (2011) 'Does discovery-based instruction enhance learning?' *Journal of Educational Psychology*, Vol. *103*, No. 1, pp. 1–18. doi:10.1037/a0021017

Kirschner, P., Sweller, J. and Clark, R. (2006) 'Why minimum guidance on instruction does not work: an analysis of the failure of constructivist, discovery, problem-based, experiential, and inquiry-based teaching.' *Educational Psychologist*, Vol. *41*, No. 2, pp. 75–86. Available from www.cogtech.usc.edu/publica tions/kirschner_Sweller_Clark.pdf (downloaded 21 May 2019).

Stockard, J., Wood, T.W., Coughlin, C. and Khoury, C.R. (2018) 'The effectiveness of direct instruction curricula.' *Review of Educational Research*, Vol. *88*, No. 4, pp. 1–29. doi:10.3102/0034654317751919. Available from http://arthurreadingworkshop. com/wp-content/uploads/2018/05/StockardDIMetaAnalysis2018.pdf (downloaded 21 May 2019).

Lipsey, M.W., Farran, D.C. and Durkin, K. (2018) 'Effects of the Tennessee Prekindergarten Program on children's achievement and behavior through third grade.' *Early Childhood Research Quarterly*, Vol. *45*, pp. 155–176.

Vygotsky, Lev S. (1967) 'Play and the mental development of the child.' *Soviet Psychology*, Vol. *5*, pp. 6–18.

Chapter 5

Ready for school?

My youngest is 4 in 2 weeks so eligible to start school this summer but I have decided to defer him till next year as I know he probably needs the next year to develop his confidence and social interactions which will help him at school. I went to school aged 4 and I know that being one of the youngest in the class has its drawbacks.

> Netmums response to a post querying whether it was possible to get a three-year-old into primary school

I still remember the discussion between my mother and grandmother about whether I should leave nursery and start school when I was four. They asked me what I thought and I told them I would love to go to school. I did and I loved it.

> Wendy Berliner, author and journalist

We now know that research tells us that the best way to make a flying start to your formal school years is by being ready for them. If things have gone well and you've had a good home learning environment and pre-school experience you should be independent, confident, curious and ready to enjoy and embrace the learning to come.

But beyond those key learning attitudes what else do you need to be ready for school and how can parents be sure their children are? Well, it's important to be mature enough to be able to sit still for a while and concentrate on what a teacher is telling you. It's good to be mature enough to follow instructions. It also helps to have had experience drawing with crayons and painting with brushes because that should have given you the dexterity to hold a pencil as you learn to write. It is also good to have developed the confidence to mix with larger groups of children and to respond to your teacher. Well-developed language and vocabulary help a lot.

But children differ so much in personality and their approach to life – as do adults – and they will have had many different experiences, educational and social, depending on what families they come from and the level of affluence and stability those families have. Some children are "young" for their age and others are "old beyond their years" so what does the research say is the best age is to start and should it vary dependent on the child? This is a contested area where policy makers and educators can disagree and researchers can come up with conclusions which, on the face of it, seem to differ until you dig a little more deeply.

To complicate it even further, there are different views about this depending on where you live in the world. Even in Europe with all its cultural links and joint history, compulsory school age can differ by as much as three years as we can see from the following list.

Primary school starting age in European countries:

FOUR: Northern Ireland, Luxembourg.

FIVE: Cyprus, Malta, UK, Netherlands, Latvia.

SIX: Austria, Belgium, Croatia, Czech Republic, Denmark, France, Germany, Greece, Iceland, Republic of Ireland, Italy, Liechtenstein, Norway, Poland, Portugal, Romania, Slovakia, Slovenia, Spain.

SEVEN: Bulgaria, Estonia, Finland, Lithuania, Serbia, Sweden.

Does the early bird catch the worm? Are children living in countries that start formal schooling earlier doing better than the rest? No, they aren't. Finland and Estonia who don't start formal schooling until their children are seven have two of the best performing school systems in the world. Poland, where children start school at six, is one of the most rapidly improved countries. All three of these European countries soundly beat the UK in the Programme of International Student Assessment (PISA), a study done every three years by the Organisation for Economic Co-operation and Development (OECD), in reading, maths and sciences, the three subjects covered by the test. The UK languishes in the middle of the table with the United States beneath.

That list of school entry ages is, of course, compulsory school ages – the latest age children must start school – and many children will be in different forms of preschools long before that throughout Europe and, indeed, the world.

In France, where some children start school at three or even two despite the mandatory age being six, President Macron said in 2018 that he wanted to drop that mandatory school age to three. That's because most children in France are in nursery schools when they are three and the ones that aren't tend to live in poorer areas or in French overseas territories and start school doubly disadvantaged. Helping the disadvantaged is one of the core arguments for an early start to school. It's an attempt to try to equalise outcomes for children whose families don't or can't support their learning in the early years.

Then there is the issue of what should be on the curriculum for these very young children. Again, politicians and educators can differ profoundly on this. Some European countries are happy to introduce formal teaching of reading later rather than early – and this includes some of the high performing school systems of Europe.

In the last PISA tables published in 2016 Finland came fourth in the world on reading and Estonia sixth. Both, remember, start compulsory school at seven years old. The Republic of Ireland came between them at fifth and children there have a compulsory school start at six. The UK which starts compulsory school at five was 22nd. The United States, where compulsory school begins at six was 24th. Topping the charts in reading, maths and science was Singapore where the children start compulsory school at six-years-old.

But we heard in the last chapter an English politician describing it as a "scandal" that children in reception classes are unable to read simple words. English schools are now being encouraged to make reading the cornerstone of the reception year (four- and five-year-olds) – the year before the formal curriculum kicks in. Your view depends on where you are sitting in the world. Early years teachers in England are horrified and say learning to read matters much less than learning independence and confidence when you are very young.

The introduction of formal learning to very young children in England worries some parents as well as educators and in England you can request that your child starts school a year later as the Mum quoted at the beginning of the chapter did. She is not alone.

In 2014, Mary Lawler, mother of three-year-old Oscar, appealed to Bradford City Council in the UK for the right to postpone his first day at school for a year. Oscar was born on August 28 and Bradford children are expected to start school in the September after their fourth birthday even if, like Oscar, they are only four and a few days.

But Mrs Lawler, who won her appeal, argued that Oscar was too young at just four years and four days. She said: "I think he needs another year at nursery to develop a bit more" (*The Daily Telegraph*).

Mrs Lawler's fears highlight the debate about the importance of play-based learning found in preschools and the introduction of formal learning in school. As we can see in most other European countries, no-one would have suggested that Oscar should start school at the age of four.

Much research supports Mary Lawler's belief that Oscar would benefit from another year of play-based education in his nursery but, crucially, not all academics agree – more to come on this later. Research studies suggest later starts don't harm learning to read and can reduce poor behaviour in class.

Research in New Zealand compared children who started formal literacy lessons at the age of five with those who started at seven. By the age of 11 there was no difference in reading ability between the two groups but the children who started at five were less positive about reading and had more difficulty understanding what they read than those who started later.

Another study of 15-year-olds' reading achievement in 55 countries found no connection between reading ability and school entry age.

A study for the National Bureau of Economic Research in the United States (2015) linked a dramatic reduction in hyperactivity to starting school a year later. Thomas Dee of Stanford University and Hans Henrik Sieversten compared children who started school at five with those who began at six. They used the Danish National Birth Cohort study to analyse responses from more than 50,000 parents about their children's mental health when they were seven and more than 35,000 when the same children were 11. Those who started school a year later had markedly better self-control and were less hyperactive.

As we said earlier, children do differ and parents are generally the best judge of whether their child is ready for school, wherever they live, and family debate about the issue is a good thing, particularly if it involves a discussion with teachers about how well they feel the child would cope, as Tristan's family in Germany did.

Tristan's story

Tristan lives in southern Germany and started school two weeks before he was six. His parents agonised about whether to let him stay in kindergarten for another year where he enjoyed drawing, craft, singing and playing outside but was not taught to read or to use numbers. However, some of his older friends in kindergarten were starting school and his kindergarten teachers thought he would cope well with more formal education so they decided that he should go too. Other parents, whose children were the same age but who found language and mixing with other children more difficult, decided that they should stay in kindergarten.

When Tristan arrived at the state-run primary school, just a few minutes' walk from his house, he was the second youngest child in the reception class. Some of his classmates were already seven. He settled in well and, in the first term, like most of the children in the class, he learned to read and to do simple sums. His favourite activity was to bring home the class penguin and to write about its weekend adventures. Like many children, he was not always hugely enthusiastic about school but he was willing to learn. His parents felt happy that they had made the right decision.

Children arrive at school with a wealth of experience already behind them. Their early years are a time of rapid development. Home and the contribution of parents are hugely important. Much evidence also points to the value of good preschools in shaping children's intellectual and social skills. But it is important to get the decision right about when to start school, particularly for the youngest in the school year.

Does your birthday matter?

As we've learned, the age you are supposed to start school varies depending on where in the world you live. But, regardless of your chronological age when you start school, does the day you are born matter? Can your birth date negatively influence your outcomes at school?

Unfortunately, yes it can, particularly if you were born very prematurely, or have a birthdate which makes you one of the youngest in the school year.

We have already seen Mary Lawler of Bradford, England winning an appeal to delay for a year the entry of her son, Oscar, to school when he would otherwise have been starting school at just four years and four-days-old. Like the netmums poster at the beginning of the chapter, she thought he was too young for formal education and needed the play-based environment of his nursery for another 12 months so that he could develop a bit more.

What's the problem?

Children are born throughout the year and there is generally a cut-off date by which you qualify for a particular school year, wherever you live in the world. Some countries are a bit more relaxed about that date, others are more rigid.

This means you can be very "old" in your school year or very "young." The youngest can be a year younger than the oldest and, developmentally, that matters a lot when you haven't been on the planet that long. Whether you arrive at school at just four or nearly five in England, for example, can make a big difference in your physical, mental and emotional development and the way you settle into school, particularly if your teachers don't know how to make sufficient allowances for your lack of maturity or even mistake the way you are for a special educational need.

For those reasons, perhaps it should not be surprising that international research tells us that children who are youngest in their school year generally don't perform as well as their older classmates – and the birth date effect seems to be strongest in countries where children start school younger and have more rigid systems.

This may all sound a bit gloomy but there are two important points to remember as you read on:

1   Not everyone is affected.
2   There are things you can do about it (and teachers can do about it).

The birth date effect was first noted in the 1960s and researchers and educators have been accumulating data since then. In the northern hemisphere where the school year often begins in autumn and the youngest children in the class are summer-born, there was a theory that the gestation period might be the culprit with summer-born children gestating in the winter months and foetuses prey to and affected by the increased number of infections that would be prevalent. This has been debunked and the finger of blame now points at your maturity levels when you take national tests and exams, possibly augmented by a lack of sufficient understanding about the impact of maturation on performance at school level.

What emerges from large scale research is that you are more likely to find the very youngest in the school year in the lowest ability sets, or identified with some kind of special need, or thinking they are not very good at learning or feeling bullied or unhappy or even indulging in riskier behaviour as they get older, because they are less grown up than their peers. Conversely, you find children who are oldest in their school year over represented in schools where they have been academically selected on the basis of test performance.

You can see why it can happen. The very young ones in the class are generally not as far ahead developmentally as the oldest when they start school. It's not just about being physically smaller, it's about how much they are able to concentrate or sit still, or how good their language skills are or whether they can hold a pencil easily.

The older ones are more likely to be more advanced in all of those things and at school that biological advantage of being older in your school year can be reinforced by praise for your quick acquisition of new skills and in turn that will benefit your self-esteem and self-image of yourself as a good learner. If you are growing up in a selective school system, you are more likely to be ready for tests to decide which school you should go to next than your younger classmates.

In England, with a school year starting in September you can start school in the school year in which you become five years old. Children who are almost five when they start school are more likely to have a flying start in the class compared to those classmates who won't be five till the end of the school year. The youngest are starting school when they are only just four – as Oscar Lawler would have been had he not stayed in his nursery for an extra year.

Think of the potential negative impact on the child's self-image as a good learner if they are less physically, mentally and emotionally developed than their older classmates, and feel they are struggling in comparison. In the case of the youngest remember, they are almost a year younger.

Whenever or wherever you are born – whether you live in the southern hemisphere and your school year starts in January or February or in the northern and have a summer or autumn start, the impact will be felt particularly in systems where formal education begins younger. Only the relevant dates will change.

But never forget that the quality of your child's preschool and how well you have been able to prepare your children for school, by reading to them, answering their questions and having lots of conversation with them, for example, will also have a positive impact that can reduce and overcome the negatives of being very young in your school year. Some very successful people were born at the "wrong" time of year for their school systems.

What's the evidence?

A large body of international research agrees that the younger you are in the year you start school, the more likely you are to be behind in performance. In countries where children start school relatively young the birth date effect is more significant and lasts longer – countries such as England. Although the children can catch up a fair bit, most of them never quite close the gap – but a significant minority do. It doesn't affect every child, this is an average effect, but it affects a lot of them and it affects the very youngest most.

Two significant pieces of research are a working paper from the London based Institute for Fiscal Studies (Crawford, Dearden and Meghir, 2010) and a report from the IFS with the Nuffield Foundation and the Economic and Social Research Council (Crawford, Dearden and Greaves, 2013). These studies found that the performance of children in tests and GCSEs in English schools are progressively affected by the birth date effect with the youngest boys affected negatively most of all and the eldest in class least affected. Every day older or younger a child was in a school year affected performance.

This was large-scale research based on several of Britain's renowned longitudinal databases, including the Millennium Cohort Study which is following the lives of nearly 19,000 children born in 2000 to 2001. It also used the Labour Force Survey which is the UK's largest household survey and provides official statistics of employment and unemployment.

The youngest in the school year, the August-borns, as a group were behind at every stage in their education. While 60.7 per cent of September-born girls and 50.3 per cent of September-born boys achieved at least 5 A*–C grades at GCSE – the expected level – only 55.2 per cent of August-born girls and 44.2 per cent of August-born boys did the same. This means that access to further and higher education, and future jobs, can be affected by the month in which you are born.

The August-born were 20 per cent less likely to go to a leading university and 20 per cent more likely to take a vocational rather than an academic route as they got older. August-born children were also more likely to be identified as having special needs and more likely to report being unhappy at school and being been bullied than autumn born children.

They were also:

- Likely to exhibit significantly poorer social and emotional development;
- Likely to have significantly lower confidence in their own ability;
- Significantly less likely to believe that their own actions made a difference;
- More likely to indulge in risky behaviour, e.g. smoking.

Yet when the research team looked at cognitive tests that take the age of the child when taking them into account, there were no differences between autumn-born and summer-born children, suggesting that different schooling experiences did not affect their cognitive development, just school outcomes; the summer-born children were generally doing less well than the average in their GCSEs, were less confident learners and were more likely to take a vocational route.

Prematurity

For premature children, this birth date effect can be compounded – particularly for the very premature, those born at 32 weeks or less gestation. Prematurity is a known risk factor in education because the child's development may be delayed or they may have special needs related to being born very early; more very premature children have autism spectrum disorders, for example.

There are almost 3,000 very pre-term children born each year in England whose birthdays fall between 1 April and 31 August (in educational terms, summer born). This group is at the highest risk of developmental delays.

As an example of the problem which exists throughout the world, although to reiterate the exact dates will differ, in England the school year begins in September and the age you are on September 1 determines which school year you belong to. Compulsory school age is five but the School Admissions Code requires school admission authorities to provide places for children in the September after their fourth birthday. If you are four on September 1 you are meant to start school the following September, when you will be almost five but it will still be the September after your fourth birthday.

If your birthday is the day before – August 31 – you belong to the previous school year and are supposed to start school that September, the September after your fourth birthday. That's a year's difference in development.

You can see the potential disadvantage of being summer-born from that. But then consider a child due to be born in October who is born prematurely in July and therefore is due to go to school a year earlier than they would have if they had been born when they were due – the other side of the school year qualifying cut off point. Combine that with potential development delays caused by prematurity and that's a double whammy.

Dieter Wolke, Professor of Developmental Psychology and Individual Differences at the University of Warwick in the UK, has spent time researching the education effects on premature children and the summer-born and believes that summer-born children should not be held back for a year but that very premature children should get extra support in school:

Dieter Wolke[1]

Professor of Developmental Psychology and Individual Differences, University of Warwick.

Research has shown that you do find a gradual effect of children younger at birth in their school year doing less well. You have to remember this is on average for a group. Some children who are summer-born do very well. I have two children – one born on 3 September and the other born on 28 August, so one was old in his school year and the other was young in hers. Both have done well academically.

For the general population of summer-born children, delaying school entry by a year is not the way to go if they do not get similar stimulation as in school. What the research shows is that it doesn't make any difference. They are better off in school getting stimulation and help if needed, particularly if they come from a disadvantaged background. They should get more help not less by being delayed entry to school. It is the age you sit tests and exams that matters.

The only children who should be held back are the very premature. If a child is due in October and is born very early, say in July, that child will face being in school a full year earlier than they should be had they been born at full-term, while also being at higher risk of school problems because of that prematurity. There should be a blanket permission for them to be held back. Pre-term children are less likely to have conduct issues – they are more likely to be shy or withdrawn – but they can have more often maths problems and attention problems.

There should be more awareness of the problems they can face being very pre-term and support given to them; they should get extra support at least for the first two years at school.

For everyone else who is young in their school year they are better off in school but getting extra support that recognises they may need it because of their lower levels of maturity. There is a lot of research discussing the longer-term poorer outcomes of pre-term children, particularly in maths, and this can continue into adulthood and affect their wealth. For exams you could use a statistical formula that recognises prematurity and being born late in the school year and correct the examination results. But that is controversial and some parents of children who have the little bonus of being older in the school year may think that's unfair.

1   The quotations in this chapter from Professor Dieter Wolke are taken from an interview with Wendy Berliner, 21 November, 2018.

Other research

Ability groups

A working paper published by the London based Centre for Longitudinal Studies at the Institute for Education in 2013 found the youngest children in a school year are far more likely to be placed in the lowest ability groups than the oldest – the autumn-born pupils. By the age of seven, September-born children were nearly three times as likely to be in the top stream as those born in the following August. If the children were not only streamed, but also grouped by ability within their class or year for specific subjects, then the age differences became even more marked.

University attendance

A study of OECD countries (Bedard and Dhuey, 2006) found younger children in the school year performing less well and also recorded the effect continuing into further and higher education. Data from Canada and the United States showed that the youngest were least likely to attend university.

In the UK this effect was confirmed by a 2010 study from the Higher Education Policy Institute which found that over a six-year period 28 per cent of August-born children went to university compared with 32 per cent of those born in September.

It's not just schools

Birth dates also affect sports teams with national teams often having players clustered with birth dates at a certain time of the year. In England, for example, top football players often have winter birthdays, perhaps a throwback to the time when they were bigger in their school year and more likely to be picked first for school teams, if they were talented, then local leagues and eventually national teams. At each step of the way more resources would have been put into their development embedding the effect of the original birth date which had benefitted them.

It's not true for all of them. David Beckham, for example, has a May birthday, but then again, his parents were fanatical Manchester United supporters travelling from London to Manchester's Old Trafford for matches and would have supported young David's ambitions to be a professional footballer every kick of the way – and he had a prodigious talent and work ethic. But Wayne Rooney, England's record goal scorer, has an October birthday and Peter Shilton, the most capped player for England, has a September one.

A 2005 study of Premiership stars by the Association of Football Statisticians found that out of 1,779 Englishmen to play at the top of the game over the previous 13 years, more than 40 per cent were born in September, October or November. According to the Football Association for the 2008–2009 season 57 per cent of players at Premier League academies were born between September and December, while 14 per cent had their birthday between May and August.

And in Australia a 2010 study from Queensland University of Technology's Institute of Health and Biomedical Innovation, found by analysing the birthdays of professional Australian Football League players, that a disproportionate number were born in the early months of the year. The Australian school year begins in January so the oldest children in the Australian school year will have birthdays in the early months of the year.

The same patterns are found in other sports – ice hockey in Canada, for example, and baseball in America, and a 2013 study looking at players in the World Junior Tennis Finals found the same age effect there.

What can be done?

In sports, the good news is that the industry is aware of what's been happening for some time and is putting measures into place to, if you will excuse the pun, level the playing field.

In education in America there is a longstanding practice often known as "redshirting" – holding children who are young in the school year or who are not developmentally ready, back for a year so that they start their education by being the oldest children in the class. The word redshirting is a 1950s one and comes from sport and practices in American high schools and colleges where young athletes would be kept out of competition for a year whilst they developed; they wore a red shirt to differentiate them from competition players – hence redshirting.

More recently the idea of holding a child back a year at the start of their education – like Oscar Lawler – has become more prevalent in England where formal education starts earlier than the European average and it is up to local authorities to decide, with input from parents and education professionals, whether a child should be held back and, even more importantly, whether they should permanently stay in the year below their chronological age.

Children are at risk of missing their school reception year and still being the youngest in class if a local authority agrees to allowing a child to be held back a year but then says they must then join their same age peers in the first year of the formal curriculum. This means they lose the reception year where schooling is more play based. Practice varies across the country with some local authorities less open to appeals.

Both in America and England the parents seeking to hold their child back a year tend to be from more affluent backgrounds and this has led to charges they are trying to get unfair advantage for their children. In the US it has been described somewhat dramatically – let alone inaccurately – as a "graying of the kindergarten."

The practice raises some obvious questions. The first is to ask, is it helpful to the education of children who are held back from starting school when in school they could get extra support? Secondly, what about the effect on very young children in their class – the summer birthday children who weren't held back from their year? Aren't they doubly disadvantaged? Somebody ends up being the youngest in any school year no matter when you start it or what you do or don't do with deferrals.

Let's try to unpick this. What we know for sure is that research in many parts of the world has confirmed a birth date effect – a phenomenon in which children the wrong side of a cut-off date for school admission can be adversely affected.

The researchers in the big IFS study were clear that their findings proved it was the *age* the children took their tests and exams that made the difference to performance. The youngest children were nearly a year younger than the oldest in their school year and it was that which made the difference.

Dieter Wolke, who we have just heard from, believes the summer-born should be in school with their age cohort and getting extra support at school if they need it, particularly disadvantaged children.

Other research, as we have already heard, finds that more children who learn to read earlier find it harder and enjoy it less, than children who learn to read later. It has also been found that children who start school later tend to behave better when they are more mature; the IFS research found the August-borns less socially and emotionally developed too.

We've also heard that children who start school when they are much younger than the other children in the school year are more likely to end up in lower ability sets or to be identified as having special educational need, which will affect their educational outcomes. The IFS research was looking at public examination outcomes and they indeed found poorer results, but to repeat it wasn't the age you started school or how much learning had been packed in prior to those exams, it was the chronological age when you took them that was the problem.

In 2015, there was a debate in the House of Commons in London which centred on these long-held concerns about the birth date effect. After it the government reissued guidelines to local authorities to ensure they understood that children could start school in the year below their chronological age but that the needs of the individual child had to be taken into account when decisions are taken. This came a year after Mary Lawler made her successful appeal to Bradford Council on Oscar's behalf.

At the same time the government also commissioned its own research into the summer birthday effect and this found delaying a summer-born child's entry to primary school has little impact on attainment. Children born in England between April and August, whose start in reception was put back a year, were doing only marginally better in Year 1 tests – so marginal that it wasn't statistically significant. It also found that where children were being held back by a year, they were generally very young children – they had July birthdays or, even more likely, August birthdays.

Perhaps most intriguingly, pupils who were not summer-born outperformed both the delayed and normal admission summer-born pupils. There is no current research that can explain that one.

Would it help to let all children start school when they are older?

It's true that the later children begin school, the smaller the developmental difference there is. Across the world six-years-old is the most common age to start school. That doesn't mean children aren't in preschool educational provision before that though.

As we have touched on before, one of the major reasons given for starting school earlier is to help disadvantaged children whose homes may not be able to provide the stimulation and early educational opportunities that more affluent homes can. For example, books and reading and attention. In England, children whose parents or carers read to them before they go to school generally have better A-level results, according to longitudinal research from the Effective Preschool, Primary and Secondary study.

If the age at which a child sits a test is the key driver of differences in educational attainment, as the IFS researchers have found, extra early support at school for the premature and the summer-born (or whoever is the youngest in the school year, regardless of where in the world the school is) is a no brainer. And whilst being very contentious, age-adjusted test scores would be a solution that would be simpler to deliver than up ending national education systems that are built on start dates buried in their culture.

An alternative would be sitting exams when you are developmentally ready – another very contentious one. Who would decide when a child was developmentally ready and would certain groups manipulate that for their children's advantage? What about the effect on teachers trying to teach a class with children taking exams at different times of the year rather than a fixed point?

The good news is that although the IFS research has found fewer young people with summer birthdays going to leading universities, it didn't find that in adulthood the summer-born were any worse off. They didn't earn less, for example, and they weren't less healthy or happy.

And there are lots of high achieving people whose birth dates give them what are known as "summer birthdays" in the northern hemisphere who prove that you are not defined by your birth date. For example, in the UK where a "summer birthday" is defined as anything from April 1 to August 31, we have:

- Sam Mendes, multi award winning film director, born on August 1;
- J.K. Rowling, author and creator of Harry Potter – born on July 31;
- David Hockney, the world's most expensive living artist – born on July 9;
- Tim Berners- Lee, inventor of the World Wide Web born on June 8.

Perhaps a key takeaway is that all teachers should know about the effect of maturation, or lack of it for the very young ones in year, in class performance and should have the resources to offer extra support that might be needed. Most of all, parents need to realise that if they support their children's mental, physical and emotional development in the home from when they are born, children have much more chance of succeeding in school whenever they are born.

References

PISA OECD (2016) *PISA 2015 Results (Volume I) Excellence and Equity in Education*. Paris: OECD Publishing. Available from https://read.oecd-ilibrary.org/education/pisa-2015-results-volume-i_9789264266490-en#page4 (downloaded 4 June 2018).

Suggate, S.P. (2009) 'School entry age and reading achievement in the 2006 Programme for International Student Assessment (PISA).' *International Journal of Educational Research*, Vol. 48, No. 3, pp. 151–161.

Suggate, S.P., Schaughency, E. A. and Reese, E. (2013) 'Children learning to read later catch up to children reading earlier.' *Early Childhood Research Quarterly*, Vol. 28, No. 1, pp. 33–48.

Dee, T.S. and Sieversten, H.H. (2018) 'The gift of time? School starting age and mental health.' *Health Economics*, Vol. 27, No. 5, pp. 781–802. doi:10.1002/hec.3638

Crawford, C., Dearden, L. and Meghir, C. (2010) 'When you are born matters: the impact of date of birth on educational outcomes in England.' Institute for Fiscal Studies with the Economic and Social Research Council. Available from www.ifs.org.uk/wps/wp1006.pdf (downloaded 26 May 2019).

Crawford, C., Dearden, L. and Greaves, E. (2013) 'When you are born matters: evidence for England.' Institute for Fiscal Studies with the Economic and Social Research Council and the Nuffield Foundation. Available from www.ifs.org.uk/comms/r80.pdf (downloaded 26 May 2019).

Crawford, C. and Greaves, E. (2013) 'When should summer born children start school?' Institute for Fiscal Studies Observations. Available from www.ifs.org.uk/publications/6856 (downloaded 26 May 2019).

Johnson, S., Hennessy, E., Smith, R., Trikic, R., Wolke, D. and Marlow, N. (2009) 'Academic attainment and special educational needs in extremely preterm children at 11 years of age: the EPICure study.' *Archives of Disease in Childhood – Fetal and Neonatal Edition*, Vol. *94*, No. 4, pp. F283–289. doi:10.1136/adc.2008.152793

de Jong, M., Verhoeven, M. and van Baar, A.L. (2012) 'School outcomes, cognitive functioning, and behaviour problems in moderate and late preterm children and adults: a review.' *Seminars in Fetal & Neonatal Medicine*, Vol. *17*, pp. 163–169.

Jaleel, J., Wolke, D., Bartmann, P. (2013) 'Poor attention rather than hyperactivity/impulsivity predicts academic achievement in very preterm and full-term adolescents.' *Psychological Medicine*, Vol. *42*, No. 1, pp. 183–196.

Campbell, T.A. (2013) 'In-school ability grouping and the month of birth effect: preliminary evidence from the Millennium Cohort Study.' Centre for Longitudinal Studies at the Institute for Education. Available from https://cls.ucl.ac.uk/wp-content/uploads/2017/04/Ability-grouping-and-the-month-of-birth-effect-T-Campbell-March-2013-FINAL.pdf (downloaded 26 May 2019).

Bedard, K. and Dhuey, E. (2006) 'The persistence of early childhood maturity: international evidence of long-run age effects.' *The Quarterly Journal of Economics*, Vol. *121*, No. 4, pp. 1437–1472. doi:10.1093/qje/121.4.1437

Clark, L. (2010) 'August-born children are 'less likely to go to university.' *Daily Mail*. Available from www.dailymail.co.uk/news/article-1246359/August-born-children-likely-to-university.html#ixzz1cSejAnbb (downloaded 6 June 2019).

McClatchey, C. (2011) 'Summer-born struggle: why August children suffer at school.' *BBC News*. Available at www.bbc.co.uk/news/magazine-15490760 (downloaded 6 June 2019).

Barnett, A. (2010) *Month of Birth Determines who Becomes a Sports Star*. Heidelberg and New York: Springer.

Cirin, R. and Lubwama, J. (2018) 'Delayed school admissions for summer born pupils.' Department for Education. Available from https://assets.publishing.service.gov.uk/government/uploads/system/uploads/attachment_data/file/707417/Delayed_school_admissions_for_summer-born_pupils.pdf (downloaded 6 June 2019).

Sylva, K., Melhuish, E., Sammons, P.Siraj, I., Taggart, B. with Smees, R., Tóth, K., Welcomme, W. and Hollingworth, K. (2014) 'Students' educational and developmental outcomes at age 16: Effective Pre-school, Primary and Secondary Education (EPPSE 3–16) project research report.' Department for Education. Available from https://assets.publishing.service.gov.uk/government/uploads/system/uploads/attachment_data/file/351496/RR354_-_Students__educational_and_developmental_outcomes_at_age_16.pdf (downloaded 6 June 2019).

Chapter 6

Starting school

My first day at school was a new adventure for me. I had to wear a school uniform: a blue dress and handmade leather sandals. Having run around all but naked for the first eight years of my life, it was very exciting.

Anonymous Australian school essay.

School's OK but I don't think I'll go again.
Michael Berliner, aged five, at the end of his second day at primary school.

Cast your mind back to when you or your children started school. It's quite likely that you remember it. Long term research shows that big life events like marriage and divorce, a spouse or a child dying, or being sacked or retiring are in the top ten of the most stressful events people have to cope with in their lives. But look a bit further down the list and there are lots of other things that can have a massive impact too. Starting school is right up there with them.

Whether your first day at school was a happy or traumatic moment may well have coloured how you felt about school for some time. You may have skipped in with barely a backward look, happy and ready to learn or you may have had to be prised sobbing off whoever brought you in and then were in no fit mental state to learn anything for a while.

If you have children of school age it's even more likely that you remember your children starting school, indeed it may be burned irrevocably into your memory with no need for helpful home videos or photographs to remind you of how you felt. Their response to it and how the class teacher dealt with it will have coloured how they first felt about school and how you felt and perhaps still feel.

Having to relinquish a wailing child who is stabbing you with baleful and yet desolate looks as a teacher firmly takes their hand and assures you they will be fine as soon as you've gone, is one circle of hell. Another is having your child cheerfully take this stranger's hand, as if you don't exist, and trot away with them as they are swallowed into a brand-new world you don't belong to and don't feel you have any locus in. Either way it can be a cue for some full-on adult sobbing.

But momentous as these first steps into formal education are – and the feelings they create – they are only one small part of the importance of the first year in education. Longitudinal research suggests that the effects of that first year can last a lifetime. We have already learned how important a good home learning environment and preschool is to children's development but settling successfully into school with effective teaching during that first year matters a lot too.

Perhaps we shouldn't be surprised given the Reception year at school coincides with a period of rapid cognitive development. As we have already learned, four and five-year-olds produce about twice as many synapses, or connections, between brain cells in some parts of their brains as adults do in the same period.

Children of this age have all the windows wide open to learning new things and brain connections used regularly will strengthen while others which are seldom, if ever, used gradually get pruned. If infant children get the right kind of education in their first year of school, that is going to keep the right highways and byways of the brain working at their optimum level and set your children up for a good education and future.

The proof comes in research published in 2017 by Durham University from a large study of English school children between the ages of four and 16. This found that it is critical to a child's educational success to receive an effective education during the Reception year – the year between the ages of four and five and the crucial year before the formal school curriculum starts in England.

We saw earlier that the definition of effective education for four- to five-year-olds can be something of a battleground that leads to clashes between those who believe research proves children this young should be learning through play and those politicians and policy makers, in England at least, who believe that although learning through play is important, direct teaching of literacy and numeracy has to form a part of daily school life – and that includes between the ages of four and five.

The Durham research team defined evidence of effective education as a class making much better progress, initially in literacy and numeracy assessments, than the average for similar classes once variables such as age on entry, gender, ethnicity, deprivation and special needs had been taken into account.

The most effective classes, where children made the best progress in literacy and numeracy during their first school year, were in the top 2.5 per cent of all the classes surveyed.

The research team also found looking at data gathered in 12 years of study that effective education, making good progress in literacy and numeracy, in that first year in school can make or break a child's educational success overall.

Good quality preschool education and a good home learning environment are important but now we have proof that so is that first year at school. Not all schools deliver the same standards of education and for the youngest children that can spell the difference between a successful education and a less successful one. The first year of school really matters to how a child does academically long term.

The first year at school is more important than any other

Durham's research found that children taught effectively in their first year of school not only make more progress in their Reception year but they are still doing better at the end of primary school than children who were taught less effectively in their first year. They also get better English and maths GCSEs than young people who had a less effective first year at school. And young people who do well in their English and maths GCSEs, which underpin access to all subjects, generally do well in other GCSEs and A-levels, which means they are more likely to get onto good university courses and have better career opportunities.

At the most basic level, good educational qualifications mean you are far less likely to end up doing work that isn't fulfilling or even worse, ending up either temporarily or permanently on society's scrap heap as unemployed or unemployable or in trouble. Government statistics from 2015 show that nearly half of people going to prison in England had literacy skills no higher than that of an 11-year-old.

The Durham researchers go so far as to suggest that the first year of school education is so important to the future of children that government policy should acknowledge it and that primary schools should consider putting their best teachers into Reception classes.

This research deserves to be taken very seriously. The study was a big one involving 40,000 English children and covered their educational journey from four to 16. It was crystal clear in its findings that if four- and five-year-olds get a good first year at school it gives them a boost in development that doesn't wash out quickly – if it washes out at all. It lasts until their mid-teens at least because the GCSE boost proves it.

The research was done by Durham University's prestigious Centre for Evaluation and Monitoring (CEM) and led by Professor Peter Tymms, formerly Director of CEM who is now developing an international project studying children starting school around the world.

The CEM study measured children's early reading and maths development at the start of school when they were four, with a well-established Durham assessment called Performance Indicators in Primary Schools (PIPS). In 15 minutes, the assessment covered name-writing, vocabulary acquisition, concepts about print, letter and word recognition, reading, and comprehension. It also checked ideas about mathematics, counting, numbers, shapes, informal number problems, and formal sums. The children's progress was assessed again at the end of their Reception year and later, at the ages of seven, 11 and 16.

By assessing children at the beginning and end of the Reception year, the research team spotted the classes where children were making more progress than average. It was then possible to follow individual children through their education and track the impact of an effective first year of school over the long term.

The research team also identified schools in which children made particularly strong progress in Key Stages 1 and 2 of the English national curriculum – between the ages of five and 11 – and then explored the long term impacts of this. This revealed that although good progress at primary school was beneficial it was still not as important as good progress in that first year at school. That was the year that had the most impact.

The researchers were careful to make sure they took account of social and economic factors that could have skewed the results. They needed to be certain that they were assessing the long-term impact of that first precious year in school, rather than things which the children brought to school with them which may have made them more or less likely to do well.

So, for example, they looked at the age the child was when they started school – we looked at that in detail in the previous chapter – their gender, ethnicity or whether they had special needs of some kind, spoke English as an additional language, or came from a deprived background. Girls get the best test and school exam results overall and white working-class boys are the largest single group of poor performers in English schools.

Interestingly, these researchers found that the positive impact of starting school when you were older in your school year faded as the years passed but what did matter was missing out on time in Reception – the year before the start of the English national curriculum.

We know from the last chapter that this is a danger for children whose entry to school is delayed for a year because they are late summer born, but whose local authority then insists they must join their chronological school year. They face missing the more informal Reception year and being tipped straight into the first year of the formal curriculum.

Some children in the Durham study didn't start Reception until the term after they were five – so they started after Christmas or after Easter. The researchers found, they never caught up with their peers in Reception who had been there from the start of the school year in September. Although they did make up some ground by the end of their primary school years, the effect was still there at the age of 16 when they generally delivered poorer GCSE results.

The team also made some other significant findings:

- Girls steadily made gains over boys in reading and English but not maths;
- Ethnic minority groups generally made similar or better progress than their white British peers;
- Children with English as an additional language made more progress. Initial rapid gains would be expected but these continued beyond the first year;
- Deprived children had poorer outcomes which accumulated till GCSE.

An important finding that underpins the importance of a good home learning environment and preschool was that measures of early reading and maths taken at the start of the Reception year – which reflect prior development – were indicative of likely success at GCSE. All those years later the early advantage of input from preschool and parents stuck. This is also confirmed by the longitudinal EPPSE study which we have referred to in earlier chapters.

Most important of all, membership of an effective Reception class between the ages of four and five- years-old – one where the children produced above average progress in literacy and numeracy – conferred higher GCSE results – again all those years later.

The research paper, 'The Long Term Impact of Effective Teaching', couldn't be clearer that the first year of school presents a golden one-off opportunity to positively impact on children's long-term academic outcomes when they are just starting their school journey.

Professor Peter Tymms[1]

Former Director of Durham University's Centre for Evaluation and Monitoring, and leader of the research study into the long-term impact of effective teaching.

> What we found is that children's progress when they start school in Reception is dramatic. And, that progress varies between children and between classes and schools. Some children start from a very low base and get to a good level, others start much further ahead and progress is modest, but progress overall is really dramatic.
>
> The class and school variation in the amount of progress is important. We followed the children through primary and up to GCSE and we saw that, although some schools and classes had quite exceptional gains in Reception, the gains tended to fade in later years but they did not disappear. From the end of Key Stage 1 the children who had had an effective Reception year maintained

1   The quotations in this chapter from Professor Peter Tymms are taken from interviews with Wendy Berliner, 21 May, 9 and 19 November, 2019.

a constant advantage over the children who had a Reception year that was less effective. This corresponds to almost half a grade more in English and in mathematics at GCSE.

The assessments that were carried out at the start of Reception are very reliable. It is quite possible to reliably assess children at age four and the results are predictive of later success and difficulties. The information generated by such assessments can help teachers bring children on in their development.

The variation that we see across classes and schools is, I think, due to the individual teacher and the quality of their teaching. It is they who are responsible for some classes making more progress than others in Reception, regardless of where they start from. You see some amazing teachers in Reception with incredible skills.

But there is no blueprint for how to do this. It is the result of the complex interactions of individual teachers with individual children, the interactions within group and with what's happening in the children's homes. What does a teacher do if a child arrives upset because of something that happened at home the night before? How does the teacher keep the children interested and motivated? The questions that we can ask and the potential answers are far too long to list.

Attempts to distil good practice from teaching have found some useful things you can do but they don't give you a manual that will work for everyone. There have been calls for better training of teachers of young children but I think primary schools should consider putting their best teachers in Reception because the impact in that year is so great.

The process of educational improvement for a nation is iterative and is a long-term project. No policy for improvement of education in the UK has yet improved basic skills of children and young people. More are getting qualifications but that is because standards have been lowered which may be a good thing but not something to shout from the rooftops.

The research team also investigated whether or not effective schools were able to reduce the gap in attainment seen between children from affluent and poor backgrounds which is a long running problem yet to be solved in UK schools or indeed other countries.

But the research showed that with this particularly knotty problem, even an effective first year of education has its limits. By analysing data of each child's home background and comparing it with attainment at school, the research team concluded that there was no significant evidence that schools in England were reducing the attainment gap between children from affluent backgrounds and their less affluent peers.

Parents and the home learning environment really do make the difference.

Other research on the first year at school

The Durham research appears to have filled an important gap in the research literature. There is much research into preschool and schooling but little specific research about the first year – until now.

Other research is limited and older but supports the Durham findings, for example:

Miss A

The earliest study appears to come from the United States and is already more than 40 years old (Pederson, Faucher and Eaton, 1978). The researchers found that a group of children who had been taught by "Miss A" in first grade seemed to have been given an initial boost which gave them an advantage throughout the remainder of their schooling.

The researchers used the school annual report cards to track the academic progress of children in the school from their arrival in first grade to their exit at the end of secondary school and it discovered 'Miss A' achieved results with her pupils in early literacy and numeracy that significantly exceeded those of her colleagues with parallel and comparable intakes.

A pleasure to teach

In 1988 the results of a study of 300 children in 33 inner London primary schools found that the Reception year had a big effect on progress. The group of infants was followed by researchers from the end of nursery to the end of infant school to understand the reasons why they had differing levels of attainment. Variables including home background, ethnicity and school were accounted for.

The researchers found that only in Reception year did some classes make statistically more progress than others and the children who made the most progress in Reception remained the highest achievers throughout infant school (aged five to seven).

Professor Barbara Tizard, the eminent developmental psychologist who was the lead researcher on the project, said at the time that the children whose teachers had high expectations of their progress, who were often children they considered a "pleasure to teach," would be introduced to a wider curriculum than children who had similar skills at the beginning of the year, but whom they did not expect to do so well. "We had evidence that the Reception year has a particularly large effect on progress," she said. Don't forget John Hattie also said it was parental expectations that had the most effect on children doing well at school in his conclusions from 15 years of research.

Play-based learning

We have discussed the importance of play to the preschool curriculum and we know early years educators in England are opposed to more formal literacy learning in the Reception year which is being encouraged by the school inspection service – more on this later in the chapter. But does play-based learning improve outcomes? Between 2000 and 2008, researchers in Northern Ireland, which at four years two months has the youngest compulsory school start age in the UK, followed the primary school careers of the first two successive cohorts of children in 24 primary schools after the introduction of the Enriched Curriculum. This new curriculum was a move away from a traditional curriculum and towards a play based one developmentally appropriate to the children. It was designed to counteract the experience of early persistent failure at school for some children.

Formal literacy and numeracy teaching were delayed for the children undertaking the Enriched Curriculum. When their progress was compared with children who had been taught using traditional methods who were now in the year above the first cohort, it was found that the Enriched Curriculum children's reading and mathematics scores fell behind in the first two years but the majority of the children caught up by the end of their fourth year. The performance of the first cohort then fell away slightly, while that of the second continued to match that of controls. Overall, the play-based curriculum had no statistically significant positive effects on reading and mathematics.

Playing catch up

Longitudinal studies indicate that children who are poor readers by the end of the first year at school almost never acquire average reading skills by the end of primary/elementary school without substantial and sustained remediation efforts.

Latest research

The international research on the effect of the first year at school being led by Professor Tymms is following studies in the Western Cape in South Africa, Russia, Brazil and Lesotho. It is early days in the research with Russia being the furthest forward in the number of years of data collected – the Russian data, however, is already following the same pattern as the English data.

Data from the Western Cape in South Africa found that the children came from a very wide range of backgrounds and poor performance at the end of the first year of formal education was associated with poorer social and financial circumstances in the home, non-attendance in the Reception year and behaviour. A surprisingly high number of the 3,000 children surveyed had behaviours associated with Attention Deficit Hyperactivity Disorder (ADHD).

As in the English research the children who were doing best in their literacy and numeracy by the end of the first year at school were those who arrived already ahead in literacy and numeracy. As in the English research, in some schools, children made more progress than in others – even after taking into account their home background.

Why is the first year so important?

Literacy is the foundation of all formal learning. If you can't read or write you can't access any of the formal school curriculum. Indeed, you can't access much of day to day normal life if you struggle to read a medicine label, or an official form or a website.

Estimates vary but, in the UK, there could be as many as eight million people who are functionally illiterate according to the World Literacy Foundation. They can read simple, familiar texts but not a lot else. That person in the supermarket asking you to read something from a label because they have "left their glasses at home" may be one of them. And demands for complex literacy skills are rising as our society becomes increasingly sophisticated, potentially pushing more to the margins of literacy.

Maths is very important too but it is literacy that is the keystone of learning and the ability to negotiate the rest of your life successfully. If you are a four- or five-year-old child struggling with your letters when your peers aren't, you can quickly get left behind in that first year. And think again about the toxic effect that could have on your self-esteem – your own opinion of whether you are a good learner or not.

It is easy to see how a vicious circle can emerge with a struggling child starting to behave badly, so they learn even less, struggle more, behave even more badly in retaliation. Older children and teenagers removed from mainstream school to alternative provision because they behave so badly in class they disrupt the learning of everyone else are often already seriously behind in their education

There is lots of literacy work done at preschool as part of the early years' curriculum but the beginning of the school curriculum itself is where children are expected to begin formally learning to read and write. Some children arrive as emerging readers and writers because their parents and their preschool have done so much to introduce them to books and games that encourage the development of reading and writing. As we learned in the genetics chapter, there also appears to be clusters of genes that some of us have that make it easier to learn these difficult things.

Other children arrive at school not knowing what a book is or how hold a pencil. Some arrive verbally fluent because their parents and preschool have encouraged their curiosity, conversation and vocabulary acquisition. Others arrive with very limited language or the social and behavioural skills needed to settle easily into a school classroom and begin to access the curriculum.

The Reception year is the bridge between the early years' curriculum and the school curriculum that begins the following year. The early years curriculum focuses on learning mainly through play and encourages the development of good attitudes to learning so you are curious, you persevere and you are self-motivated, for example. Much more to come on all of these key attributes in later chapters.

There is a great deal of research which shows that if you are falling behind with literacy and numeracy at preschool you find it hard to catch up in primary school which, in effect, means you may well lag behind till the end of your schooling.

Which all explains why that first, Reception year is so important.

What's being done?

If research shows that a good first year of effective education in school makes so much difference to how well children do in formal education, what is being done to ensure that all children get that golden first year which appears to help children from all sorts of starting points?

In England there is a panoply of government enforced assessments throughout the key educational stages ending with formal examinations at 16 and beyond, overseen by formal inspections and publicly available results which check how the system is performing. The English national curriculum was introduced in the late twentieth century by which time the "Miss A" American research study, which highlighted the importance of the first year at school, had already been published.

The children who were starting school when the English national curriculum was first introduced are well into their thirties now and many will be parents of school aged children themselves. Those children are still dependent on that golden first year of effective education at school to do well which still is not available to all – it depends on whether the school you go to is able to give it to you.

According to the latest available UK government statistics, nearly half of all disadvantaged five-year-olds in English schools – those on free school meals – are not reaching expected standards of development by the end of their Reception year. The picture for other children is better with just over a quarter of them failing to meet expected levels.

There are wide regional variations between less and more affluent parts of England. For example, the percentage of children achieving a good level of development varies between 63.9 per cent in Middlesbrough, a town with more deprived areas than anywhere else in Britain, and 80.5 per cent in Richmond upon Thames, one of London's most affluent boroughs. The percentage achieving at least the expected level in all learning is highest overall in London and the South-east of England.

During the summer term 2017, Her Majesty's school inspectors visited 41 English primary schools in which children achieved well. The schools were all ones where Reception children, including the disadvantaged, achieved well in areas such as literacy and numeracy.

Out of those visits came an Office for Standards in Education, Children's Services and Skills (Ofsted) report, *Bold Beginnings*, published in November of the same year which showed that the teaching and learning of reading was at the heart of the most successful classes. This is the report that recommended all primary schools make the teaching of reading the core purpose of the Reception year, attach a greater importance to the teaching of numbers and ensure part of every school day was kept aside for the direct teaching of reading, writing and mathematics.

This, combined with the planned government introduction of baseline testing for infants, has led to clashes with early years teachers who are concerned that the government wants to shrink the early years curriculum down to the basics of literacy and numeracy – causing harm to the overall development of very young children.

The Department for Education introduced baseline testing for infants in state run English primary schools in 2015 in a voluntary trial involving three assessment suppliers offering a mix of assessment approaches. The most popular by far with schools was based solely on observation of children rather than a test because it relied on the skills of teachers, but the government found it impossible to compare the methods and abandoned introducing any of them.

Instead a new £10m trial, this time based on a one-off test, not observation, went into trial in September 2018. The plan is for a full-scale introduction of the infants' baseline in 2020. This test will be designed to provide the baseline with which to measure a child's progress through their primary school years.

Early years professionals remain worried. Children as young as three are already known to be grouped by ability in some preschools. Professionals working in the sector believe fervently that children this young shouldn't be the subject of formal testing because they believe research shows that testing of very young children is unreliable until the age of seven – something Professor Peter Tymms would disagree with them on – when the brain enters a new phase of development. They believe that progress should be monitored by the observation of their skilled teachers, not by tests.

In an open letter to *The Guardian* published in January 2018 Keeping Early Years Unique, a grouping of teachers, parents and other education experts, complained *Bold Beginnings* was flawed because the inspectors got the results they wanted by going into schools already delivering education in the way they wanted. It called for *Bold Beginnings* to be withdrawn. It wasn't.

The Department for Education view is that the early years foundation stage framework which covers preschool and the Reception year already includes observation which helps inform the teaching and learning of the children and that the baseline tests will inform the big picture on progress in schools over time. In the tender requesting bids to provide the tests, the government was at pains to point out that the results would not be used to judge teachers or schools.

References

Tymms, P., Merrell, C., Bailey, K. (2017) 'The long term impact of effective teaching.' *School Effectiveness and School Improvement*, Vol. *29*, No. 2, pp. 242–261. doi:10.1080/09243453.2017.1404478

Sylva, K., Melhuish, E., Sammons, P.Siraj, I., Taggart, B. with Smees, R., Tóth, K., Welcomme, W. and Hollingworth, K. (2014) 'Students' educational and developmental outcomes at age 16: Effective Pre-school, Primary and Secondary Education (EPPSE 3–16) project research report.' Department for Education. Available from https://assets.publishing.service.gov.uk/government/uploads/system/uploads/attachment_data/file/351496/RR354_-_Students__educational_and_developmental_outcomes_at_age_16.pdf (downloaded 6 June 2019).

Pederson, E., Faucher, T.A. and Eaton, W.W. (1978) 'A new perspective on the effects of first-grade teachers on children's adult status.' *Harvard Educational Review*, Vol. *48*, No. 1, pp. 1–31.

Tizard, B., Blatchford, P., Burke, J., Farquhar, C. and Plewis, I. (1988) *Young Children at School in the Inner City*. London: Taylor and Francis.

McGuinness, C., Sproule, E., Bojkeb, C., Trew, K. and Walsh, G. (2014) 'Impact of a play-based curriculum in the first two years of primary school: literacy and numeracy outcomes over seven years.' *British Education Research Journal*, Vol. *40*, No. 5, pp. 772–795.

Olofsson, A. and Niedersøe, J. (1999) 'Early language development and kindergarten phonological awareness as predictors of reading problems from 3 to 11 years of age.' *Journal of Learning Disabilities*, Vol. *32*, No. 5. doi:10.1177/002221949903200512

Ofsted (2017) *Bold Beginnings: The Reception curriculum in a sample of good and outstanding primary schools*. Available from https://assets.publishing.service.gov.uk/government/uploads/system/uploads/attachment_data/file/663560/28933_Ofsted_-_Early_Years_Curriculum_Report_-_Accessible.pdf (downloaded on 4 June 2019).

Chapter 7

Organising for success

Good fortune is what happens when opportunity meets with planning.
Thomas Edison, the prolific American inventor best known for giving us the electric light bulb.

The grammar school controversy

Would you send your child to an academically selective school like a grammar school? According to a YouGov poll of 1,500 parents in 2016, 62 per cent would want their child to sit a grammar school entrance exam compared with just 15 per cent who wouldn't. A further 5 per cent of parents would not want their child to sit the exam but wouldn't stand in their way if they passed.

Nearly a quarter of those polled didn't know what they'd do, perhaps because for many parents the idea is academic as only 163 out of more than 3,000 secondary schools in England (Northern Ireland has 69) are grammars. Perhaps because they have no idea what they are like. Today's grandparents, let alone parents, are mainly products of comprehensive, not selective education in the UK.

But selective education still exercises a powerful hold over the minds of many parents and politicians. Some parents choose to send their children to grammars even though that means a long, daily journey. Birmingham's King Edward's grammars, for instance, attract children from Leicester, Derby, Stoke and Coventry which can add up to hours of commuting every day.

The debate in the media is often between individuals who feel that they have personally benefitted from grammar schools and those who think they are a way of entrenching social advantage. In 2015, a letter writer to *The Times* said: "My father was a welder in HM Dockyard Chatham; my mother was a cook at a local school. I passed the 11-plus, went to grammar school and then to St Catherine's College, Oxford. Where would I be now without the 11-plus and grammar schools? Certainly not a solicitor"

(Robert Harris letter to the *Times* 2015.) A year later, Stephen Bush, special correspondent to the New Statesman, described grammar schools as "the horror movies of public policy – they have been shot to pieces by almost every serious policy thinker from across the political spectrum, and yet they stagger on regardless" (*New Statesman*, 8 August 2016).

Grammar schools have a long history. The first grammars opened in the fourteenth century and offered a strict academic education. Reading, writing and Latin went hand-in-hand with an opportunity for the poor and clever to rise to better things. In Shakespeare's day, according to the historian G.M. Trevelyan, "clever boys of the most various ranks of society received a good Latin education, sharing the benches and floggings of the grammar school." Only later did the great, fee-paying public schools emerge. Some of those schools, such as Winchester, had started out as grammar schools.

It was not until after the Second World War that the grammar school came to be seen as the main agent of social mobility, in Britain at least. The 1944 Education Act established three types of school: grammar, secondary modern and technical. Entry to the grammar school was by 11-plus examination. A Labour Prime Minister Harold Wilson in the 1960s and 70s, one of the working-class boys who climbed the social ladder through a grammar school, said later that they would be abolished "over my dead body."

The idea, in the words of the 1944 Act, was that children would be allocated to schools according to ability and aptitude. Secondary modern schools were not supposed to be inferior, just different. But parents soon began to see them as second-rate, and with justification. (A few technical schools were founded but the idea never got off the ground because of lack of will and lack of cash.) Grammar school pupils took General Certificate of Education O-levels but there were, at first, no public exams for secondary modern school pupils. The grammar schools also had better buildings, more cash and better-qualified teachers.

By the 1960s the unfairness of the selective system was widely recognised. Children's chances of success varied sharply according to where they lived: in Wales as many as 30 per cent went to grammar school, whereas in some parts of the Home Counties the proportion was as low as 10 per cent. The 11-plus exam was seen as cruel and hopelessly flawed. Though some children from poor homes did make it to grammar school, those from middle-class backgrounds had a much better chance of passing the 11-plus and getting there.

Despite his comment about "over my dead body" Harold Wilson's Labour government in 1965 "invited" local authorities to draw up schemes for comprehensives – schools to educate children of all abilities. Significantly, the real pressure for change came not from the working classes but from middle-class parents who dreaded the stigma of 11-plus failure. Even Mrs Thatcher, later Conservative prime minister, continued to close grammar schools when she became Education Secretary.

Later, the Conservative, Thatcher and Major governments, tried to encourage more grammar schools but their efforts foundered on the wishes of parents. For example, in the English Midlands affluent Solihull parents defeated an attempt by a Conservative council in the 1980s to turn their comprehensive into a grammar for which their children would have to compete.

In 1996, the Prime Minister, John Major promised "a grammar school in every town." The Labour party rallied parents against the proposal by asking: "So which comprehensive would be the secondary modern school in this town?"

In 2016, Conservative Prime Minister Theresa May also proposed an expansion of grammar schools by promising to lift the ban on new ones. Because of opposition from MPs, including some Conservatives, she agreed instead to provide money to allow existing grammars to expand provided that they had ambitious plans to admit more pupils from poor backgrounds.

A quiet increase in the number of pupils in grammars had already begun. By 2018 there were 11,000 more than in 2010, according to a BBC analysis. By 2021, the study calculated, there would be 6,000 more, the equivalent of 24 new schools since 2010.

There are two ways of looking at the research on selective schools. The first is their effect on society as a whole. Do they promote social mobility and help to narrow the gap between the poor and the affluent? That is the question which has interested politicians most because it fits well with the popular idea of equal opportunities for all. For parents, the second question – what are the benefits for individual children – may be more important. If you have a bright child, will they be better off academically and socially at a grammar where they are with other clever children. Or would it make sense to send them to a comprehensive. Or would it not make much difference?

Parents in the 1950s and 1960s, when the solicitor quoted at the beginning of this chapter was at school, expected their children to take the 11-plus because the whole school system was divided into grammars and secondary moderns. The decision facing today's parents is more difficult. Few local authorities in England offer the 11-plus. Kent is the largest remaining selective authority in England with 35 grammars and four partially selective schools. Northern Ireland still has a grammar school system but no schools use the 11-plus to select pupils in Wales or Scotland.

A better education for your child?

Let's look first at the question most parents might ask. Would my child, whatever their ability, get better exam results if they went to a grammar rather than the local comprehensive? A major research study, led by Professor Stephen Gorard, Professor of Education and Public Policy at Durham University, published in 2018, addressed just that question.[1] It also looked at the suggestion that pupils from poor backgrounds gain particular benefit from a grammar school education.

On the face of it, grammar school pupils' performance looks better than those of their comprehensive school peers. But is that because of what happens in school or because of the nature of the children who are selected through an entrance test that measures their prior achievement?

The researchers looked at information in the National Pupil Database for England that included children's attainment before the age of 11, the type of school they attended and pupils' background (whether they were disadvantaged enough to be eligible for free school meals) for every year that they had been in compulsory schooling. The data was for students who took the GCSE examination in 2015. There were 549,203 of them with complete records so it was a large data set.

The study took into account different factors that might affect the exam results: chronic poverty, ethnicity, whether English was their first language and special educational needs. They also made allowance for a pupil's age in relation to their peers to distinguish between summer and winter-born children because, as we have seen in Chapter 5, in the northern hemisphere summer born children, on average, lag behind their older winter-born peers. They looked at how they had performed in tests earlier in their school career: Key Stage 1 national tests at seven and Key Stage 2 national tests at 11.

They found that grammars are far less likely to take pupils eligible for free school meals, just two per cent compared with a national figure of 14 per cent. Those children on free school meals who do win places tend to have been on free meals for a relatively short time, suggesting that they are from less deprived backgrounds than some of their peers. Eligibility for free school meals is the criterion often used by academics to measure poverty.

Professor Gorard's work is the first to take into account the number of years that a pupil has been on free meals, in other words whether they come from a family where poverty is short-term or longstanding. That matters because pupils' attainment at GCSE declines for every year that they have been on free meals.

Unsurprisingly, perhaps, grammar school pupils are far less likely to have special educational needs and less likely to have English as an additional language. They are also much more likely to be among the older pupils in their year group. The 11-plus examination is supposed to make

1   The information and quotations from Professor Stephen Gorard in this chapter are taken from an interview with Judith Judd, 9 January, 2019.

allowances for this but is failing to do so, the researchers say. They are more likely to be from Chinese or Pakistani families and are much more likely to live in an affluent neighbourhood.

Professor Gorard points out that all grammar research comes with caveats: the best way to measure these schools' effectiveness would be to randomly allocate pupils to selective and non-selective schools but that is clearly not practical. He does believe, however, that his research offers clear pointers to pupil performance across the system. If you take into account grammar schools' intake, their pupils are no more likely to achieve better results than they are at other types of school. Grammar school pupils come from better-off families and are already achieving more highly when they enter secondary school at the age of 11.

Whatever the research findings about the academic dividends of grammar schools, parents who are wondering whether to enter their child for an 11-plus examination are likely to have other concerns. A high-flying ten or 11-year-old may sail through the process of a competitive examination. Less able children may find it more daunting. Grammar schools in mainly comprehensive areas attract pupils from neighbouring cities and competition for them is fierce. 6,000 pupils each year sit the exam for 900 places at the six grammars in the King Edward V1 Academy Trust in Birmingham.

What effect does failing the 11-plus have on a child? Some high-profile figures still resent the experience. Michael Morpurgo, the children's author, told an interviewer:

> The word fail hits you like a dagger in the heart when you're that age. You don't forget it, and I think it somehow sends you into a spiral that you simply can't get out of. The notion is that they have thought you to be stupid, that's what it tells you.

John Prescott, the former British Deputy Prime Minister, interviewed by the Daily Telegraph in 2005, said that, 50 years on, his 11-plus failure still rankled though he added that it hadn't stopped him becoming an MP and Deputy Prime Minister.

Distance is another consideration. Because the number of grammars is small, pupils may have to travel many miles to the nearest. The six King Edward V1 grammar schools in Birmingham attract pupils from far afield. Even parents of very able children may baulk at the idea of journeys of nearly 45 miles each day for their children to a school which is far from their local community and childhood friends.

A better education for everyone?

Professor Gorard's research suggests that it doesn't make much difference to individual children's academic success whether or not they go to a selective school. But his research also looks at other big questions about selective education. Does it, as politicians and letter writers to the Times claim, help young people climb the social ladder or escape poverty?

Whatever grammars' effect on the poor children who pass the 11-plus, numerous studies have shown that only a small proportion of children from disadvantaged backgrounds attend them. Even those from disadvantaged backgrounds who succeed in passing the entrance exam don't do markedly better than their counterparts elsewhere.

Professor Gorard questions previous research that found grammar schools boosted exam results for poor children. In 2006, researchers at the Centre for Market and Public Organisation at Bristol University used the data about individual pupils in the annual school census to track test and exam results from the age of 11 to the age of 16. They found that poor pupils in grammars did exceptionally well – scoring the equivalent of eight grade points more at GCSE – or eight GCSEs at grade B rather than grade C – than pupils of similar ability who attended comprehensive schools in areas without grammar schools. But Professor Gorard says that you get very similar results if you compare these pupils' results at seven with their GCSE results, suggesting that their good performance is not simply the result of their grammar school education.

As we have seen, his is the first study to take into account the number of years that a pupil has been on free school meals. If the proportion of children eligible for free school meals in grammar schools is tiny, it is vanishingly small for those who have been on free school meals for their entire school career, just 0.4 per cent of the total. The average figure for England is 4 per cent. So, the vast majority of children in chronic poverty attend non-selective schools.

One of the reasons for the preponderance of middle-class children in grammars may be that they can afford to pay to help them through the 11-plus either by sending them to fee-charging schools or to private tutors. A small study of 212 children in two grammars carried out by Judith Ireson and Penelope Brown at London University's Institute of Education in 2013 found that seven out of ten had received some form of private tutoring to increase their chances of getting a place. A study from the Sutton Trust, an educational charity that aims to improve social mobility, also published in 2013 said that fee-charging prep schools accounted for 12.7 per cent of grammar school entrants though only around 6 per cent of all pupils attend such schools.

In 2018, Theresa May's government set about trying to encourage grammar schools to admit more pupils from poor and disadvantaged backgrounds. Ministers offered a share of £50 million to schools that were prepared to relax their admissions criteria for poor children to enable them to expand. But grammar school decisions to admit poor children who live near the school with a lower pass mark in the entrance exam than their more affluent peers have proved controversial.

Parents of pupils at the Birmingham schools mentioned earlier in this chapter protested that admission should be based on merit and that able children who lived at a distance from the school would be excluded if preference was given to poorer entrants who lived nearby. The schools already reserved 20 per cent of places for poor pupils but had no catchment areas. They wanted to give a quarter of places to poor pupils who lived near the school.

Another argument sometimes used to support the case for grammar schools is that they drive up standards in the surrounding schools. The Durham study suggests not. It found that pupils at state comprehensive schools achieve very similar GCSE results overall regardless of whether they live in an area with grammar schools or not.

This shows that the mere existence of grammar schools in an area does not seem to drive up standards or reduce the gap between pupils who are eligible for free school meals and the rest.

Selection and society

So, the Durham research suggests that selective schools are not the answer to boosting academic attainment. The researchers also examined their *social* effects and how they might affect society as a whole and the communities where grammar schools are still found. Their conclusion? Selective systems are socially and economically divisive with poorer pupils clustered together in some schools and their more affluent peers in others.

The research shows that the few local authorities in England that have retained selective systems have the highest level of socio-economic segregation. All the ten local authorities where segregation by family income is greatest have retained some selective schools. By contrast, the ten least segregated have the least selection. Professor Gorard says:

> Where children are clustered together because of poverty or special needs, schools are less likely to attract the best teachers and poor behaviour is likely to be treated differently: for example, children are more likely to be diagnosed as having special needs than if they were in a less disadvantaged area.

Selection also affects pupils' confidence and their attitude to school. Findings from a study by the Organisation for Economic Co-operation and Development that compared students' experience in 72 countries found that students were less confident and had lower expectations in countries where they were separated by academic selection or went to "different types of school."

The report was based on an analysis of the attitudes of more than 500,000 pupils as part of the Programme for International Student

Assessment (PISA). A lower proportion of pupils said they expected to go on to further education in countries where pupils were selected by ability between the age of 11 and 13. The figure was higher in school systems where pupils were selected after the age of 13.

Pupils were also more likely to have lower confidence if they were separated into different schools by ability before the age of 13. The report confirms Professor Gorard's view that the UK is one of the developed countries where poorer pupils tend to be concentrated in schools which achieve lower exam results. That, it suggests, may mean that they have lower expectations of what they can achieve.

Professor Gorard says:

> There is a lot of evidence that children's self-esteem is lower in a seg-regated system. We know that they are well aware where they come in the pecking order. Grammar schools create two sets of losers: children who do not win a place and children who would be among the most talented in another school but are less talented than many of their grammar school peers.

Selection across the world

The OECD, mentioned earlier, regularly tests pupils from different countries and publishes the results. What do they tell us about the success of selective systems in other parts of the world?

Comparisons between school systems are notoriously difficult to make. Singapore, which currently tops all the PISA rankings, does have a primary school leaving examination –which examines the children in maths, science, the English language and the child's mother tongue. The children mostly have around two hours to complete each of the subject papers.

Based on their results, children are then distributed among a system of different types of academic and technical schools, with the top ten per cent in the ability range entering schools called 'Special' which offer an accelerated track to university. The system has critics because of its competitiveness which in consequence involves stress and extra fee-paying tuition at night for children whose parents can afford it. There are pathways for children available to post-secondary institutions from the schools they are allocated, although the fastest route to university is from the "Special School".

However, if you look at countries which separate pupils on to academic and vocational tracks at 11 or earlier, for example Germany and Austria, you can see that their results in the Programme for International Student Assessment (PISA) for 15-year-olds are worse than you would expect, says Professor Gorard. Equally, countries such as Finland, Norway and South Korea that do not divide pupils at an early age do well in PISA.

Professor Gorard says:

> Dividing children into the most able and the rest does not appear to lead to better results for either group. People are fooled by the raw scores of pupils' exam results into thinking that attainment is better in grammars than in other schools. This is not to decry the schools that are currently grammars, or the work of their staff. The findings mean that grammar schools in England endanger social cohesion for no clear improvement in overall results. The policy is a bad one.
>
> If it were true that grammars got better results, you might say let social segregation go hang but a selective system is potentially very dangerous to social cohesion. Any analysis which looks at grammar schools has to look also at the four or five neighbouring schools who have had all the talented children drained out of them. In choosing a school, many parents may be thinking about the intake. That is a different issue from pupils' attainment. If you live in an area with grammar schools, a parent might decide to pick a grammar because their child will be going to school with better behaved and better motivated children. You can't blame a parent for that if their child passes the 11-plus. Otherwise, they will go to a school where all the talented children have been siphoned off and sent to the grammar.

The best type of school

For much of the last century, governments have subscribed to the belief that school organisation is a vital component of their efforts to raise educational standards. State-funded grammars and secondary moderns established in Britain in 1944 were succeeded by comprehensives, designed to educate all children under one roof, and then by a series of reforms proposed by governments who felt that comprehensives were not working.

Since the 1980s, Conservative and Labour governments have searched for ways of taking English schools out of the control of local councils, deemed bureaucratic and ineffective. In the 1980s, Margaret Thatcher tried "opting out" that allowed schools to receive funding direct from the government rather than local councils and city technology colleges financed by rich sponsors. Tony Blair, a Labour prime minister, set up academies, state-funded schools, free of local authority control and run by sponsors who had to prove their commitment by providing some cash.

The aim was to improve the worst performing schools in the poorest districts. Neither scheme attracted huge numbers. When Blair left office in 2010, there were just over 200 academies.

But the arrival of a Conservative Secretary of State for Education Michael Gove in 2010 meant revolution. His announcement that all secondary schools should become academies and relaxation of the rules so that he could speed up the changes showed that he intended to succeed where Thatcher and Blair had failed.

When he said later that primary schools whose results did not come up to scratch would be forced to convert to academy status, the death knell sounded for local authorities' educational role. By 2018, two thirds of secondary schools were academies and a quarter of primaries.

So, far more parents have the opportunity to send a child to an academy than to a grammar. As we have seen, grammar schools appear to make no difference to a child's chance of academic success. What about academies?

The research evidence so far reaches a remarkably similar conclusion to the grammar school studies. A study published in 2018 by Jon Andrews, director for school systems and performance at the Education Policy Institute, an independent research organisation, compared the progress pupils make in chains of academy schools with the progress they make in local authority schools using national test results at the age of 11 and GCSE results. It takes into account factors such as pupils' previous attainment and their background so that the results are not distorted by schools' intakes.

This study compares groups of schools rather than individual pupils but its message is clear. Overall, there is very little difference between the performance of schools in academy chains and those in local authorities. What mattered, the research found, was whether the school was in a high-performing group. Both academy chains and local authorities feature at the very top of the school improvement tables used in this study and also at the bottom.

It's important to note that the research isn't saying that all schools are the same and that children get the same opportunities whichever school they attend. On the contrary, this study found that the child in the highest performing primary school groups made a whole term's progress more than a child who was at school in one of the lowest performing groups. And a student in the highest performing secondary school groups could expect to get half a grade higher in each subject at GCSE.

The type of school makes very little difference but other factors affecting schools' performance do.

Supporters of academy schools argue that it is easier to close a group of failing academies than a group of local authority schools. Indeed, several academy trusts have been required by the Government to give up all their schools. However, the EPI report notes that the process of placing failing academies in new groups has been slow. Equally, some local authorities linger for many years at the bottom of performance tables.

Other research has looked at the effect of the academies programme on disadvantaged pupils. Governments have encouraged sponsors to support academies and to take over struggling schools as a way of raising standards for the poorest pupils. But research suggests that their efforts have been only partly successful.

"Chain Effects 2018" a five-year-analysis published by the Sutton Trust by Professor Becky Francis, Director of the University College London Institute of Education, and Professor Merryn Hutchings, visiting Professor at UCL IOE, looked at the 2017 GCSE results of pupils in 58 academy chains or groups of academies (a group of at least three academies with the same sponsor.)

They found a big variation in the attainment of disadvantaged pupils between or within chains. In 12 chains, those pupils did better than the average for disadvantaged children in all mainstream schools and in three chains they did markedly better. But in 38 chains, their performance was worse and in eight of those, markedly worse.

Interestingly, those schools that did best with poor pupils also tended to do best with their more affluent peers and those that were less successful with poor pupils were also less successful with the better-off.

While a small number of chains managed to improve each year, a small group at the bottom of the table failed to make headway. Newer chains (those included in the study for the first year) performed less well than the rest. Eight out of ten had below average results, suggesting that it takes around three years to turn around a failing school.

However, the five-year-analysis does show that while the performance of disadvantaged pupils worsened slightly between 2013 and 2016, it then began to recover. The research used the Attainment 8 and Progress 8 measures. Attainment 8 is a measure of a pupil's average grade across a set suite of eight subjects at GCSE. Once calculated, this score is compared to the average Attainment 8 score of all pupils nationally with the same prior attainment at Key Stage 2, or in national tests at the age of 11, to calculate a pupil's Progress 8 score. The analysis also used the GCSE grades for English and maths.

Private schools

Government reforms of English state education in the past half century, including the introduction of opting out and academies, have aimed to give state schools more independence, to make them more like private schools.

The combative Conservative politician Kenneth Clarke, a former education secretary, said that everyone would send their child to private school if they could afford it. (A 2013 poll by YouGov, the polling organisation, of more than 2,000 parents questioned Mr Clarke's assumption. Fifty per cent of parents said they would send their child to a state school, however rich they were.)

The schools considered so far in this chapter do not charge fees. For many parents, fee-charging schools are not an option. Only around 6,000 of the 625,000 pupils in private schools pay no fees because they receive means-tested bursaries though nearly 45,000 get some help through these bursaries. More receive scholarships but these are based on talent, academic, sporting or musical and are not means-tested (Source: Independent Schools Council). Around 7 per cent of pupils in England (6.5 per cent in the UK) attend them, though the figure rises to 18 per cent for students aged over 16.

The low percentages surprise people because former independent school pupils play such a prominent role in society. The independent reviewer on social mobility and child poverty Alan Milburn's 2012 report into fair access to the professions showed 43 per cent of barristers, 54 per cent of chief executives, 51 per cent of top medics and 54 per cent of leading journalists attended private schools.

A report from the Sutton Trust and upReach charities found that six-months after finishing university, private school graduates in high-status jobs were earning £670 per year more than those from the state sector in the same high-status positions ("Private Pay Progression" by Jake Anders of the National Institute for Social and Economic Research). In a 2018 analysis the Sutton Trust showed that independent school pupils were seven times more likely to gain a place at Oxford or Cambridge compared with those in non-selective state schools, and over twice as likely to take a place at one of the sought-after Russell Group universities.

Do private school fees buy educational and financial advantage? It is difficult to know what is driving the sheer dominance of private school pupils even though most of fee-paying schools are academically selective, some of them exceptionally selective. They are also likely to help prepare Oxford and Cambridge applicants for the exhaustive interview process they will encounter and many of the families who can afford to send their children to private school will also afford special Oxbridge preparation courses held by private companies in the summer holidays.

A number of studies over many years have shown that private schools appear to give their pupils an educational edge but the difference diminishes rapidly once social background is taken into account and most of the evidence is inconclusive.

A Durham university study carried out for the Independent Schools Council in 2016 looked at pupils' results in the Performance Indicators in Primary Schools (PIPS) assessment at the age of four and predicted their results at 16 in GCSE. It took into account students' prior attainment, their social and economic circumstances and their gender. The study looked at the average of the best eight GCSEs and found that independent school pupils gained on average two-thirds of a GCSE grade higher. The researchers estimated that amounted to a boost of about two years of additional schooling between the ages of four and 16.

On the face of it, that looks fairly conclusive but Professor Robert Coe of Durham University's Centre for Evaluation and Monitoring warned that the results should be treated with caution. He thought it unlikely that the difference was simply down to better teaching in independent schools and suggested that other factors might be at work, perhaps related to family background, that his study had not allowed for.

In particular, the measure used for deprivation was one of postcodes rather than individual children. If two families live in the same postcode, it is likely that the child who goes to a private school will come from a home with a higher income and lower deprivation. His report, which was commissioned by the Independent Schools Council, the umbrella body for independent schools, concludes: "We are unable to give a confident and precise estimate of the causal effect of attending an independent school."

Independent schools argue that parents choose them for many reasons other than their exam results. They cite the facilities that their greater resources enable them to provide and the many extracurricular activities that fee-paying parents expect as part of the educational package.

Selection *within* schools

> Their brain's bigger … it just happens. They were born like that. They were born clever
> Yolanda, aged nine, explains why some children are good at maths, quoted in research by Rachel Marks of Brighton University

> My youngest is in Year 4 in a very academic school, and she is in bottom sets for everything including sport. I am worried this is going to kill her sense of self worth and confidence. My friends with older children had a bad time, the children in the bottom sets generally stayed in the bottom sets and eventually this had a negative effect on them by year six/seven.
> Parent on the website mumsnet

> Parents should be worried if schools are avoiding teaching children appropriately, using effective methods, including ability grouping if the school judges that to be appropriate.
> John Blake, Policy Exchange think tank (BBC News, 1 December, 2017)

Schools that select pupils by ability, whether state-funded or private, are in a minority. Selection within schools, either by streaming or setting, is much more common. Streaming means grouping pupils by ability for most subjects so that they are educated with the same students in all those subjects. Setting means dividing them by ability for some individual subjects so that a student might be in one set for maths and another for English or science. Both are common in secondary schools and less common in primaries.

Labour and Conservative politicians in Britain have tried to promote ability grouping in the belief that it is popular with parents. In 2005, Jacqui Smith, a Labour Schools Minister, said: "Labour has encouraged setting and there is now more than in 1997." David Cameron, as Conservative leader of the Opposition, said: "I want to see setting in every single school. Parents know it works. Teachers know it works."

Most of the evidence, however, shows that it's much more complicated than that.

A study from London University's Institute of Education (Ireson et al. 2005) looked at the effect of ability grouping on pupils' GCSE results. The study involved 6,000 students in British secondary schools and it found that the number of years they had been divided into sets made almost no difference to average GCSE results, once the researchers had allowed for other factors that might have influenced the scores. But the practice was highly damaging to individual students of the same ability who were placed in different sets.

The researchers looked at students' scores at Key Stage 3 (at the age of 14) and predicted their expected scores at GCSE. They found that the number of years of setting in a subject between Year 7 and Year 11 had almost no effect on average GCSE performance in that subject in a school. They also looked at the results for high, medium and low scoring students separately. They found no relationship between the number of years of setting and students' average GCSE results in maths and English.

In other words, both able and less able students, did much as would have been expected. In science, setting made a small difference. Students who did better in Key Stage 3 tests achieved slightly higher grades in schools with less setting and those with lower attainment at KS3 achieved slightly higher grades in schools with more setting but the differences were so small that they were almost insignificant.

So, overall, setting offered no advantages. Yet the study shows that it does have one important disadvantage. It damages the educational prospects of individual pupils of similar ability who are put into lower sets.

The researchers found that, in most schools, pupils who achieved the *same* (intermediate) level at Key Stage 3 might find themselves in top, middle or bottom sets because teachers sometimes allocated pupils to a set for reasons other than ability – because of their behaviour or to separate them from peers. The allocation mattered because students with the same score at Key Stage 3 achieved higher grades at GCSE if they were in the top set than if they were in the middle set. Those in the middle set with the same score performed better than those in the bottom set. On average, the difference between being placed in the top rather than the bottom set in English and Maths was almost a whole GCSE grade.

One of the explanations for the findings may be that teachers expected more of the top sets. They engaged them in discussion and in more interesting work than those in the bottom sets. They also covered more of the curriculum.

Whatever the explanation, the study suggests that teachers tended to believe that the ability of a set was fixed and adjusted their expectations accordingly. Nor did they make allowance for the range of ability within sets. Since few pupils moved between sets in the course of their secondary school career, their attitude made a big difference to some pupils. Professor Ireson, Emeritus Professor of Psychology in Education at University College, London, said:[2]

> The difficulty is that there is a correlation in teachers' minds between achievement and behaviour. They see a top set student as someone getting good results and also behaving well. A top set student who is behaving badly may slide down the sets or teachers don't put some badly behaved students in the bottom set because they think that will make the bottom set horrendous to teach.
>
> The trouble with setting is that children should be able to move sets but they often get stuck. A child in the middle set may be doing well but the top set is full so the school says if this child goes up another child has to go down. Our finding that setting can make a big difference to individual pupils is a really important one.

What about primary pupils? The answer might surprise some British people whose children started school a generation ago. Streaming in primary schools *is* less common than in secondary schools but it has been increasing dramatically.

In the 1990s only around 2 to 3 per cent of classes for children aged between five and seven (Key Stage 1) were streamed. By 2014 that had increased to one in six pupils in England and one in five in Wales according to research from London University's Institute of Education. And the study, which looked at 2,544 pupils aged six and seven who took part in the Millennium Cohort Study which is following the lives of 19,000 children born in the UK in 2000–2001, found that the effect of streaming on young children helped some but not others.

While the brightest did better if they were placed in a top stream, children in middle and bottom streams did worse than if they had been in a school with mixed ability classes. Streaming widens the gap between abler and less able pupils and between those from poor backgrounds and their better-off peers, the researchers found.

In this study, 17 per cent of the sample were streamed and, of these, 8 per cent were in the top stream, five in the middle and four in the bottom.

2 The quotations in this chapter from Professor Judith Ireson are taken from an interview with Judith Judd, 21 February, 2019.

The researchers compared the reading and maths scores of the streamed six-year-olds with the results of those who had not been streamed, taking into account the children's prior ability measured at the age of five. They also looked at an overall score for both groups that included reading, writing, maths and science.

On all the measures, children in the top stream did better than if they had not been streamed but those in the middle and bottom sets fared significantly worse in reading and overall. Those in the bottom sets also fared worse in maths.

The findings fit with other research that shows that children achieve better results if they are in a class with brighter children. Bottom stream pupils were more likely to have behaviour problems, to be from poorer backgrounds and to have less educated mothers. The research took into account pupils' parents' education and other aspects of their backgrounds which might have made a difference to the results.

Overall, the message of the research is that setting may help some of the brightest students but not those who are less able. Like the mother of the Year 4 daughter struggling in the bottom set quoted at the beginning of this section, many parents worry about the ability group to which their child has been allocated. Mothers complain about the "pushy parents" of five-year-olds who think it's never too soon to fight for a child's place at the top. The research shows that they may be right: streaming and setting do make a difference to individual pupils' progress.

If you think your child has been put in the wrong set, maybe for the wrong reasons, then it is worth talking to the school. And if your child is in the bottom set it is important to make clear that you have not given up on them and to counter nine-year-old Yolanda's fatalistic belief (quoted above) that there is nothing you can do if you are not "born clever."

Choosing a school

A school's attitude to streaming and setting will play a minor role, at most, in parents' decisions about where to send their child. What about the other school characteristics reviewed in this chapter? The research shows that the *type* of school you choose is likely to make little difference to your child's academic success. As Professor Gorard says:

> There is no evidence that a particular type of school is more successful in terms of attainment than any other.

That doesn't mean that choice of school doesn't matter. Parents may want a school where well-motivated and able children are clustered together as they are in grammar and independent schools and, indeed, some neighbourhood comprehensives. If they live in an area with grammar schools, they may worry about the "segregation" caused by syphoning off brighter children so that neighbouring schools contain few able pupils.

A look at a school's "raw" exam scores, without making allowance for its pupils' backgrounds as researchers do, provides a rough guide to the sort of children who go there but not to how good the school is at boosting attainment.

It is also clear that a label such as "academy" or "grammar" doesn't guarantee a uniform standard. There are, for instance, some very good and some very bad academies just as there are some very good and very bad local authority schools.

The research suggests that schools which do well with one group of pupils are likely to do well with another. So, the way a school copes with children with special educational needs and with those from poor backgrounds may well tell you whether it will help more advantaged children to prosper.

The idea, pursued by successive governments, that you can raise standards by inventing new types of school or reviving old ones, is a myth. In the next chapter we shall look at what makes a real difference to pupils' education and what parents should look for when choosing a school.

References

Trevelyan, G.M. (1946) *English Social History*. London: Longman.

Gorard, S. and Siddiqui, N., (2018) 'Grammar schools in England: a new analysis of social segregation and academic outcomes.' *British Journal of Sociology of Education*, Vol. 39, No. 7, pp. 909–924.

ITV News (21 September 2016) '*War Horse* author Michael Morpurgo: "failing 11-plus was like a dagger to the heart".' ITV.

'Grammar schools: help or hindrance.' (2015) *The Times*. Available from www.thetimes.co.uk/article/grammar-schools-help-or-hindrance-5bzh075wfsq

Atkinson, A., Gregg, P. and McConn, B. (2006) 'The result of 11+ selection: an investigation into opportunities and outcomes for pupils in selective LEAs. ' Centre for Market and Public Organisation, University of Bristol. Available from www.bristol.ac.uk/media-library/sites/cmpo/migrated/documents/wp150.pdf (downloaded 21 May 2019).

Ireson, J. and Brown, P. (2013) 'Parents use private tutors to boost chances of a grammar school place.' *WiredGov*. Available from www.wired-gov.net/wg/wg-news-1.nsf/0/B4D814EAF9DF2D0680257BBE00491E27?OpenDocument (downloaded 8 June 2019).

Cribb, J., Sibieta, L., Vignoles, A., Skipp, A., Sadro, F. and Jesson, D. (2013) 'Poor grammar: entry into grammar schools for disadvantaged pupils in England.'Sutton Trust. Available from www.suttontrust.com/research-paper/poor-grammar-entry-grammar-schools-disadvantaged-pupils-england/ (downloaded 8 June 2019).

PISA OECD (2016) *PISA 2015 Results (Volume III) Students' Well-Being.* Paris: OECD Publishing. Available from https://read.oecd-ilibrary.org/education/pisa -2015-results-volume-iii_9789264273856-en#page1 (downloaded 21 May 2019).

'School performance in academy chains and local authorities – 2017.' (2017) Education Policy Institute. Available from https://epi.org.uk/publications-and-re search/performance-academy-local-authorities-2017/ (downloaded 5 June 2019).

Hutchings, M., and Francis, B. 'Chain effects 2018: the impact of academy chains on low-income pupils.' The Sutton Trust. Available from www.suttontrust.com/wp -content/uploads/2018/12/Chain-Effects-2018.pdf (downloaded 21 May 2019).

Milburn, A. (2012) 'Fair access to professional careers a progress report by the independent reviewer on social mobility and child poverty.' Available from http s://assets.publishing.service.gov.uk/government/uploads/system/uploads/a ttachment_data/file/61090/IR_FairAccess_acc2.pdf (downloaded 9 June 2019).

Anders, J. (2015) 'Private pay progression.' The Sutton Trust. Available from www.sut tontrust.com/research-paper/private-pay-progression/ (downloaded 9 June 2019).

Montacute, R. and Cullinane, C. (2018) 'Access to advantage: the influence of schools and place on admission to top universities.' The Sutton Trust. Available from www.suttontrust.com/wp-content/uploads/2018/12/AccesstoAdvanta ge-2018.pdf (downloaded 9 June 2019).

Ndaji, F., Little, J. and Coe, R. (2016) 'A comparison of academic achievement in independent and state schools.' Independent Schools Council. Available from www.isc.co.uk/media/3140/16_02_26-cem-durham-university-academic-va lue-added-research.pdf (downloaded 21 May 2019).

Marks, R. (2012) *Discourses of Ability and Primary School Mathematics: Production, Reproduction and Transformation.* PhD Thesis. King's College London.

Sellgren, K. (2017) 'Should young children be grouped by ability.' *BBC News* (1 December). Available from www.bbc.co.uk/news/education-42154013

Ireson, J., Hallam, S. and Hurley, C. (2005) 'What are the effects of ability grouping on GCSE attainment?' *British Educational Research Journal*, Vol. 31, No. 4, pp. 443–458.

Parsons, S. and Hallam, S. (2014) 'The impact of streaming on attainment at age seven: evidence from the Millennium Cohort study.' *Oxford Review of Education*, Vol. 40, No. 5, pp. 567–589.

Chapter 8

What works in the classroom

What happens in a classroom matters more than how large the class size is. Great teachers are able to personalize learning even in very complex settings. They find a way.
Andreas Schleicher, Director of Education and Skills at the Organisation for Economic Co-operation and Development (*Edmonton Journal*, December, 2013)

Parents pay for their child to be noticed.
Teacher at Roedean, one of England's best-known private schools for girls

Millions of words have been written by education researchers and teachers about what works best in the classroom over the last century or so. Previous practice has been turned on its head and new practices have been introduced as the years rolled by. But where are we now about what does work well on some of the bigger issues in classroom practice? You may well be surprised by some of the answers that follow starting with what the right size of a class is for optimum learning.

The class size conundrum

Many years ago, one of us visited Roedean, the Brighton fee-charging boarding school for girls and asked a teacher why parents were prepared to pay thousands of pounds for their daughters to be educated there.

"Parents pay for their child to be noticed," she said, pointing to a class of a dozen. (The average Roedean class size in 2018 was around 18.) Her answer struck a chord as it will with any parent who has worried that a not particularly confident child will be lost in a class of 30-plus or who has watched a teacher struggle to put a face to a name at a parents' evening.

Surely the benefit of smaller classes is obvious? If a primary school teacher has to hear 32 children read that will take her longer than listening to 25 children. Thirty lots of homework must take longer to mark than 20 lots. Ask most teachers and they'll agree that fewer pupils in a class means that they get more attention. The maths looks pretty simple.

That's why the issue of smaller class sizes interests politicians. In the UK, Labour based its 1997 manifesto that swept the party to power on a landslide on five pledges. One was to cut class sizes for all five, six and seven-year-olds to below 30. The promise was deemed so successful that almost 20 years later in 2015, Labour was still pledging to cap infant class sizes.

The interest is worldwide. In 2007, a survey of American adults under the auspices of the American journal Education Next and Harvard University found that 77 per cent would prefer to spend money on lower class sizes than teachers' salaries.

Yet some knowledgeable and respected figures disagree. Andreas Schleicher, Director of Education and Skills at the Organisation for Economic Co-operation and Development (OECD), the authoritative intergovernmental body that compares education in developed countries, has argued that class size reduction is not the most cost-effective way of improving schools.

Schleicher says that the countries that do best in the Programme for International Student Assessment (PISA) run by the OECD are those that emphasise teacher quality above class size. He looked at the PISA test results for South Korea and compared them with those for Luxembourg. Both spend similar amounts on education but Korea is a top performer in PISA and Luxembourg is below average. Luxembourg has invested in small classes while Korea has large classes but pays teachers better, tries hard to attract the best and invests in their professional development.

So who is right? Those who believe class size matters challenge Schleicher's view. They say that the argument that Asian countries score highly in international tests despite their big classes should be treated with caution. In places like Korea, Hong Kong and Shanghai parental aspirations, discipline and culture are very different from the US and the UK and may well explain some of the results. Many parents in these countries are extremely ambitious for their children and use out of school tutoring to improve their academic performance. Schleicher is a respected figure but his view isn't the result of research.

Indeed, credible class size research is hard to come by. Professor John Hattie, whose work we have already raised looked at 113 studies in developed nations, including the UK, the US and Europe over the past 25 years and found that cutting class sizes made only a small difference to pupils' academic progress.

The idea that you can attach a numerical figure to an effect size is questioned by some researchers but Professor Hattie has tried to do this. He suggests that effective teaching is related to nearly six times as much progress as class size reduction. The reason? Teachers don't change the way they teach because there are fewer pupils in their class so the idea that children get more attention in small classes, expressed so succinctly by the Roedean teacher, is misleading.

A government report from England's Department for Education that looked at the available evidence broadly supported the conclusion that cutting class size was not the most effective way to raise attainment. But it did draw attention to two large longitudinal studies that suggest this is not the whole story. The youngest children *do* achieve more and behave better in smaller classes though the effect of smaller classes gets less as they move up the school.

The first of these studies was done in the US state of Tennessee at the end of the 1980s. In the Student Teacher Achievement Ratio, or STAR, study, students and teachers were assigned at random to a small class with between 13 and 17 students or a normal-sized class of between 22 and 25 students. That meant the smaller classes were, on average, nearly a third smaller.

The study compared the performance of around 6,500 pupils in 330 classrooms in 80 schools and it took into account differences between schools, pupils and teachers. The researchers tested pupils in kindergarten (aged five to six), first, second and third grades in reading, maths and basic aptitude. Four years later, student achievement in the smaller classes was about three months ahead of that of students in the bigger classes. What's more, the advantages of starting school in a small class remained as pupils progressed through school and were placed in larger classes.

The second phase of the project, begun in 1989, and called the Lasting Benefits Study, showed that these children continued to outperform their peers whose school experience had begun in larger classes even in the fourth and fifth grades. The third phase, Project Challenge, looked at the effect of small classes in kindergarten, first, second and third grades in the 17 poorest school districts. These districts' end-of-year rank in reading and maths compared with neighbouring districts rose from well below average to above average.

The second important class size study mentioned in the government report was carried out by London University's Institute of Education: "The Class Size and Pupil Adult Ratio Study (CSPAR)." It followed a large cohort of pupils (20,000) from randomly selected schools who started reception between the ages of four and five in 1996/7. The researchers tested them every year in English and maths as they moved through primary school.

The study wasn't designed as a research experiment like the STAR study. Instead, it looked at existing classes but the children were from every kind of background and the schools were in cities, suburbs and the countryside. The researchers made allowance for anything other than class size that might influence their performance: social background, age, gender, pre-school attendance and so on. It collected information about how many adults were in the classroom and how qualified and experienced they were. And it asked teachers about their experience of class size and observed lessons. It defined a large class as over 30 and a small one as under 20.

Just as in the STAR study, small classes made a significant difference to reception class pupils of all abilities in literacy and maths. In literacy, the children who started school with the lowest attainment benefitted most. At the end of the second year at school (Year 1), the effect of class size on the children's progress in literacy was still clear, though not by the end of the third year. Small classes in reception didn't appear to have any long-term effect on achievement in maths.

So, the evidence suggests that smaller classes for the youngest pupils really do pay dividends and that the popularity of political pledges to cut class sizes is not entirely without foundation.

When governments think about class size, they naturally concentrate on its relationship to school standards and academic achievement. Lamar Alexander, the governor of Tennessee who commissioned the STAR study did so because he wanted the pupils in his state to get better test results and because there were some signs that class size reductions had had this effect in the state of Indiana.

But Professor Peter Blatchford, Professor of Psychology and Education at the University College of London Institute of Education, who led the CSPAR study, says that we shouldn't just think about test scores when we consider class size. His research has also found that parents are right to believe that individual pupils get more attention in smaller classes and teachers interact more with their pupils.

In many classes, there are pupils who are present but in a world of their own or paying more attention to the person in the next desk than the teacher. Professor Blatchford's research involved systematic observations in classrooms and questionnaires and interviews with teachers. He wrote in *The Guardian* newspaper:

> The focus on class size and academic performance overlooks the effect of class size on other aspects of classroom life ... careful moment-by-moment systematic observation of pupils shows that class size affects the amount of individual attention pupils receive, and their engagement and active involvement in class.

When he and his team looked at secondary schools in a follow-up study they found that the low attaining pupils were more likely to be disengaged from their work when they were in larger classes than their higher-achieving peers. In larger classes pupils spent more time talking to each other and teachers more time carrying out administrative tasks like taking the register.

He says:[1]

> There is a conundrum about class size. There is a strong view from pol-icymakers and some researchers that class size doesn't matter. Then there is an outpouring of professional angst from teachers that says that it does.
>
> If you look at class size from the point of its effect on academic attainment, that's far too limited. The negative aspects of class size on pupils may not be coming out in the test scores. If teachers can't introduce more creative, problem-solving activities because of large classes, pupils will be offered fewer non-core lessons like languages and music.

Then there's the cost to teachers and parents should care about that, he says, because it's also a cost to pupils.

> If you have 32 in a class you have 32 scripts to mark. If you have a range of attainment levels in a large class that's a management night-mare. Class size may be a very important factor in teacher retention.

He agrees with Hattie that one of the reasons research fails to show bigger benefits of class size reduction is that teachers don't adapt their practice to suit smaller classes. Teachers tend to give more one-to-one instruction in small classes but it would be more effective to use small group teaching.

> Class size changes only work if you change your teaching practice. Smaller classes can allow some really good teaching practice. Teaching isn't just about delivering a lesson or making a presentation as the proponents of large classes tend to think.

It isn't a matter of choosing to reduce class sizes or to make this or that intervention, it's about what constitutes effective teaching. It's what you do in smaller classes that matters, he says.

You can't, of course, measure behaviour or daydreaming in the way that you can measure maths and reading but both the Tennessee and the London studies suggest that teachers in small classes have more time to build up relationships and interact with pupils. Even if, as Hattie and Schleicher say, the key to a good education is excellent tea-chers, it looks as though small classes make a real difference to the youngest pupils and they may help all pupils have a better experience at school.

1   The quotations in this chapter from Professor Peter Blatchford are taken from an interview with Judith Judd, 1 May, 2019.

References

Schleicher, A. (2012) 'Use data to build better schools.' TED talk. Available from www.ted.com/talks/andreas_schleicher_use_data_to_build_better_schools/tra nscript?language=en#t-249101

Howell, W.G., West, M.R. and Peterson, P.E. (2007) 'What Americans think about their schools'. *Education Next*. Available from www.educationnext.org/what-am ericans-think-about-their-schools/ (downloaded 9 June 2019).

Word, E.R., Johnston, J., Bain, H.P. and Fulton, B.D. (1990) 'The state of Tennessee's student/teacher achievement ratio (STAR) project, technical report 1985–1990.' Available from www.classsizematters.org/wp-content/uploads/2016/09/STAR-Technical-Report-Part-I.pdf (downloaded 23 May 2019).

Blatchford, P., Bassett, P., Goldstein, H., and Martin, C. (2003) 'Are class size differences related to pupils' educational progress and classroom processes? Findings from the Institute of Education Class Size Study of children aged 5–7 Years.' *British Educational Research Journal*. Available from https://core.ac.uk/ download/pdf/82606.pdf (downloaded 23 May 2019).

Hattie, J. (2015) *What Doesn't Work in Education: The Politics of Distraction*. London: Pearson. Available from www.pearson.com/content/dam/corporate/global/p earson-dot-com/files/hattie/150602_DistractionWEB_V2.pdf (downloaded 23 May 2019).

Department for Education. (2011) 'Class size and education in England evidence report'. Available from https://assets.publishing.service.gov.uk/government/ uploads/system/uploads/attachment_data/file/183364/DFE-RR169.pdf (downloaded 23 May 2019).

Mosteller, F. (1995) 'The Tennessee study of class size in the early school grades.' *The Future of Children*, Vol. 5, No. 2. Available from www.jstor.org/stable/i273896

Blatchford, P. (2003) 'A systematic observational study of teachers' and pupils' behaviour in large and small classes.' *Learning and Instruction*, Vol. 13, No. 6, pp. 569–595. Available from http://dx.doi.org/10.1016/S0959-4752(02)00043–00049

Blatchford, P., Edmonds, S. and Martin, C. (2003) 'Class size, pupil attentiveness and peer relations.' *British Journal of Educational Psychology*. Available from http s://pdfs.semanticscholar.org/3777/a9287d88ac42b14aeec37e3a5e7ee3c52035.pdf

Learning to read

> Reading involves far more than decoding words on the page. Nevertheless, words must be decoded if readers are to make sense of the text.
>
> Jim Rose, leader of an English government review of reading, 2006

> No matter how brilliant at "decoding" we are, it doesn't guarantee we can read for meaning.
>
> Michael Rosen, former UK Children's Laureate

Reading is fundamental to education. Children who can't read struggle to make progress in other school subjects and, if they arrive at secondary school without sound reading skills, they are in trouble. So, it is not surprising that reading has provoked some of the fiercest controversy among educationalists and that governments have been reluctant to leave this part of the curriculum to teachers. The result for the past 70 years has been a succession of hotly-debated approaches.

At its simplest, the argument is between those who say that children need to be able to decode the letters of the alphabet before they can read and those who fear that, unless they are introduced to interesting books early on, they will be turned off reading for good.

Today's grandparents learned to read mostly using a method called analytic phonics which puts the emphasis on learning letter sounds and then points to words that are similar. They had specially-written reading books with vocabulary that mattered more than a good story. Their children were taught with a mixture of methods, including some phonics but also whole word recognition (look and say) and encouragement to guess words from context and pictures.

For the past 20 years, the emphasis on phonics has been growing again, particularly on synthetic phonics, a system that emphasises identifying and pronouncing sounds rather than letters. In synthetic phonics, children are taught to sound out the smallest units of sound (phonemes) and how to blend these together to read a word and they are taught all this very quickly: 42 letter sounds at six a day in eight days.

At the same time, they are taught to identify letters in the initial, middle and final positions in words and to sound and blend words using magnetic letters. Blending comes much later in analytic phonics, which starts from a whole word and breaks it down. In this method, children are taught to recognise common letters at the beginning (or end) of words e.g. pan, pig, park. It also encourages the use of rhyme in learning to read.

A study carried out in Clackmannanshire in Scotland is the basis for the popularity of synthetic phonics. The study, commissioned by Clackmannanshire Council and funded partly by the Scottish Office, was published in 1998.

It involved 300 pupils and 13 classes in eight schools. Researchers Dr Rhona Johnston of the University of Hull and Joyce Watson of the University of St Andrews divided them into three groups. The group taught with synthetic phonics rather than other methods far outperformed the other groups. After 16 weeks, children in the former group had reading ages which were, on average, seven months ahead of their chronological ages, while the latter groups had fallen slightly behind their chronological ages. By the end of the first year, the synthetic phonics group was a year ahead of its reading age and 14 months ahead in spelling.

Disadvantaged children who might have been expected to be further behind were not and boys, who tend to lag behind girls, had also kept pace with their peers. The researchers continued to track the children in a seven-year longitudinal study and concluded that at the end of that time, the synthetic phonics children were three and a half years ahead of their chronological age in reading accuracy and three and a half months ahead in reading comprehension. Boys and disadvantaged pupils performed particularly well.

The study was hugely influential and in 2006, an English government review of primary education led by Jim Rose, a former Ofsted Director of Inspection, said that synthetic phonics offered "the best route to becoming skilled readers."

Politicians have pursued his advice enthusiastically but teachers and other researchers are more sceptical. Researchers point to weaknesses in the Clackmannanshire study that failed to take into account other factors that might have influenced children's progress. They were particularly critical of the claim that synthetic phonics improved children's reading comprehension. Some researchers also argued that the use of rhyme (not part of the synthetic phonics programme) is particularly useful in teaching reading in the English language where an estimated 20 per cent of spelling is irregular. (Think of words such as light and right.)

In 2006, the Labour government asked researchers at the universities of York and Sheffield to look at the best evidence about phonics teaching. They concluded that it improved reading accuracy but could find no strong evidence that it boosted reading comprehension. Their review suggested that it didn't make much difference which type of phonics was used – analytic or synthetic – if the teaching was consistent. It also said there was not enough evidence to decide what effect synthetic phonics had on children's ability to understand what they read.

Politicians' enthusiasm for phonics continues. In 2012, the Coalition government in England introduced a phonics screening check for all primary pupils at the end of Year 1. Six-year-olds are asked to read some real words and some pseudo-words to make sure that they are able to "decode" language.

It's clear that phonics of whatever variety does have a role to play in helping children learn to read and it seems to be particularly important for pupils who come from homes where books and reading may be uncommon. The benefits for the most disadvantaged pupils were confirmed in 2018 by a study of 270,000 children in 150 local authorities from the Centre for Economic Performance at the London School of Economics.

The study is the first large-scale analysis of the effects of the government decision to promote synthetic phonics in schools. It looked at children's progress at the age of 11 and not just after they had completed the phonics programme. Researchers used national test scores to measure children's performance in reading at the ages of five, seven and 11. Those taught using synthetic phonics had made better progress at the age of seven than those taught using other methods. For children from poor families or whose second language was English, the benefits persisted until they were 11 – they were still ahead of similar children who hadn't had synthetic phonics instruction. But for the average child, the advantages had disappeared by the end of primary school.

Most children, it seems, learn to read eventually whatever method their teachers use. Phonics helps to narrow the gap between the poorest children and their more affluent peers but it offers no lasting benefit to the latter. It is not a panacea.

There is plenty of evidence from research on both sides of the Atlantic that supports the idea that a mixture of methods is the best way to encourage and promote reading. That includes coupling understanding with decoding, paying attention to individual children's interests and experience, careful monitoring, an early introduction to wonderful story books and plenty of interaction with good teachers.

The late Professor Michael Pressley of Michigan State University studied first grade classrooms in the US and found that the most successful teachers of literacy used a variety of techniques. They promoted reading and writing for pleasure and meaning and encouraged reading across the curriculum alongside phonics. Classroom discipline was also important. He insisted that good literacy instruction should balance the teaching of skills with a broad experience of reading and writing.

In a review of evidence about reading published in the Journal of Literacy Research in 2002 Professor Pressley also referred to evidence we have considered earlier in this book about the vital importance of parents in helping children learn to read. He didn't mean by that that parents should go on a crash course in synthetic phonics but that they should read stories, read cereal packets, read advertisements and talk about books with their children. In the same article he said: "Good reading instruction, begins at home."

And he argued that parents could carry on supporting their children's literacy after they had started school by, for example, talking to them about books and by keeping family journals.

There is plenty of evidence in the UK, too. Professor Greg Brooks of Sheffield University reviewed family literacy programmes for the government and noted that courses for parents of children aged between three and six reduced the proportion of children who struggled with reading from around two-thirds to a third.

The debate about how far early literacy teachers should concentrate on the "decoding" techniques of reading and how much they should emphasise a love and understanding of the written word will go on. No-one, however, disputes that parents play a vital role in helping their children become enthusiastic and confident readers.

References

Rosen, M. (2012) 'Michael Rosen's letter from a curious parent'. *The Guardian*, 4 June. Available at www.theguardian.com/education/2012/jun/04/michael-rosen-phonics-screen-test

Pressley, M., Wharton-McDonald, R., Allington, R., Block, C.C., Morrow, L., Tracey, D., Baker, K., Brooks, G., Cronin, J., Nelson, E. and Woo, D. (2001) 'A study of effective first grade literacy instruction.' *Scientific Studies of Reading*, Vol. 5, No. 1, pp. 35–58.

Watson, J.E. and Johnston, R.S. (1998) 'Accelerating reading attainment: the effectiveness of synthetic phonics'. Interchange, Scottish Executive Education Department, Edinburgh. Available from https://eric.ed.gov/?id=ED427284 (downloaded 23 May 2019).

Johnston, R. and Watson, J. (2005), 'The effects of synthetic phonics teaching on reading and spelling attainment: a seven-year longitudinal study.' Scottish Executive Education Department, Edinburgh. Available from https://dera.ioe.ac.uk/14793/1/0023582.pdf (downloaded 23 May 2019).

Machin, S., McNally, S. and Viarengo, M. (2018) 'Changing how literacy is taught: evidence on synthetic phonics.' *American Economic Journal: Economic Policy*, Vol. 10, No. 2, pp. 217–241.

Brooks, G., Gorman, T.P., Harman, J., Hutchison, D. and Wilkin, A. (1996) *Family Literacy Works: The NFER evaluation of the Basic Skills Agency's Family Literacy Demonstration Programmes*. London: Basic Skills Agency.

Maths anxiety and how to end it

> The myth is that there is such a thing as a maths brain.
> Jo Boaler, Professor of Mathematics Education at Stanford University, USA

> I'm sorry sire, but there is no royal road to geometry.
> Greek mathematician Euclid's response to a busy king who wanted to learn geometry

The teaching of maths has provoked less controversy than the teaching of reading but that does not mean that it is less complicated. Much research concentrates on an issue that barely arises in the debate about literacy, fear of maths, or as it is called in the US, math.

A glance at the internet shows the extent to which attitudes to maths are the starting point for much research on the subject. Wikipedia has an entry on Mathematical Anxiety, Wikihow on How to Cope with Maths Phobia and numerous websites offer to test whether you suffer from maths anxiety and provide tips on how to overcome it.

We know from our own experience that people are ashamed if they struggle with literacy but are not afraid to admit that they are "rubbish at maths." We know, too, that we can pass on our fears about maths to our children and that may affect their ability to handle numbers confidently.

Parents make a vital contribution in this as in every other sphere of education.

Researchers in maths education are grappling with the need to combat fear of maths among adults and children. Their work overlaps with research covered elsewhere in this book: the importance of a growth mindset developed by Professor Carol Dweck and also with new discoveries about how the brain works.

Professor Jo Boaler, quoted at the beginning of this section, is one of those leading the quest for a different type of maths education. She suggests that one of the reasons for common anxiety about maths is the tendency for maths teachers to ask closed questions that require right or wrong answers. She points to research into the role of mistakes in how we learn.

Jason Moser, a psychologist from Michigan State University, studied the neural mechanisms in the brain when people make mistakes and he found something amazing (Moser et al., 2011). During MRI scans of children's brains, he observed that when we make a mistake synapses fire – synapses are electric signals that move between parts of the brain when we learn. *More* synapses fire when we make a mistake than when we get the right answer and they fire even if we don't know that we have made a mistake. Professor Boaler writes: "Mistakes are not only opportunities for learning, as students consider their mistakes, but also times when our brains grow."

Research in the classroom, she suggests, reinforces her argument. Dr Gabrielle Steuer and her colleagues at the University of Augsburg in Germany found that children performed better in maths classes where they were not afraid to make mistakes.

The logic of these findings, Professor Boaler says is that teachers should ask more open-ended questions and pupils should be rewarded for asking good questions, reformulating problems, explaining, justifying the methods they have used in a calculation and looking at a problem in a different way.

Further evidence that how children feel about maths makes a difference to how well they learn comes from a 2018 study from the Stanford University School of Medicine led by Dr Lang Chen. He found that a "can do" attitude to maths made a big contribution to success in the subject. The researchers gave 240 children, aged between seven and ten, questionnaires and assessed their IQ, reading ability and memory capacity. The children then answered arithmetic questions, including problems. Their parents were questioned about their child's level of maths anxiety and the children also answered a survey that assessed their attitude to maths. A positive attitude to maths led to better functioning of the hippocampus, part of the brain associated with memory, while students were trying to solve arithmetic problems.

Perhaps the importance of attitude in maths helps to explain some of the findings of researchers at Johns Hopkins University in the US who are investigating what works in maths teaching. Marta Pellegrini from Florence University in Italy spent nine months with a team at Johns Hopkins reviewing evidence about the most effective way to teach primary school maths. The review looked at 78 high quality studies of maths programmes. They were divided into eight categories tutoring (extra help for individual or small groups of children), technology, professional development of teachers to improve their knowledge about maths and teaching methods, classroom management, whole-school reform, social and emotional support, textbooks and assessment.

Tutoring made the biggest difference and it didn't have to be one-to-one tutoring. Small-group tutoring was just as effective. Surprisingly, it made very little difference whether the tutors were qualified teachers or teaching assistants. (As we shall see in Chapter 10, other researchers have found that teaching assistants are less effective than teachers in supporting struggling pupils.) The second most effective category was classroom organisation and management that led to better behaviour. That included co-operative schemes such as the Good Behaviour programme. (In that programme the teacher divides pupils into teams for a maths or reading activity and they get penalty points for bad behaviour, for example, interrupting or leaving their seat. Teams can lose a fixed number of points and still win.)

Interestingly, the type of maths taught and the methods used (pedagogy), seemed to make little difference to pupil achievement. Professional development courses for teachers did not lead to better maths results. At the end of a year-long study in which 80 teachers received 90 hours of first-class in-service training to improve their teaching, children in classes taught by teachers in a control group who had *not* received the training did better than children in the classes whose teachers had.

What is going on? Robert Slavin, Director of the Center for Research and Reform in Education at Johns Hopkins, suggested in his blog that tutors provide a "human element" to teaching: a child wants to see the teacher's eyes light up and to earn their praise. And it turns out that children who are more sociable and better behaved are also better at maths.

He says in the blog, which begins with the quote from Euclid at the head of this section:

> We need breakthroughs in mathematics teaching. Perhaps we have been looking in the wrong places, expecting that improved content and pedagogy will be the key to better learning. They will surely be involved, but perhaps it will turn out that math does not live only in students' heads, but must also live in their hearts.

References

Boaler, J. (2015) *Mathematical Mindsets: Unleashing Students' Potential Through Creative Math, Inspiring Messages and Innovative Teaching.* San Francisco, CA: Jossey-Bass. https://www.youcubed.org/evidence/mistakes-grow-brain/

Moser, J.S., Schroder, H.S., Heeter, C., Moran, T. P. and Lee, Y.H. (2011) 'Mind your errors evidence for a neural mechanism linking growth mind-set to adaptive posterror adjustments.' *Psychological Science*, Vol. 22, No. 12. pp. 1484–1489. doi:10.1177/0956797611419520

Steuer, G., Rosentritt-Brunn, G. and Dresel, M. (2013) 'Dealing with errors in mathematics classrooms: Structure and relevance of perceived error climate.' *Contemporary Educational Psychology*, Vol. 38, No. 3, pp. 196–210. Available from http://dx.doi.org/10.1016/j.cedpsych.2013.03.002

Chen, L., Bae, S.R., Battista, C., Qin, S., Chen, T., Evans, T.M. and Menon, V. (2018) 'Positive attitude toward math supports early academic success: behavioral evidence and neurocognitive mechanisms.' *Psychological Science*. Available from https://med.stanford.edu/content/dam/sm/scsnl/documents/Chen_Positive-Attitude-Toward-Math.pdf (downloaded 5 June 2019).

Pellegrini, M., Inns, A. and Slavin, R. (2018) 'Effective programs in elementary mathematics: a best-evidence synthesis'. Paper presented at the annual meeting of the Society for Research on Educational Effectiveness, Washington, DC.

Slavin, R. (2018) 'What works in elementary math.' Blog available from https://robertslavinsblog.wordpress.com/2018/10/11/what-works-in-elementary-math/ (downloaded 9 June 2019).

Slavin, R. (2019) 'A mathematical mystery'. Blog available from https://robertslavinsblog.wordpress.com/2019/02/14/a-mathematical-mystery/ (downloaded 9 June 2019).

Why marking matters

> We're addicted to grades. I've nothing against grades at the end of the school year. But telling students, after every piece of work, that they're at levels 5, 6 or whatever is bizarre, perverse.
>
> Dylan Wiliam (*The Guardian*, 18 January, 2011)

> My parents are pressuring me to get perfect grades.
>
> US student on the website familyeducation.com

In the previous two sections we've looked at how teachers approach literacy and numeracy. They measure their success – and parents see the results of that measurement – by awarding marks or grades for pieces of work.

In England, the past three decades have seen an increase in the number of national tests that pupils are required to take. Even the performance of the youngest schoolchildren is measured as we have seen, for example, in the introduction of a "phonics" check for six-year-olds' progress in reading. A baseline test for five-year-olds is planned from 2020. Throughout their schooling, teachers judge whether children have reached the "level" expected for their age. So seven-year-olds are expected to reach Level 2, 11-year-olds Level 4 and 14-year-olds Level 5.

For parents, it is reassuring to know what their children have achieved. Teachers, too, need to check what their pupils have learned. But research tells us that this assessment *of* learning (sometimes called summative assessment) is not enough. If students are to make the best possible progress, teachers also need to employ assessment *for* learning (or formative assessment).

At its simplest, this means that instead of teachers writing 6/10 on a maths test or essay, they should suggest how it might be improved. But they should also help their students to understand the aim of their learning, how far they have progressed towards their goal and what they should do next.

Teachers have, of course, been using assessment for learning for many years but it first received widespread acceptance after an authoritative piece of work published in 1998 by Professors Paul Black and Dylan Wiliam of King's College, London.

Inside the Black Box analysed 600 assessment studies involving 10,000 pupils from all over the world and concluded that traditional 5/10 marks and comments such as "could do better" and "satisfactory" should be the exception rather than the rule. They found that pupils who have the same teachers progress further if they receive comments on their work than if they receive just marks or even marks and comments. The right kind of feedback could raise standards by as much as two GCSE grades, the study suggested.

The findings held good for children of all abilities. If those at the bottom of the class received poor marks without constructive comments they tended to give up. Very able children who always received high marks might just coast along without making the effort required to do even better if they kept receiving good grades without comments about how they could progress.

But, though Black and Wiliam's research won huge popularity and thousands of copies of their book were sold, both have said that its principles have not been introduced in most classrooms. The idea of assessment for learning was adopted by the government of Labour prime minister Tony Blair in the first decade of this century but it focussed on measuring pupils' progress rather than helping them take control of their own learning.

Although teachers know that providing good feedback is important, it isn't easy to achieve. A review of research in 1996 (Kluger and DeNisi) found that in more than a third of well-designed studies, feedback actually led to worse performance from students. Kluger and DeNisi also argued that even if a type of feedback led to significant progress in students it shouldn't continue if students became dependent on it.

Professor Wiliam argues that we have to look at what feedback does to students because the only good feedback is feedback that is used so it is vital that students understand why they are receiving feedback and how to use it.

In a paper on the secret of effective feedback (2016) he says that there is no point in a teacher suggesting, for instance, that paragraphs three and four in a story should be reversed because the teacher has done the work and the student will have learned little.

By contrast, he says that effective feedback in maths might involve a teacher returning 20 solved equations to a student with the comment that five of them are wrong. "Find them and put them right." This kind of "detective work" encourages analysis and builds understanding.

Professor Wiliam says the amount of feedback teachers can give will always be limited so it is important to encourage students to assess themselves. Self-assessment is commonplace among adults. Most bosses begin an appraisal with their employees by asking: "How do you think you are doing?" We should encourage young people to think about their progress in the same way.

Professor Wiliam says that his work with instrumental music teachers has reinforced his belief in the importance of self-assessment. They have only between 20 and 30 minutes a week with their pupils so they have to spend the time making sure that they are going to make good use of their practice time in between lessons – and that means evaluating their own performance, thinking about what they found easy or difficulty and what they might do differently next time.

Professor Wiliam has designed resource materials to support formative assessment. The Education Endowment Foundation, a charity that aims to break down the link between educational achievement and family income ran a project that examined the effect of introducing these into teachers' professional development. The foundation recruited 140 schools and gave half of them the materials and used the rest as a control group. Those who were given the materials received minimal support and their teachers had a single day's in-service training.

Many did not implement the materials as the authors had intended but the results were still significant. Two years later the students in the schools that received the materials had made the equivalent of two months' extra progress across eight GCSE subjects compared with students in the schools that did not.

Getting feedback right is one of education's great challenges but the potential rewards are huge.

References

Wilby, P. (2011) 'Teaching guru is optimistic about education.' *The Guardian*, 18 January. Available at www.theguardian.com/education/2011/jan/18/tea ching-methods-government-reforms

Kluger, A.N. and DeNisi, A. (1996) 'The effects of feedback interventions on performance. A historical review, a meta-analysis, and a preliminary feedback intervention theory.' *Psychological Bulletin*, Vol. *119*, No. 2, pp. 254–284. doi:10.1037/0033–2909.119.2.254

Wiliam, D. (2016) 'The secret of effective feedback.' *Educational Leadership*, Vol. *73*, No. 7, pp. 10–15.

Speckesser, S., Runge, J., Foliano, F., Bursnall, M., Hudson-Sharp, N., Rolfe, H. and Anders, J. (2018) 'Embedding formative assessment, evaluation report and executive summary.' Education Endowment Foundation. Available from https://dera.ioe.ac.uk/32012/1/EFA_evaluation_report.pdf (downloaded 23 May 2019).

Black, P. and Wiliam, D. (1998) 'Inside the black box: raising standards through classroom assessment.' *Phi Delta Kappan*, Vol. *80*, No. 2, pp. 139–148.

Homework

> Homework is part of the traditional parents' mindset about what makes a good school.
>
> Headteacher of an Essex comprehensive school

This remark by a headteacher gives you some idea that homework is a hotly debated subject. Parents expect a good school to set lots of it, he says. But that's not the same as providing evidence that it raises educational standards. Listen to Professor John Hattie, mentioned earlier, who has spent many years analysing what works in education. He told interviewer Sarah Montague on a BBC Radio 4 programme the Educators:

> Homework in primary schools has zero effect. In high schools, it's larger.... If you try and get rid of it in primary schools many parents judge the quality of the school by the presence of homework so don't get rid of it. Treat the zero as saying it's probably not making much difference so let's improve it. Certainly, I think we can get over obsessed with homework. Five to ten minutes is as good as one or two hours.

He is right about the popularity of homework with parents but they expect the hours their children spend doing homework to pay off. Some politicians have tapped into this expectation by putting pressure on schools to set regular homework for their pupils. Tony Blair's Labour government laid down homework guidelines in 1997 for the amount of homework all pupils, even the youngest, should do.

Below we look at some of the questions that researchers have asked about homework.

Does more mean better?

It might seem obvious that doing more school work leads to better test and exam results. Surely practice makes perfect? But the link is not straightforward. As Professor Hattie suggests, most research shows that homework has little or no effect in primary schools though it does make some difference in secondary schools.

Caroline Sharp of the National Foundation for Educational Research did a study for Ofsted, published in 2001, that looked at research for the previous 12 years in the UK and the United States. She found a link between secondary pupils' achievement and homework for those who did a reasonable amount, but doing lots of homework didn't necessarily boost performance: underachievers included those who did a lot and those who did a little. She found no conclusive evidence that homework boosted achievement for primary pupils.

The important EPPSE (Effective Pre-School Primary and Secondary Education) longitudinal study for England's Department for Education mentioned earlier was more positive about homework than the Sharp study when it reported its findings on the subject in 2012.

Researchers from London University's Institute of Education, Oxford University and Birkbeck College, London, tracked 3,000 pupils over a period of 15 years. When they reached secondary school, students were asked to report how much time they spent on homework on a typical school night. Spending more than two hours a night on homework in English, maths and science led to better GCSE results for secondary pupils even when pupils' backgrounds were taken into account. Students who reported in Year 9 spending between two and three hours on homework on an average weeknight were almost 10 times more likely to achieve 5 A*–C grades at GCSE than students who did not spend any time on homework. A similar result was found for the time spent on homework reported in Year 11.

However, a study of nearly 7,500 Spanish 14-year-olds agreed with Caroline Sharp that too much homework was pointless. Students who did more than 90 minutes in maths and science got worse exam results than those who did the allotted amount of between 60 and 70 minutes a night. Again, students were asked to say how often and for how long they did homework.

Are homework battles worth it?

Most parents think they are, according to the Sharp study. Parents want their children to have homework even if that leads to conflict about playing online games, spending time on social media and going out with friends.

But care is needed. In 1999, Dr Susan Hallam and Dr Richard Cowan of London University's Institute of Education published a review of half a century's research on homework that suggested that tensions between parents and their children caused by homework could be counter-productive, alienating children from school and leading them to switch off from school altogether.

Quality not quantity

Professor Hattie told Radio 4 that his review suggested that the type of homework matters. It should be used to reinforce learning that has taken place in class rather than to do open-ended projects where the student has to start from scratch.

> The worst thing you can do with homework is give kids' projects. The best thing you can do is to reinforce something that they've already learnt.

Some schools have begun to experiment with "flipped learning". In this process, students study the core content of a lesson online (the information that a teacher would usually impart in the classroom) outside class and then do activities in class that reinforce what they have learned at home. The idea is that questioning, discussing and deepening knowledge is a better use of classroom time than instruction in basic facts. It is too early yet to say how effective this approach will be.

Should parents help?

It's tempting for a supportive parent to leap into action when a child arrives home with a difficult set of maths questions, a tricky English essay or a project on the Romans that requires a trip to the local library or museum. The Sharp study found no clear relationship between the amount of parental help students received with homework and their achievement though it thought encouragement to do homework and the provision of a quiet place to study might help.

The 2015 study of the Spanish students concluded that parents who helped their children with maths and science did them no favours. Those who did 70 minutes of homework with parental help achieved lower scores than those who worked independently. Indeed, the absence of parental support was more important than the amount of time spent.

One of the main aims of homework is to encourage children to work on their own and to know when they need to set aside their mobile phones and get down to their maths. The technical term used for this is self-regulation. It means setting your own goals, planning how you are going to achieve them and deciding how well you are progressing – the same skills that good feedback tries to promote. For parents, the trick is to know how to support and encourage homework without provoking a nightly fight and to resist the temptation to do the work for them.

References

Sarah Montague interview with John Hattie, The Educators, *BBC*. Available from www.bbc.co.uk/sounds/play/b04dmxwl (downloaded 9 June 2019).

Sharp, C., Keys, W. and Benefield, P. (2001) 'Homework: a review on recent research.' Slough: National Foundation for Educational Research. Available from www.nfer.ac.uk/homework-a-review-of-recent-research/

Sammons, P., Sylva, K., Melhuish, E.C., Siraj, I., Taggart, B., Smees, R. and Toth, K. (2014) 'Influences on students' GCSE attainment and progress at age 16: effective pre-school, primary & secondary education project (EPPSE).' Department of Education, London, UK. Available from https://dera.ioe.ac.uk/20875/1/RR352__Influ ences_on_Students_GCSE_Attainment_and_Progress_at_Age_16.pdf (downloaded 23 May 2019).

Fernández-Alonso, R., Suárez-Álvarez, J. and Muñiz, J. (2015) 'Adolescents' homework performance in mathematics and science: personal factors and teaching practices.' *Journal of Educational Psychology*. Available from www.apa. org/pubs/journals/releases/edu-0000032.pdf (downloaded 23 May 2019).

Cowan, R. and Hallam, S. (1999) 'What do we know about homework?' University of London, Institute of Education.

Teachers make a difference

> It's remarkable how much power one good person can have in shaping the life of a child.
>
> Bill Gates, founder of the Microsoft Corporation, on Blanche Caffiere, the teacher who inspired his love of learning.

This chapter has outlined some of the ways in which what happens in the classroom affects students' achievement. Teachers are a vital part of that classroom experience. It is no accident that successful people often point to a teacher who helped them turn round their lives or inspired in them a passion for literature or science.

Professor John Hattie synthesised 500,000 studies of the effects of different factors on student achievement. These included the students themselves, their home, their peers, the aims and policies of the school, ability grouping, class size, the school's finances and the contribution of teachers, for example, feedback and the quality of instruction.

He estimated that, as we have seen earlier in this book, students and their home environment mattered most but teachers, particularly excellent teachers, accounted for 30 percent of the variance in students' progress.

He concludes: "It is what teachers know, do and care about which is very powerful in this learning equation."

The point about *good* teachers is important. A report from the Sutton Trust in 2011 reviewed the international evidence about teachers' effectiveness and showed just how dramatic the difference between a good and bad teacher could be.

Even having a very effective rather than an *average* teacher raises each pupil's attainment by a third of a GCSE grade, the trust's report says. Just one year with an excellent teacher increases a pupil's maths score by between 25 per cent and 45 per cent of a school year, according to this review.

For pupils from poor backgrounds the difference is even more remarkable. An excellent rather than a poor teacher adds a whole year to their learning. Teachers' performance was measured by the progress their pupils made using a value-added score. About one in every six teachers was very effective and about one in six poor.

For policymakers, the big question is not whether teachers make a difference but how to improve them. The Sutton Trust report warns that value-added scores based on test and exam results are not always a robust measure of teaching quality. However, they do give parents some indication of how good a school's teaching is.

We discussed in the section on selection the difference that a school's intake makes to its test and exam scores. If you are choosing a school for your child you should look not just at the raw scores that its pupils achieve in their test and exam results but at the progress they have made. Home is hugely important in boosting achievement but the quality of your child's teachers really matters.

References

Hattie, J.A.C. (2003) 'Teachers make a difference: what is the research evidence?' Paper presented at the Building Teacher Quality: What does the research tell us ACER Research Conference, Melbourne, Australia. Available from https://research.acer.edu.au/cgi/viewcontent.cgi?article=1003&context=research_conference_2003 (downloaded 23 May 2019).

'Improving the impact of teachers on pupil achievement in the UK.' (2011) The Sutton Trust. Available from www.suttontrust.com/wp-content/uploads/2011/09/2teachers-impact-report-final.pdf (downloaded 23 May 2019).

Chapter 9

Children who struggle

A child with no mind.
> A doctor describes Felicity Fryd, an autistic child, born in 1938

There exists, therefore, a clear obligation to educate the most severely disabled for no other reason than that they are human. No civilised society can be content just to look after these children; it must all the time seek ways of helping them, however slowly, towards the educational goals we have identified.
> The Warnock Report on children with special educational needs, 1978

In the middle of the nineteenth century they were "lunatics" or "idiots." For the first half of the twentieth century they were "mentally deficient." In the 1930s the eugenics movement, as we have already heard, suggested that the world would be better off without them and in Germany Hitler honed the gas chamber techniques he would later use in the Holocaust by killing thousands of them.

Even those who campaigned to improve their lot used labels that would be unthinkable today. Judy Fryd, whose autistic daughter is mentioned at the start of this chapter, founded the National Association of Parents of Backward Children – later Mencap – in 1946. The 1944 Education Act described them as "ineducable." By 1959, legislation referred to them as "subnormal" or "severely subnormal." As late as the 1960s, electric shock treatment was seen as a "cure" for autism.

Today we talk about children with special educational needs and disabilities (SEND). The big change in attitudes in the UK began in 1978 with the publication of the report of a government committee of inquiry into the education of handicapped children and young people by Mary Warnock. It was a milestone moment. The report argued that we should consider including all children in "the common enterprise of learning" and the 1981 Education Act that followed the report said that all children should be educated in mainstream schools wherever possible. Since then, researchers have tried to distinguish different types of learning disability and to investigate the best ways of helping these children to receive the best possible education.

Government figures show that there are 1.3 million children with SEND (around 14.5 per cent of the total) and one million of these are receiving some kind of support. A quarter of a million have Education, Health and Care Plans. These plans, which replaced "statements" of special needs from September 2014, are legal documents that summarise the extra help a child may need over and above the special educational needs support normally available in schools. Parents of children with these plans may be able to get a personal budget to support them. Ninety-three per cent of children with SEN are in state-funded mainstream schools and 46 per cent of those with plans are in special schools.

The children in this group have different and sometimes complicated needs that have been given different labels: general learning difficulty, specific learning difficulty, emotional and behavioural difficulty, dyslexia, ADHD (Attention Deficit Hyperactivity Disorder) and autism.

All these are complex but here are a few basic definitions:

Autistic people have difficulty with social interaction, communication and imagination and often show repetitive patterns of behaviour.

Dyslexia, sometimes called word blindness, means that you have difficulty in learning to read or interpret words or letters.

ADHD children find it very hard to concentrate and are hyperactive. Some are also very impulsive.

Most people have heard of some of these disabilities but misconceptions persist. Here are a few common myths:

Autism

All autistic people are geniuses – MYTH. Just under half of all people with an autism diagnosis also have a learning disability. Others have an IQ in the average to above average range. "Savant abilities" like extraordinary memory are rare.

Everyone is a bit autistic – MYTH. While everyone might recognise some autistic traits or behaviours in people they know, to be diagnosed with autism a person must consistently display behaviours across all the different areas of the condition. Just having a fondness for routines, a good memory or being shy doesn't make a person "a bit autistic" (*National Autistic Society*).

ADHD

Parents can cause or cure ADHD – MYTH. A 2017 study led by Dr Martine Hoogman at Radboud University in Nijmegen in the Netherlands, published in the *Lancet,* analysed the brain volumes of more than 3,200 people and noticed that those of patients with ADHD were underdeveloped in five ways.

Areas governing emotion and motivation were smaller than in the general population, regardless of whether the participants were taking brain medication. Researchers measured the differences in the brain structure of 1,713 people with ADHD and 1,529 without, all aged between four and 63. An MRI scan measured their overall brain volume and its size in seven regions thought to be linked to ADHD. The hippocampus, which may contribute to the disorder through its role regulating emotion and motivation, was one of the regions found to be under developed in people with ADHD.

Dr Hoogman said that the results showed that people with ADHD had different brain structures and suggested that ADHD was a brain disorder. She told a newspaper that she hoped the findings would counter the idea that ADHD was just a label for naughty children or caused by poor parenting. (*The Daily Telegraph*, 16 February 2017).

Dyslexia

Dyslexics are usually very intelligent/Dyslexia is a sign of low IQ – MYTH. Dyslexia affects a cross section of people regardless of race, ethnicity, gender, age, intellectual level etc. It is not an indication of low or high intelligence (*The Dyslexia Association UK*).

Some of these myths go back to the scientists who first identified the disability. Sir George Still, a British doctor, identified ADHD in 1902. He described it as "an abnormal defect of moral control in children." Leo Kanner identified autism syndrome in 1943 and follow-up studies to his work found it mostly among children with special needs and disabilities.

However, in 1944, Hans Asperger, an Austrian paediatrician, produced a study that suggested that children of average or above average ability displayed the same behaviour that Kanner had found. His ideas were developed in the 1980s by a British psychiatrist, Lorna Wing.

The term dyslexia was first coined in 1887 by Rudolf Berlin, a German ophthalmologist, but it was British contemporaries working in the late nineteenth and early twentieth centuries who first used it in relation to children. William Pringle Morgan, a GP, and James Hinshelwood, another ophthalmologist, noticed that bright and intelligent children among their patients were having difficulty learning to read. So, we can see how some of the misleading ideas about these disabilities arose.

One final point. Dyslexia is supposed to be more prevalent in more creative people. Some very creative people in history, and today, such as Leonardo Da Vinci, Thomas Edison, Richard Branson, the celebrity chef Jamie Oliver, Kath Kidston, Keira Knightly and Pablo Picasso are among the exceptional and varied talents said to have displayed at least some symptoms of dyslexia or have publicly admitted the diagnosis. Small-scale research has established a link but whether some people with dyslexia enjoy the arts or entrepreneurialism and then excel in them because they find the written word harder and therefore compensate by concentrating on other things remains unclear.

Are labels helpful?

Labels for physical or mental disabilities can be comforting and may be useful in identifying necessary help and support but they also pose problems and cause controversy. Drugs are often used to treat ADHD and academics from Australia and the Netherlands have argued that children are being diagnosed with the condition when they are developing normally. They raise concerns that drugs to treat them are being prescribed unnecessarily.

Some people have described dyslexia, particularly the idea that you can be intelligent and have difficulty with reading, as "a middle-class myth" promoted by parents who don't want to admit that their children are struggling. The idea that dyslexia is associated with a high IQ has gained traction because some famous people have talked about having the dis-ability. Orlando Bloom, the actor who starred in the blockbuster film *Pirates of the Caribbean*, said in the 2010 Adam Katz memorial lecture: "I was first diagnosed with dyslexia at the age of seven. I had a pretty high IQ but I struggled with reading and spelling."

The idea that some of the traditional labels may mask complex pro-blems is supported by some research. A study at the UK's Cambridge University in 2018 questioned the accuracy of many of the diagnoses given to parents of children with special needs. Duncan Astle and his colleagues at the MRC Brain and Science Unit at the university studied 520 children aged between five and 18 years (average age nine) who had been referred to a research clinic at the unit.

Sixty-four per cent of the children had been referred for problems with attention, memory, difficulty processing sounds or poor school progress in reading or maths, and the rest because they had a specific diagnosis of ADHD, autism or dyslexia. The study assessed their performance in working memory, word and sound recognition, spelling, reading and maths. The researchers also measured their communication skills. A parent or carer reported on each child's behaviour, for example how well they could control their impulses and emotions.

The team fed the results into an artificial neural network, a computing system that mimics the brain, and looked for any patterns in the data from the learning assessments, grouping children with distinct similarities into clusters. One hundred and eighty-four of these children also had MRI brain scans and these were compared with 36 typically performing children so that the researchers could look for differences in communication between regions of the brain.

The children *did* fall into four distinct groups but those groups bore no relation whatsoever to either the original reason for their referral or their diagnoses. The researchers said:

> Children referred primarily for problems with attention, poor learning or memory were equally likely to be assigned to each group.... The four groups cut across any traditional diagnostic groupings that existed within the data.

At the extremes were two groups. One group consisted of children who did not have learning difficulties but who did have behaviour problems that presumably accounted for their lack of progress. Children in the other group had severe and multiple learning difficulties. They were in the bottom 5 per cent of the population for spelling, reading and maths and struggled with communication. The scans showed reduced connectivity between areas of the brain involved in higher order thinking skills such as problem solving.

A third group found phonological processing – dealing with sounds in words – and verbal short-term and working memory (the ability to remember and use relevant information) difficult. The scan showed reduced connectivity between parts of the brain involved with language. A classic case of *dyslexia* you might think? But it turned out that these children were also poor at maths. It looks, the researchers suggested, as though difficulties with processing sounds may be a sign of more general learning problems.

For the fourth group, memory was the main problem. These children had poor spatial short-term memory and poor verbal and spatial working memory often associated with *dyscalculia* (trouble with maths). What's more, though they appeared to have distinct difficulties, both groups scored almost identically on the reading and maths measures. Children who had difficulty concentrating who had been diagnosed with ADHD were found in all four groups.

This research chimes with the thinking of other researchers who argue that we need to move beyond the labels if we are to work out how best to help struggling children progress. We need to look at what works in the classroom for individual children rather than trying to tailor an educational programme to a particular diagnosis. Lani Florian, Professor of Social Educational Inclusion at the University of Aberdeen said in a 2008 review:

> The key point is that, while there are differences between learners, the salient educational differences are found in learners' responses to tasks and activities, rather than in the medical diagnostic criteria that

have been used to categorise them in order to determine their eligibility for additional support.

It's also clear that some teaching strategies that work with students who don't fall into the SEND category are just as effective with those who do according to a review of specialist teaching in 2003 (Cook and Schirmer). Another study (Lewis and Norwich, 2005) suggested that it would be better to look at the high or low *intensity* of a strategy than at whether it was appropriate for a particular type of need.

In other words, offering children who struggle, for example, more phonics in the teaching of reading, more frequent feedback, more teacher-led rather than independent learning and short-term rather than long-term goals. All these strategies might be used for teaching all children but are particularly important for this group.

So, the evidence shows that labels have their limits and most parents will agree that what matters for their children is not the label but the measures schools can take to help them. If your child is hyperactive and distracted, you want them to concentrate better. If they can't read, for whatever reason, you want them to learn. The Cambridge study concludes that it is important to secure an accurate assessment for a child with special needs and that diagnosis needs to improve.

All together

We have seen how dramatically the Warnock report changed attitudes to the inclusion of many of the children described in the section above in mainstream UK classrooms. That was in 1978. Yet the debate goes on. Some parents of children without SEND and some teachers still question whether the presence of these pupils holds back their more able peers.

In 2017, an Australian senator Pauline Hanson said it would be better for teachers if students with autism and disability were put in special classrooms. She argued that children with autism should not be in mainstream classrooms because "it is taking up the teacher's time." She later said that her remarks had been misconstrued by the media. A review of 280 studies by researchers at Harvard University's Graduate School of Education shows how wrong she was (Hehir et al. 2012). This looked at international studies on the inclusion of SEND students in mainstream classrooms. One, from the University of Manchester in the UK in 2007, found that 81 per cent of studies showed that the SEND students made no difference to the progress of their classmates without disabilities and in some, the effect was positive. Differences between schools, the Harvard review says, are much larger than differences between inclusive and non-inclusive classrooms. As we have seen earlier in this book, the overall quality of teaching in a school is hugely important in students' progress and it is much more important than whether pupils with and without disabilities are taught together.

But what about children with severe emotional and behavioural problems? Surely, they have a disruptive effect on their classmates? The research surveyed in the Harvard review suggests that the education of a class would be held back only in the unlikely event that there were two or more of these children.

There is some evidence, cited in this report, that non-disabled children actually progress better in classrooms that include children with learning disabilities. One of the reasons for this may be that teachers with positive attitudes towards inclusion are more likely to adapt the way they work to benefit all of their students so that teaching is better tailored to individuals.

The social benefits of inclusion are also well-documented. Numerous studies suggest that non-disabled pupils educated alongside their disabled peers are more likely to have friends who are disabled and are more likely to tolerate differences in others. A Canadian study found that disabled students were teased and rejected less in inclusive schools.

Senator Hanson said that it wasn't just the students without disabilities who were better off if disabled students were assigned to special classes. The disabled students themselves would also make more progress. That claim is challenged by research which offers many examples of the benefits of inclusion for these students.

A 2012 study, again by Dr Thomas Hehir and colleagues from the Harvard University Graduate School of Education, examined the performance of more than 68,000 primary and secondary school students with disabilities in the United States state of Massachusetts. Once other factors that might influence a child's academic performance (family income, school quality and proficiency in English) had been taken into account, they found that, on average, students with disabilities who spent a larger proportion of their school day with their non-disabled peers performed significantly better on tests in language and mathematics than students with similar disabilities who spent a smaller proportion of their school day with their non-disabled peers.

This finding chimes with research on setting we discussed earlier which found that children of similar ability spread among different sets had different academic outcomes. If they were in the top set, they performed better than children of *similar* ability allocated to middle or bottom sets, possibly because of behaviour issues. It's thought the teaching in the top set, which would have been more challenging, benefitted everyone in the set even though some might have been of lower ability than others.

The evidence about SEND is not confined to the US. Researchers in Norway followed nearly 500 secondary school students with disabilities over six years. They also took into account other factors related to student achievement and found that included students were more than 75 per cent more likely to earn a vocational or academic credential than students who were educated in special classes. It is likely that there will be a minority of children for whom special schools may prove to be the best solution but that is not the case for the majority.

What about Hanson's claim that children with learning disabilities are taking up too much of the teacher's time? Two studies from University College London's Institute of Education challenge her assumption. The SEN in Secondary Education (SENSE) and Making a Statement (MAST) of primary pupils, studies spent 1,340 hours observing SEN pupils with Education and Health Care Plans, previously known as statements. They are the largest ever observational studies of such pupils in the UK. They found that in secondary schools these pupils were usually taught together with other low-ability children. They weren't just separated from the most able pupils but also from average pupils who were taught in different groups from them by a different teacher in middle ability groups. There were very few mixed ability classes.

In primary schools, pupils with statements got less time with the teacher than their peers. What's more, these two studies show how the presence of teaching assistants, who are widely used to support these pupils, reduces the opportunities for them to interact with teachers. The research on teaching assistants in the next section, carried out by the same researchers, confirms how wrong Hanson was. Far from taking up too much teacher time, SEND children are not getting a fair share of it.

The role of teaching assistants

Once a child has a diagnosis of special needs, schools will try to find ways to support them, whether or not they have an Education and Health Care Plan (EHCP). If they are in a mainstream school, it is likely that they will spend some of their time supported by a teaching assistant. Indeed, it is a common response from schools to organise help from an assistant particularly for children with EHCPs. As a parent you might well be grateful. Surely that extra help is a good thing? Unfortunately, research tells us, the answer is not straightforward.

The Deployment and Impact of Support Staff study (DISS) from London University's Institute of Education is the biggest ever study of teaching assistants and covers the period from 2003–2008. Researchers surveyed more than 6,000 schools, more than 4,000 teachers and nearly 8,000 teaching assistants (TAs). It observed teachers, TAs and pupils and 34,400 interactions between TAs and their pupils and analysed the effects of TAs on pupils' attitude to learning, their academic progress and their achievements in tests and exams. The study didn't just look at SEND pupils but because schools deploy support staff so often to work with these pupils it is highly relevant to them.

Even the researchers were surprised by their findings. The study showed that pupils who received the *most* support from TAs made *less* progress in English, maths and in science than similar pupils who spent little or no time with TAs.

The difference between those who received the least support and those who received the most was significant. Pupils with a medium level of support made less progress than those with no support. The negative impact was most marked for pupils with SEND.

What could explain this? How could it be that in every year group studied (Years 1, 2, 3, 6, 7, 9 and 10) extra support had a negative effect on attainment?

The study was longitudinal so it didn't just look at pupils' attainment at the end of a year but at their progress. It also took account of the fact that the pupils receiving the most help were likely to be those who were struggling academically or who had SEN. One explanation, the researchers suggest, is that these pupils spend much of the time separated from their classmates, for example on special programmes designed to help them catch up in reading and writing, and therefore do not benefit from the skills and knowledge teachers have to offer in their daily interaction with other pupils. Some teachers deliberately devolve responsibility for these pupils to support staff. The study says:

> We query the way in which lower attaining pupils can now get less of the teacher's attention. It would seem appropriate to argue that all pupils should get at least the same amount of a teacher's time, and, indeed, that those in most need are most likely to benefit from more, not less.

Another explanation for the report's findings may be that TAs treat children differently. They are less formal and more "chummy" than teachers. The researchers' question whether saying "darling" or "my love" to pupils is conducive to better learning even if it does mean that children behave better and get on better with adults and their classmates.

Teachers observed in this study also spent more time than TAs on making sure that pupils were learning and understanding a task. TAs tended to focus on getting the task done. They were more likely than teachers to tell pupils the answers and to finish the work for them. Some pupils became too dependent on the teaching assistants working with them even though the school was trying to turn them into independent learners. The report raised questions about how well-prepared TAs are and how communication between them and teachers is organised.

Researchers didn't just look at the academic progress pupils made. They also investigated the effect of teacher assistants' support on eight different measures of pupils' attitude to learning such as how easily they were distracted, how independently they worked and how motivated they were.

There was little evidence that more time spent with support staff improved pupils' attitude on any of the measures except in the case of Year 9 pupils where extra support made a difference on all of the attitudes measured. The main effects were between the pupils with a high level of support and those with a low level of support. The report says:

> The largest effect was an increase in good relationships with peers which was ten times more likely with high levels of additional support compared to low amounts of support. High levels of additional support also lead to pupils being eight times more likely to be less distracted, not disruptive and be independent. Pupils were six times more likely to improve in following instructions when they received high levels of support, five times more likely to become more confident and four times more likely to become motivated and complete work.

The researchers suggest that the difference between the findings for primary and Year 9 pupils may be because support tends to be more individual at this age with the TA forming a closer relationship with the pupil.

Teaching assistant numbers increased sharply between 2011 and 2016 – by around 40,000 or 30 per cent. Given the bleak picture of their effectiveness painted in the DISS report, was this a huge mistake? Should parents be alarmed if their child is spending a big chunk of their schooldays with an assistant? Not necessarily.

More recent research from the Education Endowment Foundation (2015) has looked at ways in which schools can deploy teaching assistants so that they do make a positive difference to struggling pupils. This found that where TAs provide short, structured help to small groups of pupils they can boost these children's progress. But they do need to be trained in how best to provide this help. Pupils also make better progress when their work in class is explicitly linked to their work outside class with the teaching assistants.

Professor Peter Blatchford, Professor of Psychology and Education at the University College London Institute of Education, who directed the study says:[1]

> We were shocked when we saw the findings (of the DISS report): the more support a child received from a teaching assistant, the less well they did. And it wasn't that the kids who struggled most were being taught by teaching assistants. The findings were independent of any characteristics of the pupils themselves.

1   The quotations in this chapter from Professor Peter Blatchford are taken from an interview with Judith Judd, 1 May, 2019.

It was a government-funded project and the findings were so surprising that the steering group asked us to do the study again. So we
did. First time round the effects of spending more time with a teaching assistant were overwhelmingly negative. Second time, they were
entirely negative. And it was the children with SEND who were most
likely to make less progress.

After his initial surprise, he decided the results made sense.

Why would you expect anything else? Put crudely, the children most
in need tended to be supported by the people with the least training.
Given that SEND children require sophisticated teaching skills that
seemed to be a mistake. And the more support a child received from a
teaching assistant, the less they received from a teacher. In many of
the classrooms we looked at, it wasn't additional, it was an alternative. The answer isn't to get rid of teaching assistants but to ask
how they can add value to teachers.

Since the DISS report was published, he and his colleagues have
worked on ways that the deployment and training of teaching assistants
can be improved.

You have to think strategically about how you use them. You can't
have the inclusion of SEND children in mainstream classrooms on the
cheap. There has to be something *small* about the support for SEND
children. Teaching assistants have a big role to play but very much in
concert with teachers.

His research hasn't probed whether some children would be better off
in special schools but he suspects there are some with complex needs
who would benefit from that kind of environment. He has seen examples
of children with complex needs doing well in mainstream classrooms but
mainstream education for SEND pupils is still variable.

Inclusion is a very commendable idea but we haven't thought
through how to implement it. In mainstream classrooms in schools
which haven't thought it through, SEND children may be getting a
bad deal.

What works best

The search for strategies that will help this group of pupils is an international one. As we have seen, some of the strategies that work for pupils
without disabilities are also relevant to those who struggle.

It's clear from research that separating children into ability groups is unlikely to increase academic achievement and it is important that all children have plenty of opportunity to interact with teachers. Methods such as phonics should be part of the process of teaching every child to read though they may be particularly useful for struggling or disadvantaged children. Independent learning is important for any student's academic progress as Professor Dylan Wiliam has already suggested and those with special educational needs should not become too dependent on teaching assistants.

Yet many of these pupils will need additional support. The Education Endowment Foundation is a grant-making charity set up by the Sutton Trust dedicated to breaking the link between family income and educational attainment. Children from poorer homes generally do less well at school. The foundation also analyses research into the needs of children with learning disabilities because the two are linked. It looks at different interventions and produces a 'toolkit' for teachers based on its findings. It evaluates the strength of research evidence and compares it with the cost to schools. Here are some of its conclusions.

One to one tuition

This emerges as one of the most effective ways of helping pupils catch up with their peers. Short sessions of around 30 minutes three to five times a week over six to 12 weeks seem to work best. There is some evidence (see Chapter 8 on teaching maths) that small group tuition works, too. Yet again, this suggests that the quality of teaching may be the key to academic progress rather than the precise size of the group. And one to one tuition appears to be more effective if teachers rather than teaching assistants provide it. The Foundation says:

> Overall, the evidence is consistent and strong, particularly for younger learners who are behind their peers in primary schools, and for subjects like reading and mathematics.

Four recent evaluations in the UK of one-to-one tuition interventions – Catch-up Numeracy, Catch-up Literacy, REACH and Switch-on Reading – made an average difference of between three and six months' additional progress for children in a school year. It is, however, a relatively expensive option.

Behaviour

Better behaviour does lead to improvements in academic performance, the Foundation's analysis finds. But the programmes that are designed for individual students work better than ones aimed at improving the behaviour and discipline in a whole class or school. Helping teachers to improve discipline and students to learn more effectively and relate better to their peers both boost attainment.

But better behaviour doesn't necessarily improve academic performance. One meta-analysis of anger management studies found that these programmes reduced bad behaviour but did not lead to better learning.

Daily report card

Teachers monitor and record on the card how the student is doing and this tells them immediately whether they are doing well or need to change course. At the end of the day, the student takes the card home for parents or carers to read or sign. Parents offer a reward at home for good behaviour, for example, more time on a computer game or playing with friends. In a trial where a group of pupils were randomly selected and compared with another similar group who were not given cards, a year-long use of report cards led to a significant improvement in pupil behaviour. The study did not, however, find any significant difference in academic achievement. It made little difference whether teachers or parents provided the rewards, suggesting that immediate feedback from the teacher was the most important element in this approach. The idea of giving rewards to motivate behaviour is challenged by other research discussed in the following chapter.

Managing emotions

Social and emotional learning aims to help students get on better with their peers and to control their emotions, the EEF says. It isn't principally about raising academic performance but the right type of intervention can work. It can make a difference to pupils' motivation and to their relationship with their classmates.

However, the outcome of different approaches is variable. An evaluation of government attempts to introduce this type of learning in UK secondary schools (SEAL – Social and Emotional Aspects of Learning) found that it had no positive impact on learning though the authors said there was evidence that this approach could be useful. These programmes work best when they are carried out by committed teachers who have been trained for the task in hand. Here is one such programme:

Incredible Years (IY) Classroom Dinosaur Programme

Primary teachers use this to improve emotional wellbeing and social skills. There are 30 lessons a year on learning school rules, success at school, emotional literacy, empathy, interpersonal problem solving, anger management and social and communication skills.

They involve videos, role playing, discussion and circle time and practice of the skills learned.

For example, children are shown pictures and videos of different emotions – sad, happy, angry. They are asked to check their own bodies for tense or relaxed muscles and to match their own feelings to the pictures. They use 'detective' skills to work out what other children are feeling.

Wally, a child-sized puppet, teaches them some of his 'secrets' for calming down. In role play, they take the part of a child, parent or teacher who has a problem.

In the US, a trial where the participants were randomly selected and compared with a control group in Head Start schools for disadvantaged children found that the programme improved children's control of their emotions and their social skills. There are also Incredible Years child and parents' programmes. All three have been tested in the UK and found to have some effect, particularly when they are used together.

Literacy

Talk with adults and other pupils is a good basis for literacy, the Education Endowment Foundation says. That might mean discussing a book or specifically trying to increase pupils' vocabulary by relating it to real objects and events. Remember the boys in the preschool chapter who left their bikes to come and look at the snails when one of their classmates suggested snails could hear sounds?

Technology – the use of IT – is a good way of getting children to talk to each other because they discuss what they see on a screen. It is less effective as a tutoring tool. Strategies to help children understand what they are reading seem to work better with older than with younger pupils but all the evidence suggests that there is no single solution to teaching struggling readers to read. Phonics, as we have seen, should be part of the mix but it needs to be used alongside other approaches.

Reading recovery

This is one of the most successful programmes for struggling readers and has been running since the 1970s when it was developed in New Zealand. It isn't directed specifically at SEND children but they are often included in its participants who are in the bottom 5 per cent of readers aged around six. These are children who, for example, cannot write their own name or read the simplest book after a year at school.

They receive a series of daily one-to-one lessons of 30 minutes for 20 weeks with a specially trained teacher. It starts with an assessment of what the child knows and is different for every child. The teaching of letters and words is combined with teaching to help understanding of the text.

Although Reading Recovery carries on longer, you'd be right in thinking it has similarities in terms of the intensity with which it is delivered, with the approach the EEF found worked best in helping children who fall behind in class mentioned earlier. That involved 30-minute sessions up to five times a week, for up to 12 weeks.

Eight out of ten children who complete Reading Recovery catch up with their classmates. What is more, the effects last. A 2018 study from University College London found that the progress made was still evident ten years after pupils took part in the programme. The Reading Recovery group were more than twice as likely as a comparable group who had not taken part to achieve five or more good GCSEs including maths. They also had significantly higher point scores across eight GCSEs than the comparable group. Only 2 per cent of the group passed no GCSEs compared with 7 per cent of the second group.

Children who were given one-to-one tuition did better than those on a Reading Recovery programme that used small groups. A four-year study of nearly 7,000 children in 1,200 US schools also in 2018 confirmed previous studies of the intervention's effectiveness and said that it could be successful if it was rolled out nationally.

The programme does have its critics. Phonics advocates say that its use of a variety of approaches detracts from schools' efforts to teach synthetic phonics. But the research evidence for its effectiveness is powerful. The drawback is the cost of training teachers and funding one-to-one tuition. It is one of the most expensive ways of supporting struggling readers.

However, research by the charity Pro Bono Economics, published in 2018 suggested that it had the potential to bring a saving of £1.2 billion over the lifetime of children who have so far been supported by it because they will go on to earn more and will need less special educational needs help.

Evidence from the Education and Endowment Foundation suggests that tackling behaviour and social and emotional difficulties are important in the support of SEND students. That is reinforced by Dr David Mitchell, of the University of Canterbury, New Zealand, who listed 27 such strategies in his book *What Works in Special and Inclusive Education* (Routledge 2014). He also includes:

- Direct instruction – teacher-directed, well-structured lessons based on pre-scripted lesson plans;
- Self-regulation – helping learners to work out their own goals and how to reach them;
- Improving memory – through mnemonics, breaking up material into manageable chunks and reviewing it regularly;
- Peer tutoring – encouraging pupils, including SEND pupils, to teach each other supervised by a teacher.

Many of these strategies, of course, work equally well for all pupils but they may be particularly important for this group.

Memory and mnemonics

Mnemonics uses links to help remember basic facts, for instance, 'Never Eat Shredded Wheat" or NESW for the points of the compass. Another memory strategy might link different types of information: a sad face alongside the word sad. Or breaking down information, for example a telephone number, into more manageable chunks. Some phonics programmes use mnemonics to teach letters and sounds. For example, each finger of a child's hand has a colour to match a sound and the child chants each sound in turn as they extend the appropriate finger.

A striking feature of research into the education of pupils who struggle most is the array of different schemes that are being tried and the inconsistent findings of much of the research. There is no single answer to many of the difficulties they encounter.

A combination of approaches, often involving parents and teachers, is needed. Support has to be based on a careful assessment of individual children and, as we have seen, those assessments are not always accurate. Parents know their children better than anyone so their help is vital in explaining to teachers' children's difficulties and needs.

Professor Peter Blatchford was indignant when he discovered that the most vulnerable children were receiving the least attention from teachers. Good teaching and strong support from parents are the key to success for all children and particularly for this group. Researchers, educators and parents are desperate to play their part but find it hard to work out how. Yet many studies show that the right kind of help can make a difference.

The content of the next chapter is particularly relevant to these children, as well as many others. How do you stop those who struggle to succeed from giving up? How do you persuade the little girl who says she hasn't got a 'maths brain' to carry on trying? For that matter, how do you persuade a bright but lazy child to put the effort into their school work. Motivation – the appetite for learning and perseverance in the face of failure – matter enormously to the progress of all children.

References

Warnock, H.M. (1978) *Special Educational Needs. Report of the Committee of Enquiry into the Education of Handicapped Children and Young People*. London: Her Majesty's Stationery Office. Available from https://webarchive.nationalarchives.gov.

uk/20101007182820/http:/sen.ttrb.ac.uk/attachments/
21739b8e-5245-4709-b433-c14b08365634.pdf (downloaded 10 June 2019).

Hoogman, M. et al. (2017) 'Subcortical brain volume differences in participants with attention deficit hyperactivity disorder in children and adults: a cross-sectional mega-analysis.' *The Lancet Psychiatry*, Vol. 4, No. 4, pp. 310–319. doi:10.1016/S2215-0366(17)30049–30044

Thomas, R., Mitchell, G.K. and Batstra, L. (2013) 'Attention-deficit/hyperactivity disorder: are we helping or harming?' *British Medical Journal*, 347, p. f6172.

Cancer, A., Manzoli, S., Antonietti, A. and Besson, M. (2016) 'The alleged link between creativity and dyslexia: Identifying the specific process in which dyslexic students excel.' *Cogent Psychology*, Vol. 3, No. 1. doi:10.1080/23311908.2016.1190309

Kapoula, Z., Ruiz, S., Spector, L., Mocorovi, M., Gaertner, C., Quilici, C. and Vernet, M. (2016) 'Education influences creativity in dyslexic and non-dyslexic children and teenagers.' *Plos One*, Vol. 11, No. 3, p. e0150421. doi:10.1371/journal.pone.0150421

Child Mind Institute. (2010) 'Orlando Bloom on dyslexia.' Available at https://childmind.org/article/orlando-bloom-on-dyslexia/ (downloaded 25 May 2019).

Astle, D.E., Bathelt, J., the CALM team and Holmes, J. (2018) 'Remapping the cognitive and neural profiles of children who struggle at school.' *Developmental Science*, Vol. 22, No. 1, p. e12747. doi:10.1111/desc.12747

Florian, L. (2008) 'Inclusion: Special or inclusive education: future trends.' *British Journal of Special Education*, Vol. 4, pp. 202–208.

Cook, B.G. and Schirmer, B.R. (2003) 'What is special about special education? Overview and analysis.' *Journal of Special Education*, Vol. 37, No. 3, pp. 200–205.

Lewis, A. and Norwich, B. (eds) (2004) *Special Teaching for Special Children? Pedagogies for inclusion*. Maidenhead: Open University Press.

Hehir, T., Grindal, T., Freeman, B., Lamoreau, R., Borquaye, Y. and Burke, S. (2016) 'A Summary of the evidence on inclusive education.' Instituto Alana. Available from https://alana.org.br/wp-content/uploads/2016/12/A_Summary_of_the_evidence_on_inclusive_education.pdf (downloaded 25 May 2019).

Kalambouka, A., Farrell, P., Dyson, A. and Kaplan, I. (2008) 'The impact of placing pupils with special education needs in mainstream schools on the achievement of their peers.' *Educational Research*, Vol. 49, No. 4, pp. 365–382.

Hehir, T., Grindal, T. and Eidelman, H. (2012) *Review of Special Education in the Commonwealth of Massachusetts: A Synthesis Report*. Boston, MA: Massachusetts Department of Elementary and Secondary Education. Available from www.doe.mass.edu/sped/hehir/2014-09synthesis.pdf (downloaded 25 May 2019).

Webster, R. and Blatchford, P. (2017) *The Special Educational Needs in Secondary Schools (SENSE) study*. The Nuffield Foundation. Available from www.nuffieldfoundation.org/sites/default/files/files/SENSE%20FINAL%20REPORT.pdf (downloaded 25 May 2019).

Webster R. and Blatchford P. (2013) *The Making a Statement Project Final Report*. The Nuffield Foundation. Available from www.nuffieldfoundation.org/sites/default/files/files/mastreport.pdf (downloaded 25 May 2019).

Blatchford, P., Bassett, P., Brown, P., Koutsoubou, M., Martin, C., Russell, A., and Webster, R. with Rubie-Davies, C. (2009) 'Deployment and Impact of Support Staff in Schools.' Institute of Education, University of London. Available from file:///C:/Users/User/Downloads/Deployment_and_Impact_of_Support_Sta ff_in_Schools_.pdf (downloaded 25 May 2019).

Sharples, J., Webster, R. and Blatchford, P. (2015) *Making Best Use of Teaching Assistants Guidance Report*. Education Endowment Foundation.

Education Endowment Foundation (2018) 'One to one tuition.' Available at: http s://educationendowmentfoundation.org.uk/evidence-summaries/teaching-lea rning-toolkit/one-to-one-tuition/#closeSignup (downloaded 25 May 2019).

Carroll, J., Bradley, L., Crawford, H., Hannant, P., Johnson, H. and Thompson, A. (2017) 'SEN support a rapid evidence assessment'. Department for Education. Available from https://assets.publishing.service.gov.uk/government/uploads/ system/uploads/attachment_data/file/628630/DfE_SEN_Support_REA_Rep ort.pdf (downloaded 25 May 2019).

Humphrey, N., Lendrum A., Wigelsworth, M. (2010) 'Social and emotional aspects of learning (SEAL) programme in secondary schools: national evaluation.' Department for Education. Available from https://dera.ioe.ac.uk/11567/1/ DFE-RR049.pdf (downloaded 25 May 2019).

Webster-Stratton, C., Reid, M.J. and Stoolmiller, M. (2008) 'Preventing conduct pro- blems and improving school readiness: evaluation of the Incredible Years Teacher and Child Training Programs in high-risk schools.' *Journal of Child Psychology and Psychiatry*, Vol. 49, No. 5, pp. 471–488. doi:10.1111/j.1469–7610.2007.01861

Hurry, J. and Fridkin, L. (2018) 'The impact of Reading Recovery ten years after intervention.' UCL Institute of Education. Available from www.ucl.ac.uk/readin g-recovery-europe/sites/reading-recovery-europe/files/the_impact_of_reading_ recovery_ten_years_after_intervention_hurry_and_fridkin.pdf. (downloaded 25 May 2019).

Sirinides, P., Gray, A. and May, H., (2018) 'The impacts of reading recovery at scale: results from the 4-year external evaluation.' *American Educational Research Association*, Vol. 40, No. 3, pp. 316–335.

Chapter 10

Motivation

In ancient times scholars worked for their own improvement; nowadays they seek only to win the approval of others.

Confucius, Analects 14.24 (551–479 BCE).

The proper question is not, "How can people motivate others?" but rather, "How can people create the conditions within which others will motivate themselves?"

Edward Deci, Professor of Psychology and Gowen Professor in the Social Sciences at the University of Rochester, New York.

I think most people that are able to make a sustained contribution over time – rather than just a peak – are very internally driven. You have to be.

Steve Jobs, Co-founder of Apple Inc.

One of the more fascinating and important motivation experiments of the twentieth century involved two groups of psychology students being given Soma puzzles – a precursor to Rubik's cube – to solve. The two groups were in different rooms. There were three sessions and in the second session one group of students was told they would be paid for each finished puzzle. The other group was not offered any reward. In the third session neither group was offered payment but some students carried on still trying to solve the puzzles when time was up. Who do you think they were? The ones previously offered a reward or the ones who weren't?

It was the ones who *were never* offered money who carried on trying to solve the puzzles. The ones who had been offered a reward abandoned the puzzles and started to read magazines, left for both groups, as the researcher asked the students in each group to hang around for a few minutes while he recorded some data and came back with a questionnaire. What he was actually doing was noting what the students in the room did next.

The young researcher, Edward Deci, concluded that the students who had been paid for solving puzzles had lost intrinsic motivation for the task – a desire to do it for the interest, value and enjoyment of it. For Deci it was the beginning of a life-time study, along with colleague Richard

Ryan, which was to lead to the motivational theory of self-determination which has spread across the world today.

And for anyone who is offering treats to little children to congratulate them on doing anything from eating their greens to getting full marks in spelling tests, or paying older children in money or computer games to hit certain exam grades, this matters a lot because in the long run, that approach can be damaging if you rely on it. There are better ways to motivate your children.

A brief history of motivation

Some people appear to be more motivated than others. While some are happy to lie on the sofa watching television or streaming box sets after work, others are at choir rehearsal or working as a volunteer for the local branch of the political party they support or pounding the streets in preparation for a half marathon. Some people are happy to be watching that television in a house that's untidy and dirty; others would even have trouble sleeping in a house that wasn't in order.

Google the words "motivation coach" and you will get 152m results in less than a second. Google "how to motivate yourself" and you only get 104m results in just over half a second suggesting a lot more people are motivated to ask other people to get them motivated than want to do it for themselves! Google oozes motivational speeches, songs and videos. Charismatic leaders can motivate people just by opening their mouths. No top sports team would be complete without psychological input. There is a big industry in motivation suggesting a lot of us must feel we are a bit lacking.

But all of us are motivated to varying degrees. At the very least we need the motivation to get out of bed unless we are very ill or physically constrained. We need to meet our own physical needs before we can do anything else. If we couldn't be bothered to eat and drink, we'd soon be dead unless someone stepped in with a feeding tube. But what else motivates us? Protecting our children? One would hope. Pleasing others? That definitely works for some. Fulfilling ourselves? What does that even mean?

What motivates human beings was clearly on the mind of the great Chinese philosopher and teacher, Confucius 2,500 years ago when he made the comment quoted at the beginning of the chapter, and for the last 150 years psychologists have studied it with increasing sophistication. By and large they have explained motivation in two ways – either in terms of our instincts (hardwired behaviours we're born with) – or our response to stimuli (things that happen to us that we learn from).

That second approach is known as behaviourism and for much of the second half of the twentieth century it was the behaviourist explanation of human activity that led the field with researchers producing many studies proving a link between reward and punishment to condition – or motivate – human behaviour

If you are offering pudding to a sweet-toothed child to eat their greens or cash for good grades, or the opposite – less time on the computer if you don't finish your homework/tidy your room/walk the dog, or no stars on your motivational chart if you are too young for any of that, you are employing a tactic that goes back a long way. You are conditioning somebody to do something by doing something to them.

This was first recorded scientifically by a Russian physiologist called Ivan Pavlov working in St Petersburg, Russia, in the late nineteenth and early twentieth century. His discovery was an accidental offshoot of an experiment to work out how much dogs salivate in response to food. He predicted they would start to salivate when the food was placed in front of them, but tiny test tubes in their cheeks collecting their saliva proved they were salivating as soon as they heard the footsteps of his assistant bringing their food.

Pavlov was intrigued and experimented using other things, such as the ringing of a bell, to herald to the dogs that food was on its way and found that also caused them to salivate before the food was placed in front of them. The ringing of the bell told their saliva glands that dinner was about to be served. Salivation was a hard-wired response to food because the dogs needed saliva to help their food go down their throats but an external stimulus they associated with food – such as a ringing bell – could start if off as long as they were then fed soon after. It was to become known as *classical conditioning*.

Research into whether humans could be similarly conditioned was soon to follow at Johns Hopkins University in the United States. In an experiment (Watson and Rayner 1920) that makes for hard reading in the more enlightened times of the twenty-first century, a nine-month-old baby known as Albert was shown a white rat, a dog, a rabbit, a monkey – all of them alive – and various furred masks and, because this is what babies encountering new things do, showed no fear of them. He particularly liked the white rat. However, the scientists were able to startle Albert and make him burst into tears – an unconditioned response – if they made a noise by hitting a hammer loudly on a steel bar out of his sight but within his hearing.

Two months later the experiment continued with the white rat being reintroduced to Albert and just a few seconds later the steel bar being hit by the hammer again. Albert cried in response to the sound. For the next seven weeks the same experiment was repeated once a week with the same response from Albert. By the end of the series of experiments he would cry just at the sight of the rat and he would try to crawl away. The researchers wouldn't have to hit the steel bar because Albert was associating the noise he didn't like with the rat in the same way Pavlov's dogs had associated something they did like, their dinner, with the ringing of a bell.

The theory of classical conditioning was further developed in the 1920s and 1930s by an American psychologist and behaviourist, Burrhus Frederic Skinner. Known as *operant conditioning*, his theory was based on an earlier theory from 1898 – Thorndike's Theory of Effect. Thorndike's theory said that behaviour that gives you a pleasant response is more likely to be repeated than behaviour that gives you a response you don't like. You are more likely to stroke a purring kitten again than one that scratches you.

Skinner's theory went further and said that it was behaviour that was reinforced that was most likely to be repeated. Behaviour that wasn't reinforced was less likely to be repeated. It was to be known unsurprisingly as reinforcement theory. Skinner did not believe in the existence of free will in humans – he believed in reinforced behaviour.

To give one example. Skinner experimented with pigeons that he kept underweight and hungry. He found that he could condition – or motivate – them to peck a small metal disc on the side of their box which could open a chute that gave them some food before closing again. Importantly, pecking the disc didn't provide food every time but often enough to deliver food and make it worth the pigeon's while to try it. Gambling machines work on the same variable schedule. If they never paid out, no one would play them. The fact that they sometimes do pay out produces a conditioned response to keep on playing for gambling addicts who, Skinner would have argued, are exhibiting reinforced behaviour not free will.

Reinforced behaviour in a classroom would typically involve a child being praised for putting their hands up, regardless of getting questions right to begin with, and also for good work and behaviour. Gradually, the praise would be diminished as the child became conditioned to make the right responses in class and only outstanding work would eventually be praised. Bad behaviour would be ignored.

The same thing would apply in the home. Only the child who did what the parent wanted – did their homework, tidied their room – would be praised. Naughty behaviour would be ignored because to acknowledge it was to reinforce it. If the child wanted more attention, for example, they would be conditioned into learning that breaking a vase wouldn't work but doing their homework would. Or at least that was the theory. Presumably parents might have to ignore a lot of smashed vases with some children before it would work.

But over the years there were critics. Some thought the theory didn't account for inherited learning abilities so wasn't a complete theory of learning. Later, social learning theorists pointed to humans learning automatically from watching things rather than from their own experience of reinforcement.

In the middle of this debate came Abraham Maslow's 1943 book – *A Theory of Motivation*. This argued that certain basic needs have to be met before an individual can start focussing on fulfilling themselves. Maslow's Hierarchy of Needs made him one of the most influential and famous psychologists of the twentieth century.

Maslow argued that humans are motivated to achieve certain needs but that some take precedence over others. Usually expressed in a five-tier triangle, the most basic of these needs at the bottom of the triangle are physiological and are around survival – the need for food, warmth, sleep and shelter. Next up are the needs for safety and security and above that come psychological needs for belonging, intimate relationships and friendships. Above that comes the need for esteem which evokes feelings of self-respect and accomplishment and only then do you get to the apex of the pyramid which relates to fulfilling your potential. You can think ambitious thoughts when your life circumstances have you further down the pyramid but you can't enact them until the basic layers of needs are met.

Nonetheless, operant conditioning was the major theory of motivation in place when Edward Deci, a young American experimental psychologist with a mathematics background, published the results of his experiment with the psychology students and the Soma puzzle cubes in 1971. In doing so he had broken the ground for the development of new theory which would eventually largely demolish the reward and punishment theory as the best way of motivating people.

Self-determination theory

Six years after he first published the results of his Soma cubes experiments Deci met Richard Ryan, a fellow academic at the University of Rochester in New York where they both worked. They got on well and soon began to collaborate. At the time Deci had a Masters in business administration but was teaching experimental psychology and Ryan had a background in philosophy but was on the university's clinical graduate programme. Their distinctive areas of work and expertise meant they used different methods and approaches but crucially they both had a strong and shared interest in high quality motivation.

Together they developed their theory of self-determination, initially laid out in 1985 in a co-authored book called *Intrinsic Motivation and Self-Determination in Human Behavior*. At its heart was the notion that the best quality of motivation came from within an individual, not from external influences. It didn't go down well at all with the behaviourists who believed external influences were the key to motivation and pointed to copious research to prove it.

Self-determination theory is split into two major areas. The first is that there are two types of motivation – autonomous and controlled, also known as intrinsic and extrinsic motivation. Autonomous motivation comes from within an individual. They are motivated to do something because they are interested in it and enjoy it. They understand the full value of it and are willing to do it. These are the kinds of people who do things for the love of it and for its value. The child who loves swimming and joins their local swimming squad and wants to go to bed early so that they can get up at dawn to train for competitions before they go to school is autonomously motivated; no-one is having to persuade them with rewards to do it.

Controlled motivation comes from outside the individual. Someone else is making demands of them, they are being obliged to do something or pressured to do it – rewards are offered. The little child who loves the sounds they can make on their toy xylophone and is quickly drawn to the piano which they relish to learn is autonomously motivated. The little child whose parents decide they need to learn the piano and who does the minimum of practice with the promise of an ice lolly, more screen time, etc. is being subjected to controlled or extrinsic motivation with rewards.

The critical thing that Deci and Ryan discovered is that you do something better if your motivation is autonomous. Indeed, you do your most creative work possible because you feel more engaged in what you are doing and you feel good about yourself.

It's the quality of the motivation that matters, not the amount. You may be able to motivate yourself every New Year's Day to start that diet because the magazines are full of "new year, new you" articles, but there is nothing in the world that will make you stick to eating habits that will keep you at a healthy weight unless you are intrinsically motivated to.

The opposite is true of controlled or extrinsic motivation. You don't perform as well and you feel less good psychologically. That's why there are "new year, new you" articles exploding from magazines and online every January. People haven't stuck to the rules suggested by strangers last January. If, however, last January you had internalised an image of yourself at a certain weight, enjoying long walks in the countryside every weekend and enjoying the food which maintains that lifestyle, you may well have autonomously motivated yourself to do just that. You never needed a magazine to tell you how to stick to your ideal weight and never will again. Or that's the theory.

But, and it's a big but, in the right circumstances, controlled motivation can be internalised by an individual who understands the value of the task and thus becomes autonomously motivated.

The individual who internalises the "new year, new you" ideas and makes them their own has become autonomously motivated. The individual who internalises those ideas because they want to live long enough to enjoy being part of their grandchildren's lives as they grow up may be even more strongly motivated. The teenager who understands their parents' arguments about the importance of getting good grades at school to the establishment of a worthwhile and interesting career, may internalise those arguments and do their homework willingly because they see the value of doing so; they have become autonomously motivated.

The other major part of the theory relates to the conditions that are needed to motivate us best. In turn that relates to the human needs that have to be satisfied before we can produce our best performance and remain psychologically well. If these needs are not met, there will be negative psychological consequences. The needs, which share some similarities with Maslow's Hierarchy but also include big differences, are:

1   **Competence** – we need to feel confident and effective in what we are doing – we have a human need to build our skills.
2   **Relatedness** – we need to feel a sense of belonging to others, to feel cared for and to care for others, to be cared for by groups that are important to us.
3   **Autonomy** – we need to be able to decide what we do rather than be coerced by others.

What does this mean for parents or teachers? You need to be supporting these basic psychological needs of children and teenagers to get optimal outcomes. Forget the bribes and the threats as a modus operandi, they may work in the short term but not in the long term if you want children to grow up capable of their most creative work.

That underlying finding of the initial research that Deci published in 1971 is significant. By offering rewards you can damage someone's feelings about the value of the task itself and undermine their intrinsic motivation to do it. Remember the group that was offered money for completing the Soma puzzles? They were perfectly happy to keep trying in the first session without being paid. But once they had been offered money in the second session for completing the puzzles, they were less interested in doing so in the third session when they weren't paid. The ones who weren't paid for any of the sessions just kept on trying because their interest had been piqued.

And if you were wondering whether this is just something that operates for university students, or older children who know the value of money, think again because there have been similar findings with young children.

In one well known study (Lepper, Greene and Nisbett, 1973) three groups of pre-school children, aged between three and five-years-old, were given coloured markers to play and draw with by researchers. After they had been observed playing with the markers the researchers told one group they would get a certificate with a gold seal and ribbon if they played with the markers, a second group was offered no reward and a third group was given a reward as a surprise.

Children who expected to receive the reward for playing with the markers were significantly less interested in playing with the markers after they had been told about the certificate, whereas the levels of interest in playing with the markers remained consistent in the two other groups.

A 1999 meta-analysis of hundreds of studies by different researchers testing the same idea in different ways found that offering rewards always undermines intrinsic motivation for the activities under review (Deci, Koestner and Ryan, 1999).

Turning from education briefly to the world of work that children will grow up to be in, it sounds counter intuitive but these results also find an echo in research into how much pay motivates people. A meta-analysis of studies into the relationship between pay and job satisfaction (Judge et al., 2010), which reviewed 120 years of research, found only a very weak link between pay and job satisfaction. It was a finding repeated across cultures. There was no significant difference between the findings for the United States, India, Australia, the UK or Taiwan.

A Gallup study published the following year reported that the majority of American workers – 75 per cent of them – were not engaged by their work. The highly educated and the middle aged were the least likely to be enthusiastic about what they did, even though they were more likely to earn more than younger and less educated people. Which is bad news for whoever they work for because research also links the most successful businesses with the most positive work forces.

Finally, while we are talking about work motivation a study which looked at the part managers, work goals and pay played in job satisfaction (Cho and Perry, 2011) found people who were most pay focussed enjoyed their jobs less than the people who focussed more on the work they actually did. Money doesn't buy you everything.

None of this is to suggest that no one can be motivated by external factors like money or grades in school or a desire for social approval, but reward and punishment do not always change people's behaviour over time. If they did prisons would not be full of recidivists, businesses would be full of people who love their jobs and magazines wouldn't run "new year, new you" pieces.

What self-determination theory is saying is that the best motivation, in terms of producing the best performance of whatever type, and the best psychological feelings, comes from within an individual.

You are not teaching children the value of learning or hard work by giving them Amazon vouchers for doing their homework. You are teaching them to dance like some Pavlovian dog. They may stop dancing in a future devoid of Amazon vouchers (or their equivalent) because they haven't actually internalised the value of what they are doing.

Edward Deci is now Professor of Psychology and Gowen Professor in the Social Sciences at the University of Rochester, New York and Richard

Ryan is a professor at the Institute for Positive Psychology and Education at the Australian Catholic University and a research professor at the University of Rochester. They are among the world's leading theorists in human motivation.

Blooming children

When it comes to motivation the personal motivation of individual children matters hugely, but the motivations of the people around them, their parents and their teachers, can have an enormous impact on them. That's why Deci and Ryan's list of conditions needed before autonomous motivation can blossom is so important.

Just one example: if parents haven't done well at school and don't expect their children to either, that's not very motivational for their children who won't have their needs for feeling they are (or can be) competent met. If parents have done very well at school and don't think their children are doing well enough, that's hard for the child too.

There is research on what's known as the "golem" effect in which children (and adults) who have low expectations of themselves – or their teachers or bosses have low expectations of them – fulfil the prophecy and underperform (Babad, Inbar, and Rosenthal, 1982).

Again, this chimes with the earlier research we discussed on setting which shows pupils of the *same* tested ability performing differently subsequently. Those placed in the top set did better than the children placed in the middle set and those placed in the bottom set performed worst of all. The theory is that teacher expectations, and thus their teaching, was tailored to whichever set they were teaching, and they didn't alter their teaching to meet the varying abilities existing within sets.

Where teachers have high expectations of all the children in their classes a positive and motivational atmosphere is created for everyone. And if parents, regardless of their own background, expect their children to do their very best at school, encourage them to be spurred on by problems not deterred, and take it as read they will aim for higher education, they are creating a wonderfully motivational background against which their children can prosper. It feels good to be believed in.

But are those fine words or is it truly motivational to have someone believe in you if you believe them? Do high expectations really make a difference? In 1965 two researchers decided to find out in an experiment with Californian elementary school pupils which involved a daring sleight of hand. The researchers were Robert Rosenthal, a professor of social psychology at Harvard University and Leonore Jacobson, an elementary school principal in San Francisco.

In their experiment young children starting school in 18 different classrooms were given intelligence tests by researchers who then gave the class teachers lists of the 20 per cent of their pupils who would "bloom" over the next year because they had "unusual potential for intellectual development."

Eight months later all the children were retested and the ones identified by the researchers in the earlier test were indeed blooming. They scored significantly highly in the second test. Then the sleight of hand was revealed. The names of these "intellectual bloomers" had been picked randomly by the researchers out of the class lists. Their choice was nothing to do with test results yet they bloomed – they fulfilled the expectations placed on them. Their teachers – who in turn perhaps had been prompted by the research that had "identified" the "brightest" and, consciously or unconsciously, treated them differently – gave them more challenging tasks perhaps, because they expected them to be capable of them which meant they developed more quickly.

It was dubbed the "Pygmalion effect" named after the mythical story of the Greek sculptor who fell in love with a statue he had sculpted from ivory of a beautiful woman. Aphrodite, the Goddess of love, granted his wish for a wife just like "my ivory girl" by bringing the statue to life. George Bernard Shaw's play of the same name, about the transformation of a street flower seller into an elegant lady, became the hit musical *My Fair Lady*.

Rosenthal and Jacobson produced a book in 1968 called *Pygmalion in the Classroom* but their research methods and the inability of other researchers to repeat the results was criticised soon after publication. However, in the years since many other studies have confirmed the existence of what subsequently became known as the "teacher expectancy" effect.

Why do teacher expectations matter? If you think a child is limited or advantaged intellectually, and treat them differently, perhaps giving the less able student simpler work and the more able one more challenging work, or just being nicer to them, you can see why one child might do better in class than the other. Remember the research on setting and have faith in your children.

It's all in the mind

Teacher expectations matter, parent expectations matter but so do student expectations, exemplified by their mindset or their approach to learning. Mindset can slow down the brightest and speed up the less cognitively able. We know this from work of academic Carol Dweck who has been mentioned earlier in the book. Dweck is the Lewis and Virginia Eaton Professor of Psychology at Stanford University in the United States and a world leader in the field of student motivation. Her studies have revealed that there are two types of mindset when it comes to learning – a fixed mindset and a growth mindset. This applies to adults as well as children and teenagers.

Someone with a fixed mindset believes their abilities are immutable, that they are born with a certain amount of intelligence and aptitude and they cannot improve on that. If they hit a problem when they are learning something, they can struggle and give up to easily because they believe they have reached the limits of what they are capable of. Their mindset is demotivating them.

We've already learned earlier in the book that children who don't do well at maths are the most likely to think they don't have a "maths brain" even though no such thing exists. Remember Yolanda who was fatalistically resigned at nine-years-old to the "fact" that some children – not her – were better at maths because they had bigger brains – they were "born clever."

Someone with a growth mindset doesn't think like that. They believe that with enough effort and training they can do better, that they can grow their intelligence and their aptitudes, whether it's maths or anything else. If they have a problem, they see it as an opportunity to keep trying and keep learning and not to give up. Their mindset is motivating them.

It's thought that about 15 per cent of us are somewhere in the mindset middle but the rest fall into either the fixed or the growth camps. To be clear this is an attitude of mind and not about your IQ or aptitudes. Some very able children can have fixed mindsets even though they get top grades, whilst other children who have to work much harder to learn can have growth mindsets.

Clever children with fixed mindsets are motivated by feedback only when it reinforces their feelings of being clever. They don't see their academic success as being down to hard work and they generally fear failure and don't cope well with it. Less able children with fixed mindsets see their lack of success as being down to their own in born limitations.

By contrast all children with growth mindsets see feedback as an opportunity to learn, not to underline anything about their limitations or potential. They don't fear failure because they see it as an opportunity to redouble their efforts and improve.

Parents can inadvertently encourage both attitudes. For example, they might say to a child who is finding maths difficult that they were rubbish at maths at school too and still are. That is telling the child that your ability is fixed and you can't improve. They are feeding feelings of incompetence even though they might be trying to make the child feel better.

Or a parent might constantly praise a child for being clever when they do well at school. That is telling the child that they are only doing well at school because they are clever, that hard work doesn't come into it. When a child like that fails for the first time, they can be completely floored because they have no mental strategies for working round the problem. They aren't "clever" enough.

When parents and teachers go out of their way to make sure they praise the effort a child makes, regardless of how able they are, they are more likely to be encouraging a growth mindset, particularly if they remind the child that it is the work and practice they've done at school and in homework that is making them do better in class; the child that believes that is less likely to stumble at learning hurdles because they know it is in their power to learn how to jump them.

Dweck published a book which brought her ideas to a wider public, *Mindset. The New Psychology of Success,* in 2006. Commercial companies pounced on the ideas soon after they were published and developed programmes to encourage growth mindset which have proliferated in schools and elsewhere since. It's not difficult to see why the idea has taken off. At heart it is a simple explanation for the differences between humans when it comes to motivation – differences we can all see.

But doubts about the efficacy of these mindset programmes exist. There have also been complaints from other academics that they cannot replicate Dweck's findings which Dweck has rebutted by saying they haven't accurately replicated the conditions of her study. A joint study published in 2018 by two American universities, Michigan and Case Western Reserve, pressed a different point. Researchers there found that mindset programmes had only a weak effect for most students in most cases.

Their research comprised two meta-analyses of the results of hundreds of studies of growth mindset programmes in schools and found only one group, the disadvantaged and youngsters at high risk of failing at school, clearly benefitting from them – in itself surely a very good thing.

But Dweck, in a robust response published in *The Conversation* (26 June 2018), soon after the Michigan and Case Western Reserve research was published, said that the researchers had got it wrong. The data they'd collected had shown effect sizes that were large when set beside the impact of other, often much more expensive, programmes to improve the education of children and young people.

Dweck, who makes it clear she has no financial relationship with anyone selling mindset programmes, was awarded the inaugural $4m Yidan Prize in 2017 and said it would be spent on developing even more effective mindset interventions for children in school and materials for teachers.

Dweck was looking at motivation for learning in children long before she fully set out her mindset ideas in her 2006 book. During the 1980s and 1990s she published a series of research papers testing out ideas with other academics.

In 1992 when she was at Columbia University she published with a fellow psychologist, Gail Heyman from San Diego University, a paper which looked at the relationship between intrinsic or autonomous motivation and the use of learning goals – goals that are aimed at helping an individual improve their personal skills in anything they want to improve. Once they hit the goal – perhaps of playing a piano piece with no errors – they move on to a harder piece until they can play that perfectly and then to the next harder piece and so on as they gradually get better and better.

What Dweck and Heyman found was that having specific learning goals actually encouraged the development of prized autonomous motivation – the stuff that comes from within an individual that is central to Deci and Ryan's self-determination theory discussed earlier in the chapter. But they also found that performance goals – the evaluation of those skills – actually discouraged personal motivation. Evaluation could be test or exam results but it could also be pudding for eating your greens, extra screen time for finishing your homework, performance indicators at work and so on. Put simply, rewards diminish interest in the task, as Deci and Ryan had said.

Specific learning goals are also at the heart of the idea of deliberate practice developed over 40 years and through numerous studies by Anders Ericsson, a Swedish psychologist and Conradi Eminent Scholar and Professor of Psychology at Florida State University in the US. He is a world leader in research into expert performance and believes the people who are best at what they do get there because they always push themselves out of their comfort zone in the practice they undertake for any endeavour whether it's sporting, academic, creative, scientific or anything else. They take expert advice on what the next rung of the ladder should be and aim for it and they use expert feedback to improve and get themselves to that next stage. Their personal motivation is undeniable because experts are built steadily and solidly over time. They don't flash in a pan.

The idea of specific incremental goals also accords well with brain science because it is dopamine, the feel good hormone, that both encourages us to act and then rewards us with feeling good when we accomplish something – like getting up and making a cup of tea and enjoying drinking it, or getting on with a piece homework and having the pleasure of finishing it.

In summary

If you could bottle motivation and sell it in the supermarket, you'd be very rich. But you can't. The truth is that the most motivated people are motivated from within – Steve Jobs quoted at the start of this chapter was right. That teenager who resists doing homework but will happily spend hours on a computer game is motivated from within, just on the wrong thing if they are to do well at school; they'll probably get very good at playing computer games with all that practice.

Rewards or treats can work in the short term to motivate but the effect doesn't last unless the children, teenagers or adults concerned become personally convinced of the value and enjoyment of whatever they are doing. Repeated use of rewards and punishment run the risk of permanently deterring motivation for the task at hand.

As a parent, your job is to encourage effort and specific learning goals but above all develop the right conditions in which autonomous motivation can thrive. And for that you can ditch the bribes and rewards but instead help your children and teenagers towards becoming competent in what they do and ensure that they live in an environment in which they are cared for and have a sense of belonging but also are allowed to make their own choices about what they do. You just have to work with them so that they learn to make good choices of their own.

References

Deci, E.L. (1971) 'Effects of externally mediated rewards on intrinsic motivation.' *Journal of Personality and Social Psychology*, Vol. *18*, No. 1, pp. 105–115. doi:10.1037/h0030644

Pavlov, I.P. (1897/1902) *The Work of the Digestive Glands*. London: Griffin.

Watson, J.B. and Rayner, R. (1920) 'Conditioned emotional reactions.' *Experimental Psychology*, Vol. *3*, No. 1, pp. 1–14.

Skinner, B.F. (1948) '"Superstition" in the pigeon.' *Journal of Experimental Psychology*, Vol. *38*, pp. 168–172.

Skinner, B.F. (1951) *How to Teach Animals*. San Francisco, CA: Freeman.

Maslow, A.H. (1943) 'A theory of human motivation.' *Psychological Review*, Vol. *50*, No. 4, pp. 370–396. doi:10.1037/h0054346

Deci, E.L. and Ryan, R.M. (1985) *Intrinsic Motivation and Self-Determination in Human Behavior*. New York and London: Springer Science & Business Media.

Deci, E.L. and Ryan, R.M. (2008) 'Self-determination theory: a macrotheory of human motivation, development, and health.' *Canadian Psychology/Psychologie canadienne*, Vol. *49*, No. 3, pp. 182–185. doi:10.1037/a0012801

Lepper, M.R., Greene, D. and Nisbett, R.E. (1973) 'Undermining children's intrinsic interest with extrinsic reward: a test of the "overjustification" hypothesis'. *Journal of Personality and Social Psychology*, Vol. *28*, No. 1, pp. 129–137. doi:10.1037/h0035519

Deci, E.L., Koestner, R. and Ryan, R.M. (1999) 'A meta-analytic review of experiments examining the effects of extrinsic rewards on intrinsic motivation'. *Psychological Bulletin*, *125*, pp. 627–668.

Judge, T.A., Piccolo, R.F., Podsakoff, N.P., Shaw, J.C. and Rich, B.L. (2010) 'The relationship between pay and job satisfaction: a meta-analysis of the literature.' *Journal of Vocational Behaviour*, Vol. *77*, No. 2, pp. 157–167.

Blacksmith, N. and Harter, J. (2011) 'Majority of American workers not engaged in their jobs.' *Gallup News*. Available from news.gallup.com/poll/150383/majority-american-workers-not-engaged-jobs.aspx

Cho, Y.J. and Perry, J.L. (2011) 'Intrinsic motivation and employee attitudes: role of managerial trustworthiness, goal directedness, and extrinsic reward expectancy'. *Review of Public Personnel Administration*, Vol. *32*, No. 4, pp. 382–406.

Babad, E.Y., Inbar, J. and Rosenthal, R. (1982) 'Pygmalion, Galatea, and the Golem: investigations of biased and unbiased teachers.' *Journal of Educational Psychology*, Vol. *74*, No. 4, pp. 459–474. doi:10.1037/0022-0663.74.4.459

Rosenthal, R. and Jacobson, L. (1968) *Pygmalion in the Classroom: Teacher Expectation and Pupils' Intellectual Development*. New York: Holt, Rinehart & Winston.

Dweck, C.S. (2012) *Mindset: The New Psychology of Success.* New York: Constable & Robinson Limited.

Dweck, C.S. (2000) *Self-theories: Their Role in Motivation, Personality, and Development.* New York: Taylor & Francis Group.

Deci, E.L. and Ryan, R.M. (2008) 'Self-determination theory: a macrotheory of human motivation, development, and health.' *Canadian Psychology/Psychologie canadienne*, Vol. *49*, No. 3, pp. 182–185. doi:10.1037/a0012801

Sisk, V.F., Burgoyne, A.P., Sun, J., Butler, J.L. and Macnamara, B.N. (2018) 'To what extent and under which circumstances are growth mind-sets important to academic achievement? two meta-analyses.' *Psychological Science*, Vol. *29*, No. 4, p. 549. doi:10.1177/0956797617739704

Dweck, C.S. (2018) 'Growth mindset interventions yield impressive results.' *The Conversation.* Available from https://theconversation.com/growth-mindse t-interventions-yield-impressive-results-97423

Heyman, G.D. and Dweck, C.S. (1992) 'Achievement goals and intrinsic motivation: their relation and their role in adaptive motivation.' *Motivation and Emotion*, Vol. *16*, pp. 231–247.

'Stanford psychologist recognized with $4 million prize for education research.' (2017) *Stanford News.* Available from https://news.stanford.edu/2017/09/19/ stanford-psychologist-recognized-4-million-prize/

Chapter 11

It's curious

We keep moving forward, opening new doors, and doing new things, because we're curious and curiosity keeps leading us down new paths.
Walt Disney, pioneer of the animation industry, winner of a record 22 Oscars as a film producer, founder of Disneyland and Disneyworld

Curiosity is one of the most permanent and certain characteristics of a vigorous intellect.
Dr Samuel Johnson, compiler of the Dictionary of the English Language published in 1755

I have no special talents. I am only passionately curious.
Albert Einstein in private correspondence in 1952

If you've read this book through, you should now have a much better idea of what matters most to encourage learning – how and why children do really well at school – and the research that underpins what we can be sure of.

You will know that a child who feels emotionally, socially and physically secure is more likely to develop their learning potential when they are young because they have the basic tools needed to grow strong internal motivation and become a good learner.

But you will also now know that our brains are not going into irreversible decline from our late teens as we once thought. Unless we damage them, we can all learn new and complex things well into old age – if we want to. If your children don't do well at school, it's not all over for them. They have time on their side – if they wish to use it – to have a second crack at formal learning when they are adults. You should also know by now that rewards and punishment might work in the short term to get the homework done, but at a cost. You won't change negative attitudes to learning in the long term by quick fixes.

What else do we know? The type of school your children go to, paying fees or sending your children to selective schools makes little or no difference to how they turn out academically. Bright children do well in selective schools because they were doing well before they got there – that's why they passed the entrance test – and they should continue to do well unless something bad happens. Leading fee-paying schools select their pupils, as do grammar schools and other forms of academically selective schools. The pupils arrive well equipped to continue succeeding.

That is not, of course, the same as saying all schools are the same – they are not. Some are better than others. But good teaching in lively but orderly environments matters more than school structures – that's good teaching that gets the best out of all children, regardless of their ability.

When it comes to class size, smaller is better for the youngest children but, within reason, class size isn't that important when it comes to attainment, although children may well have better relationships with teachers – and behave better and be more engaged in the lesson – in smaller classes.

The attitudes to learning that children bring to school with them and the quality of their teachers impacts on how well they do at school. Countries like South Korea have some of the most successful schools in the world despite having large numbers of pupils to a class. But they also invest in high salaries for good teachers and the country has a parental culture which generally understands the importance of education. Some parents are so ambitious for their children they hire after school tutors so that their children do even better at school – and they expect their children to behave well in class. That cannot be said for all parents in the West.

Streaming and setting by ability matter because of a tendency for many teachers to believe in ability being fixed and to teach accordingly. Children of similar ability spread among upper and lower sets perform differently in public examination. Those in the top sets do best, those in lower sets worst even though their ability is broadly the same.

Teacher expectations really matter because when teachers expect the children in their care to do well, they tend to do well and when they don't, the opposite can be true. And while we are on the subject of expectations, they matter across the board. A child who thinks they are no good at school, perhaps because their parents tell them they were no good at school either, sets themselves up to fail unless someone challenges that assumption.

Teacher feedback is only useful if it helps a child improve and focus on the overall goals of the curriculum they are working on. Comments like "Could do better" or marks like 10/10 without explaining the reasoning behind those comments and marks are nigh on useless. It can allow poorer performing pupils to give up because they don't know what they need to do to 'do better' or high performing pupils to simply coast without challenge. The only good feedback is feedback that is used constructively by the pupil.

As for homework, in primary schools it has little or no effect but in secondary schools it is associated with better performance in public examinations as long as it's of the right type – reinforcing learning – and there's not too much of it. If it creates too much tension between parents and children, it's dangerous – it can put kids off school learning altogether. It's a delicate balance which needs care, empathy and patience to get right.

How young you are in the school year matters because you are more likely to lag behind older classmates if you are less mature than the others in your class. Having a good first year at school is crucially important to ensure you have the best opportunity for a successful time at both primary and secondary school, whenever your birthday is.

Genes matter up to a point because some learning abilities appear to be transmitted genetically but there is no single gene for intelligence and our attitudes are of crucial importance to what we end up using our lives for.

Our genes are not responsible for our destiny – we are. The most intelligent person in the world will not be successful in anything if they lack the motivation to use their intelligence. Someone less intelligent but more diligent is always going to get more out of their life.

There are, of course, many more things we've covered in this book which are important but we'd like to end by reminding you what the research shows matters most of all in education and also to introduce to you one unsung superhero of learning before we close.

Parents matter most

It's a no brainer really when you think about it but, in most cases, it is parents and those all-important attitudes they develop to learning in their children that matter most of all to how well a child does at school. Can do attitudes which mean the children don't give up when learning gets difficult but who keep going, looking for ways to understand and move forward.

Some children seem to be able shrug off poorer parenting of all types and do very well at school but they are outliers. Most disadvantaged children don't do as well at school as their more affluent classmates. We saw that earlier in the book when we looked at the yawning attainment gap between children coming from more affluent homes and those suffering from socio economic deprivation. At the end of the day, the home a child grows up in still matters more than the schools they go to.

If it's a home where learning is enjoyed and valued and effort encouraged, the children in it will have a far better chance of flourishing at school. If it's a home where children are read to, sung to, played with and talked with before they go to school, they are likely to hear millions more words and learn many more things than their more disadvantaged contemporaries before they first set a small foot inside a nursery, let alone a school.

Because of this they will generally learn to read more quickly and embrace new ideas and the curriculum with more ease and do better in key examinations at the end of their school life. All these are facts established by years of research by the best academic minds in education from across the world.

And what else do the homes that produce children who do well at school do? What else do these children begin to learn in the very earliest days at their mother's breast and in their father's arms? It's curiosity – the superhero of learning. Something that all children are born with but something that is not encouraged in all homes indeed it's actively discouraged in some.

Without curiosity, learning is a laborious chore. With it, our minds soar into unexplored areas of thought that make learning that much easier, that much better. It certainly worked for all those people quoted at the beginning of this chapter, and many, many millions more men and women down the ages.

Curiosity killed the cat – really?

The old proverb "curiosity killed the cat" implies that a luckless feline will soon lose all nine lives if it is curious and, by inference, that any human who asks too many questions, opens too many doors is asking for trouble if not the same demise as the cat. You could imagine it as the kind of thing that could be said to children in times when they were supposed to be seen and not heard.

But it's not a very old proverb. It's thought to be a nineteenth century corruption of a phrase from a Ben Jonson play written in 1598, *Every Man in his Humour*. The line said "Helter skelter, hang sorrow, care will kill a cat, up-tails all, and a pox on the hangman" the context of the line being that care meant worries or sadness for other people. William Shakespeare used a very similar phrase with the same meaning the following year in his play *Much Ado About Nothing*. This suggests one of two things, it was common currency as a saying at the time or Shakespeare simply lifted the phrase. We'd probably support the former explanation.

The first time "curiosity killed the cat" actually gets recorded as a proverb is in the 1898 edition of Ebenezer Cobham Brewer's reference book *The Dictionary of Phrase and Fable*, a peak moment for certain types of adults to believe children should be seen and not heard, particularly at school. Albert Einstein, quoted at the beginning of the chapter, was at school during the late nineteenth century and he was to say later that it was "a miracle that curiosity survived formal education." Surely schools are doing better now though? We'll come to that in a moment.

First, what does the research show about curiosity and learning? The most recent is very clear that children who are more curious than others are more likely to perform well at school – whatever their economic or social background. This was spelled out by a research team at the University of Michigan C.S. Mott Children's Hospital and the Center for Human Growth and Development who published their findings in *Pediatric Research* (April 2018).

How did they find out? They looked at the curiosity levels and school performance of 6,200 kindergarteners who are part of the US Department of Education sponsored Early Childhood Longitudinal Study, Birth Cohort. The cohort is a nationally representative, population-based study which is following the lives of thousands of children born in 2001.

The children's parents were interviewed during home visits to enable researchers to fill in a behavioural questionnaire about the curiosity the children were showing when they were babies of nine months, toddlers of two years old, and when they started preschool and kindergarten. Reading levels, maths skills and behaviour were measured when the children started kindergarten.

The researchers then crunched all the data and found that the children who showed the highest levels of curiosity were also the highest performers in reading, maths and behaviour. They also found something else so astonishing that it has implications for family policy across the world.

As we've already said, children from poorer homes generally perform less well at school than children from better off homes where there can be more resources to support early learning. But this research found children from poorer homes who had scored highly on the curiosity questionnaire were performing as well on maths and reading assessments as the children from wealthier homes. In fact, the connection of curiosity with better school performance was even more noticeable in the children from less well-off homes than everyone else.

The project says:

> Our results suggest that while higher curiosity is associated with higher academic achievement in all children, the association of curiosity with academic achievement is greater in children with low socioeconomic status.
>
> Curiosity is characterised by the joy of discovery and the desire for exploration and is characterised by the motivation to seek answers to the unknown. Promoting curiosity in children, especially those from environments of economic disadvantage may be an important, under recognised way to address the achievement gap.

The researchers also checked the children to see how good they were at staying focussed in class –a skill known as effortful control – because the ability to stay focused in class at school is also linked with high academic achievement, as is good behaviour, a skill known as self-regulation. They found that even if the children with higher levels of curiosity were less good at staying focused in class, they were still doing better academically. Curiosity mattered more than focus to how well they did at school.

The report also said:

> Currently, most classroom interventions have focused on the cultivation of early effortful control and a child's self-regulatory capacities, but our results suggest that an alternate message, focused on the importance of curiosity, should also be considered. Promoting curiosity is a foundation for early learning that we should be emphasising more when we look at academic achievement.

The results confirm with practical research the most popular academic theory about the value of curiosity – that it is there to stimulate learning. Humans are not alone in using it to learn – other animals do too – but we appear to be alone in using curiosity for so much more than to ensure our basic needs are met. We are curious about more than where the next meal is coming from. We ask a lot of questions – once our basic needs are met.

Some scientists have even described humans as informavores – rather than carnivores – because of our appetite for information.

The link between curiosity and learning was first demonstrated in the 1950s by Daniel Berlyne, the British born psychologist who spent much of his academic career in the US and Canada and became a leading theorist on curiosity in the twentieth century. He died at the height of his powers at the age of 52 in 1976 with a hotly anticipated book on curiosity and education unfinished.

In one of his studies participants were read lists of facts and were allowed to ask questions about the ones that piqued their curiosity. Later they were asked to recall the fact lists. The facts that encouraged them to ask questions and seek more information, were the ones they remembered most easily.

And this doesn't just work for adults, babies play longer with toys that have interested them before – they are curious and want to learn more about them. Older children or teenagers are more likely to remember something they have read, and to more deeply understand it, if something about it is a bit baffling or unexpected and piques their interest (Garner, Brown, Sanders and Menke, 1992).

George Loewenstein (1994) theorised that curiosity was similar to other drives, such as hunger, that need to be met. In the case of "curiosity," the "food" it consumes is information of which, Loewenstein thought, a small amount would first tickle the palate – like an hors d'oeuvre – and sharpen the appetite for much more information, the main course if you like. That would then be consumed enjoyably to the point at which the person was sated and they would then become less interested if they were offered even more information. Their curiosity – or appetite for information – was satisfied at this point.

His ideas were backed up by more recent work (Kang et al., 2009) in which participants in the study were asked trivia questions. The people who proved to be least curious about the answers came from opposite ends of the knowledge spectrum – they either had no idea what the answer was or they were pretty confident they did know. The most curious to know the answers were the people in the middle, the ones who thought they might know the answer but were not confident they were right. Min Jeong Kang and colleagues went on to conclude that curiosity made you learn better, consistent with the theory that the primary function of curiosity is to enable learning to take place.

In the past a great deal of time was spent by academics to define theoretically what curiosity is, something that proved harder than you would think. Attempts have also been made by education academics to build systems which can be used to work out how curious a child is but it is difficult to do.

However, where it has been studied, all research is unequivocal in linking curiosity to learning so you would assume that it is built into the way teachers teach and schools function. Except that perhaps you can tell that it is not necessarily so from the earlier comment of Prachi Shah at the University of Michigan who spoke of the importance of emphasising curiosity more in the classroom as a route to academic achievement. The brutal truth is that there isn't enough time for unbridled curiosity in the classroom and it takes a hit at school.

Susan Engel is Senior Lecturer in Psychology and Director of the Program in Teaching at Williams College in Williamstown, Massachusetts, and a leading authority on curiosity. What she has found in her studies in the classroom is shocking. When she and her student, Hilary Hackmann, gave teachers a list of things that were most important to acquire at school it all started rather well. They would often circle the word 'curiosity' if it appeared in that list but when they were asked to name what was most important to acquire at school – with no list provided – they invariably never mentioned it. And this, despite decades of academic work which has proved the crucial importance of curiosity to learning.

What is worse, in 2006 when Engel and her students did observations in an American suburban elementary school classroom, they found a chilling absence of curiosity among the children. The youngest would ask only between two and five questions in any two hours in class. Questions were asked but mostly by the teacher as s/he kept the children on task for whatever they were meant to be learning.

In the most active classrooms children were able to get involved in hands on activities but they were doing things the teacher told them to do, not exploring things that made them curious. Even when the activity was designed to teach through experience the teacher was very clear about what they wanted the child to get out of the activity and so the child had to stay on task, at the expense of high-quality learning.

In a talk on the origins of curiosity given for Williams College in 2011 Engel recalled a science class of ten and 11-year-old children who were learning about ancient Egypt. They had been given dowels, small bars and a device called a Newton meter to measure force during a group activity. The idea was that they would learn that by using the dowels as rollers it would take less force to move the little bar – that would then give them an insight into how the Egyptians moved massive pieces of stone to build the Pyramids. They were also meant to be filling in a work sheet which was telling them what to do as they moved through the activity and answering questions on what they observed.

The children were split into small groups of three and four and part way through the class it became obvious that one group had forgotten the work sheet and were doing experiments of their own with the equipment. They were using the dowels as a conveyor belt, using the bar and dowels to build a pyramid and dangling the bar from a string attached to the measuring device to see what that did.

At this point the children were told by their teacher: "Now, now kids enough of that. There will be time for experimenting at recess. This is time for science."

The fact that the children were absorbed in "doing science" by experimenting to answer questions of their own – the best form of learning – had escaped the teacher who needed the learning task she had set to be completed. Yet these were children carried away by curiosity and were still "on task" for the general scientific area they were looking at.

Remember the research we mentioned earlier from the University of Augsburg in Germany which found that children performed better in maths classes where they were not afraid to make mistakes? These American children could well have learned from the response of their teacher that to deviate from an experiment in class was a mistake.

Remember the research from Professor Jo Boaler, the leading maths expert, who argues that teachers should ask more open-ended questions and pupils should be rewarded for asking good questions, reformulating problems, explaining, justifying the methods they have used in a calculation and looking at a problem in a different way? These children were certainly reformulating the problem and looking at it in a different way – and then being told that they could use their free time, not class time, to continue and to stick to the work sheet in class.

Perhaps the teacher could have taken an interest in what they were doing and asked open ended questions about what they were finding before encouraging them back to the work sheet. It wouldn't have taken that long and the group's curiosity would have been rewarded and they wouldn't give up asking their own questions in the future.

Because most children of this age, ten to 11-years-old, have largely given up asking questions – being curious – in class according to Engel's research. In the elementary school where the amount of questions asked in class was being logged, there were two hour stretches of time in the 5th Grade classrooms where the ten and 11-year-olds failed to ask their teacher a *single* question.

This is not the first time the paucity of questions from children in school classrooms has been noted. In the 1980s the distinguished British researchers Professors Barbara Tizard and Martin Hughes, fitted 30 working class three and four-year-old girls with smocks into which had been sewn small tape recorders. Each little girl was recorded for two and a half hours at home and five hours at preschool in a study into the development of learning. The children asked an average of 26 questions an hour when they were home with their mothers – although one child was recorded asking 145 questions an hour when she was at home.

At home their conversation was rich and varied as they attempted to make sense of the world with their questions. But once inside the school building these lively little girls seemed suddenly to lose their tongues and only asked an average of just two questions an hour.

In her book, *The Hungry Mind*, Engel contrasts this lack of curiosity in school with the behaviour of the typical pre-school child who has a voracious appetite for knowledge and who will seek to satisfy it by asking hundreds of questions every day. She cites research into the questions four children asked between the ages of 14 months and five years (Chouinard 2007) which found the children were asking, on average, 107 questions per hour. That's well over one a minute. So why do children stop asking questions so suddenly when they get to school? Perhaps because they learn not to.

The transcripts of the observations noted by Engel and her students did occasionally note a child asking a question that might lead the discussion in another direction, but when that happened the teacher would not answer it to keep the lesson on track. Sometimes they would put the child off kindly, sometimes less so.

Writing in the journal *Education Leadership* (2013) Engel says:

> Although it's hard to discourage the investigations of a 2-year-old, it's all too easy to discourage those of 7-, 11-, or 15-year-olds. In one classroom I observed, a 9th grader raise her hand to ask if there were any places in the world where no one made art. The teacher stopped her midsentence with, "Zoe, no questions now, please; it's time for learning."

How long would it have taken to answer that wonderfully interesting question which illustrated curiosity and a desire to learn? Or to suggest

Zoe researched the answer and came back to class and told everyone what she had found? How long would it have taken to validate Zoe's curiosity, to light the fuse rather than snuffing it out? How angry does that make you feel?

Perhaps the teacher didn't know the answer and was embarrassed to admit it, particularly with a researcher in the room. Perhaps s/he was a less confident teacher and felt the only way to keep the children on task and complete the download of information s/he was expected to make was by not allowing questions that were not directly on topic.

To some extent you can understand where the teachers are coming from. They have targets to meet, curricula to deliver and if they encourage questions about things that are not specifically under discussion in class by answering them, the children won't get the injections of formal learning they need to eventually pass tests, examinations and have qualifications that allow them to fulfil themselves in adult life.

But ... we know curiosity is at the heart of all quality learning and to deny it a genuine role in the classroom is to deny the opportunity for deeper learning in favour of the superficial that can be regurgitated in tests and exams and then largely forgotten. Unless or until schools change their practices to allow more genuine curiosity in classrooms, how can we as parents or grandparents or people working with children continue to encourage them to be curious after they go to school? By continuing to answer the questions that, we hope, we've been answering since the day they first started articulating them.

Zoe, that ninth grader, who was so curious she was willing to ask an off-piste question about humanity and art, may come from a home where her questions get answered because she is still asking them at school regardless of the response.

But not all children are getting their questions answered out of school. Not all children are growing their curiosity and developing their learning skills. Those four children we mentioned earlier whose monitored conversations between the age of 14 months and five years revealed just how many questions toddlers and young children ask were already showing individual differences by the age of three in the numbers of questions they asked.

One of the children, Abe, asked 69.6 questions an hour. It sounds like a lot doesn't it – it's more than one a minute. But another little boy, Adam, was asking an average of 198 questions per hour – *three times* the number Abe was asking. Adam was asking an average of more than three questions a minute!

Was Adam having to ask more questions to get the answers he needed to meet his curiosity or was Abe asking fewer because he was already adapting to the lack of answers? What do you think?

Remember the study on children's talk from earlier in the book which found that middle class parents generally talk differently, and much more, and in longer more complex sentences to their children than many parents do in poorer homes?

Less advantaged children are more likely to hear shorter sentences and are generally hearing more language in the form of instructions– "Stop that!" "Put your shoes on," etc. rather than discussing with their parents where rainbows come from or being told the reason they had to put their shoes on – "We're going for a walk in the park to look out for those squirrels and we want to keep your feet warm and dry while we're walking."

Cue potential questions about why squirrels don't have to wear shoes, or any other thing that occurs to the extraordinarily curious being that is a child. Poorer children in that study had heard 30 million fewer words by the time they were four, were behind when they got to school and were more likely to be still lagging behind at school by the time they were nine.

Obviously, three-year-olds will ask more questions than 11-year-olds. Anyone who has ever loved a small child and spent time with them will be familiar with the sheer volume of why, where, what, when type questions they can ask in a very short time. It is breath taking. But the world is a big place and they are very little and new and very curious and have much to learn. The only way you can stop that curiosity and that learning in its tracks is by not answering them. So, answer them and if you don't know the answer, look it up – preferably with the child – and learn something yourself.

They may be asking fewer questions by the time they are seven or 11 because they know a lot more by then but, if you let them, they will ask the bigger questions – like Zoe did about art – and it should be your profound privilege to try to help them find an answer.

And don't believe, as Susan Engel discovered (Engel, 2011), in an earlier study of adult attitudes to curiosity that curiosity is something that only certain people have – other adults or other people's children. We are all born curious. And don't believe that, of course, children will remain curious in all but the most restrictive circumstances. They won't unless you help them to keep the light of curiosity alive.

And it's not just about the questions your children ask. If you show curiosity in things that are new to you, that is role modelling curiosity to your child. Another of Engel's studies has found that young children introduced to an unusual object with an adult will look at the adult to see how they react. If the adult is curious about the object, the child is also curious. You can swat curiosity flat, or you can encourage it to blossom.

To do well at work when they are adults, children are going to need curiosity because increasingly that's what the best firms are looking for as part of the skill set when they hire people. It's only companies that are going nowhere in the long run that want drones who don't question the status quo or look for better ways of doing things.

The future

New education research is emerging all the time. Nothing ever stands still. Professor Michael Thomas, Director of the Centre for Educational Neuroscience at Birkbeck College, part of the University of London, quoted earlier in the book believes neuroscience may eventually benefit the development of teaching and learning in the way that public health benefitted enormously from the huge strides in the study of biology during the nineteenth century and early twentieth century.

Genetics research is still in its infancy but the advent of more powerful computers and relatively cheap DNA testing, is making the difference as it gives scientists more and more data to crunch. Trends may emerge which will provide us with deeper understanding of human genetic inheritance that will also give a boost to ideas of how we teach and learn.

This book has provided you both with a road trip around some of the very best and most pertinent research about the education of children and young people that is out there – and a manual to make sense of it. Use it as a combined guide and map but use your own intelligence when applying it, just as you should do with a manual for anything else.

A guide book or sat nav is meant to complement your own thoughts and your own knowledge, not just to tell you where to go and what to do and for you to follow that blindly. Think of the owner of a £96k Mercedes-Benz who faithfully followed the instructions of her GPS even when it told her to drive into the aptly named River Sence in Leicestershire in England. The car was dragged 200 metres down river. The driver was OK but the car was a write off.

Our children are precious and no-one knows them better than their parents do. Help them make the best of their school days by ignoring the fake news, the myths and the misunderstandings. Always ask yourself: "What's the evidence?" And if there isn't any or it isn't peer reviewed research from well-known institutions or organisations, or reported by trustworthy mainstream media – ignore it and move on using this book as your guide. Good luck!

References

Shah, P.E., Weeks, H.M., Richards, B. and Kaciroti, N. (2018) 'Early childhood curiosity and kindergarten reading and math academic achievement.' *Pediatric Research*. doi:10.1038/s41390–41018–0039–0033

Berlyne, D. (1954) 'A theory of human curiosity.' *British Journal of Psychology*, Vol. 45, pp. 180–191.

Garner, R., Brown, R., Sanders, S. and Menke, D.J. (1992) '"Seductive details" and learning from text.' In K.A. Renninger, S. Hidi and A. Krapp (Eds), *The Role of Interest in Learning and Development* (pp. 239–254). Hillsdale, NJ: Lawrence Erlbaum Associates, Inc.

Loewenstein, G. (1994) 'The psychology of curiosity: a review and reinterpretation.' *Psychological Bulletin*, Vol. *116*, No. 1, pp, 75–98. doi:10.1037/0033-2909.116.1.75

Kang, M.J., Hsu, M., Krajbich, I.M., Loewenstein, G., McClure, S.M., Wang, J.T.Y. and Camerer, C.F. (2009) 'The wick in the candle of learning: epistemic curiosity activates reward circuitry and enhances memory.' *Psychological Science*, Vol. *20*, pp. 963–973. doi:10.1111/j.1467–9280.2009.02402.x

Engel, S. (2006) 'Open Pandora's box: curiosity in the classroom.' Occasional Paper. Bronxville, NY: Child Development Institute, Sarah Lawrence College.

Engel, S. (2011) 'The hungry mind: the origins of curiosity.' Talk delivered July 18, 2011, as part of the Williams Thinking lecture series. Available from www.youtube.com/watch?v=Wh4WAdw-oq8

Engel, S. (2011) 'Children's need to know: curiosity in school.' *Harvard Educational Review*, Vol. *81*, No. 4, pp. 625–645.

Engel, S. (2013) 'The case for curiosity.' *Creativity Now!* Vol. *70*, No. 5, pp. 36–40.

Engel, S. (2015) *The Hungry Mind*. Cambridge, MA: Harvard University Press.

Tizard, B. and Hughes, M. (1984) *Young Children Learning*. London: Fontana.

Chouinard, M.M., Harris, P.L. and Maratsos, M.P. (2007) 'Children's questions: a mechanism for cognitive development.' *Monographs of the Society for Research in Child Development*, Vol. *72*, No. 1, pp. i,v,vii–ix, 1–129.

Index